Residential Crowding in Urban America

Residential Crowding in Urban America

 Mark Baldassare

University of California Press
Berkeley · Los Angeles · London

University of California Press
Berkeley and Los Angeles, California
University of California Press, Ltd.
London, England
Copyright © 1979 by
The Regents of the University of California
ISBN 0–520–03563–1
Library of Congress Catalog Card Number: 77–83102
Printed in the United States of America

1 2 3 4 5 6 7 8 9

to Heidi

Contents

Tables and Figure

Tables

Figure

Preface

In 1974 I prepared a research proposal on the social and psychological consequences of household crowding and neighborhood density. It was highly critical of work that was taking place on a topic attracting a great deal of publicity. To put it simply, I was not convinced that crowded humans were "like" crowded animals, and thus I did not support the rush to the laboratory or to census and deviance data to discover the link between population density and pathology. Moreover, I was disturbed by the lack of theoretical guidance in these studies and the fact that some fundamental and important issues concerning residential crowding in urban America had been overlooked. The research proposal was funded by the Department of Housing and Urban Development, and it resulted in my doctoral dissertation in Sociology at the University of California at Berkeley. This book is a revision and extension of that earlier work.

Its task is to make some general statements about the existence and effects of residential crowding in urban America. The study is necessarily broad. It asks questions about individuals' experiences with housing, neighborhoods, family life, socializing, and overall well-being. The evidence for the impact of household crowding and neighborhood density on these factors comes from respondents' evaluations in recent national surveys. In the process of examining these issues, I relied not on assertions from animal studies but on sociological thinking about the home, the neighborhood, and interpersonal relations. The attempt is thus to develop a comprehensive approach to residential crowding that, I think, is more relevant to real-world problems and existing social theories.

The risk of this approach is sacrificing depth for variety. Each of the substantive issues addressed in this book obviously deserves closer attention. It should be kept in mind that my overall purpose is to provide some basic knowledge about and guidelines for the study of residential crowding in the United States for an audience of concerned laypersons, planners and policymakers, and academicians. The book provides data and ideas that, in my opinion, lay the groundwork for much needed and exciting research; I hope others and myself will conduct that research in years to come. In a broad sense, I hope that this book serves the purpose of placing crowding studies in their proper perspective: eliminating myths and misunderstandings, establishing some basic facts, and providing (theoretical and substantive) justifications for future (and redirected) research. I strongly disagree with those who think that "overcrowding doesn't make a difference," or that the topic has been overstudied; rather, I believe that past conceptions were simplistic and that researchers are only now beginning to ask the really important questions.

The book is composed of four parts. In the first, I introduce the general topic of crowding and talk about methods that have been used to investigate the impact of overcrowding. Toward the end of this section (in chapter 2), I present the issues, methods, and hypotheses of the present study. The second part is concerned with crowding in the home, operationalized in terms of persons per room. It presents information on the existence of household overcrowding in the United States and provides evidence on the impact of this form of residential crowding on family life and satisfaction with the dwelling. The third part concentrates on neighborhood density, measured in terms of persons per residential acre. It reviews data on levels of areal crowding experienced by Americans and on the relationship between high density and various complaints about the neighborhood and its attributes. Another major concern in that portion of the book is whether residential crowding results in social withdrawal and disruption of important relationships. The fourth part reviews the most popular topic in the crowding literature, pathology, and summarizes the general findings in the present study, while making numerous suggestions for future research.

During various stages of this project, I received valuable assistance and advice from numerous individuals and organizations. While I am responsible for the content of this book, the suggestions given by John Clausen, Claude Fischer, and Donald Foley at Berkeley were especially helpful. I was also aided by comments from William Goode, Allan Jacobs, Richard Ofshe, Carol Silverman, and Guy E. Swanson. The two manuscript reviewers for the University of California Press, Robert E. Mitchell and Daniel Stokols, provided me with some very concrete and valuable advice. Martin Wachs generously gave of his time on the eve of his sabbatical to read the entire manuscript and made numerous comments that I incorporated in the present version of the book. My editor, Grant Barnes, provided a supportive and calm background through all of this.

Financial support came from several sources, though the major portion was supplied by the Department of Housing and Urban Development Doctoral Dissertation Research Grant (H–2365–G) that allowed me to pursue research and writing undisturbed for one year. Small grants from the National Institutes of Mental Health Program in Social Structure and Personality Development in the Sociology Department at the University of California, Berkeley (MH–08268), and the Graduate Dean's Office at the same institution helped to get the initial research under way. A revision of the entire dissertation took place while I held an NIMH Postdoctoral Fellowship in the Sociology Department at the University of California at Los Angeles (MH–14583), and I am grateful for the support and patience that Program Director Ike Grusky showed for this project.

Preparing the data for analysis was not a simple task, as I explain later, and I received generous assistance from these individuals at the Institute for Social Research (University of Michigan) and the National Opinion Research Center (University of Chicago): Angus Campbell, Ann Robinson, Norman Bradburn, Patrick Bova, and David Cook. The National Planning Data Corporation (Ithaca, New York) provided the neighborhood density data in an accurate and efficient manner. On the Berkeley campus, Susan Feller prepared the census data for one set of survey respondents and checked census materials collected by NORC. I received computer assistance from Tracy Cameron, Patsy Fosler, Cathy Janes, and the Computer Center staff.

I cannot end without mentioning the encouragement, support, and toleration I received from friends, family, and colleagues. Their interest in crowding, and the insights and observations they continue to provide help to motivate my work in this area.

M. B.

Los Angeles, California
December 1977

Part I—The Study of Crowding: Theory and Methods

1. Issues and Concepts in the Study of Crowding

The ratio of people to space in residential settings is a topic that has attracted great interest in recent years. Especially in the last two decades, scientists, policymakers, and laypersons have been engaged in serious discussions about the wisdom of exposing urban dwellers to high densities. A general concern has also been raised through the mass media, making the public sector wonder whether overcrowding threatens both individual well-being and the social order. Policymakers and applied scientists, long using density as a yardstick of urban development, have taken to more detailed discussions of the association between overcrowding and the quality of urban life for residents. Social scientists, after years of neglect, are at last addressing the relationships between human beings and their environment, turning their attention to one of the allegedly simplest and most easily measured ecological phenomena—the density of populations.

Most of these interest groups have been reflecting broader concerns, raised since the turn of the century, about the consequences of urbanization and its resultant housing patterns. These issues can be seen, for example, through a series of new towns and social work movements in the western world that have criticized the existence of overcrowded slum homes and high density city life. A long-standing concern has thus been the effect of residential crowding on the family and the community. There is a presumption that basic social units such as these have been endangered by the pressures of urban life (e.g., overcrowding), making the attainment of human well-being and satisfaction more difficult.

In this study, I shall concentrate on the effects of household crowding and neighborhood density on *personal attitudes* and *social life*. In particular, I am interested in factors such as

3

residential satisfaction, family relations, interpersonal relations, and reported well-being. This introductory chapter demonstrates that these four factors are major themes or areas of interest discussed throughout the crowding literature. By concentrating on the measurement of subjective responses and social patterns of urban residents, through the use of national social surveys, the present study provides only limited information on related topics, such as the costs of growth, economic life, and general health. The contribution of this book is thus largely sociological and psychological, though the findings will have significance for all those concerned with urban individuals' experiences and reactions to dense living conditions.

This chapter discusses the general debate concerning the effects of residential crowding, as raised in popular literature, professional schools, and academic communities. At first glance, the concerns of these groups may seem unconnected. I emphasize their converging interests in an attempt to determine the major questions concerning density in urban America. The general finding is that, while the terms used by these three groups often differ, the crowding issues and problems they have addressed are actually related. This examination of the history of ideas takes on even greater significance because there has been much cross-fertilization in this new field, since public fads become policymakers' concerns and, in turn, become subjects of the scientific study of crowding. A review of the influential ideas that run through the literature on this topic uncovers the information needed to separate serious concerns with residential crowding from the less critical or in some instances unfounded problems. This chapter thus serves to define the areas to be studied in the rest of the book, as much as the data will allow, and builds an orientation for studying the impact of residential crowding.

I begin with a review of the "popular" or mass interest in overcrowding that has recently emerged, in an attempt to discover why this subject has captured the public's imagination. Next, the attention given to density by "applied" fields is reviewed, along with reasons for their more sophisticated attempts to define and measure residential crowding. "Profound" interests or social theorists' assessments of the causes and consequences of high densities in modern societies provide the most fully explicated ideas that guide the present work. Classical sociological theories, in particular the so-called Chicago School of urban sociology, are carefully searched for frameworks that can guide specific formulations. More recent theoretical arguments by social psychologists studying crowding are reviewed to determine their contributions above and beyond past theories.

By synthesizing these diverse concerns, I present some *central issues* in the study of crowding. I then develop a sociological approach to understanding the effects of high density environments on residential satisfaction, family relations, interpersonal behavior, and reported well-being. This view emanates from the weaknesses and strengths of the theoretical discussions reviewed in this chapter, and thus I do not proceed with "faddish" notions of the effects of density or, worse yet, aimless searches for significant relationships, as many other studies on crowding have. This sociological approach is presented in general terms at the end of the chapter. It is fully operationalized (i.e., presented in the form of hypotheses) by the end of chapter 2 and then used throughout the analyses of the national surveys in the substantive parts of the book.

Popular Interests

There are a number of reasons why the public turned its attention to discussions of overcrowding during the last two decades. Best-sellers issued dire warnings of impending doom to the American way of life, while major national magazines carried stories on the impact of overcrowding. A review of the ways in which the topic of density came to receive mass attention can stimulate a better understanding of the development of this interest, in terms of its primary issues. For the time being, I will not painstakingly critique the "evidence" presented through the mass media but instead attempt to survey the concerns being voiced about over-

crowding. The issues I review were raised through a variety
of current events and public queries: urban unrest and decay;
poverty and family disorganization; the population explosion; the environmental and no-growth movements; and
"pop" ethology.

Perhaps there has always been a bias against high density living in American society. There seems to be evidence
that this nation of immigrants with heterogeneous life-styles
and values needed spatial separation of its groups, who had a
strong desire for personal privacy. Various historical facts
point to this demand: "manifest destiny" and the migration
that followed in the vast, underpopulated western segment
of the North American continent; the rapid suburbanization
and deconcentration of population that has taken place since
World War II; an almost fanatical attachment to the single
family home; and reluctance to use more economical forms of
transportation in favor of the privacy and freedom afforded
by the automobile.

Anyone who lived in the United States during the
1960s, however, is well aware that this was a period of great
unrest in the cities. The urban centers, rocked by racial and
political disturbances, seemed on the verge of anarchy. Problems coincidental to modern urban life, such as poverty,
crime, and collective violence, seemed unmanageable. The
situation was getting out of control, and, as presidential
commissions and the public searched for reasons, urban
crowding came under review. Perhaps, some wondered, the
violence in urban America was not caused by the values of a
"sick" society or economic inequalities, as certain critics had
suggested. Instead, the force at work could be the "unnatural" concentrations of individuals in our cities. People
could thus be seen as "going berserk" because they lacked
adequate space for healthy living (physical, psychological,
and social). The close interpersonal distances and overstimulation that are supposedly characteristic of dense urban life
were the culprits creating conflict and disorganization. The
scenario was clearly seen by Edward T. Hall, in his widely
read book *The Hidden Dimension,* when he talked about the

inevitable and dangerous struggle for space domination among ethnic groups in crowded urban America (1966: 165–66). In a sense, crowding became the nonsocial explanation of the society's social problems; no solution short of a mass urban exodus seemed likely to alleviate the problem. Of course, the argument that urban crowding leads to social decay could easily be extended to internal housing situations, and it was. In-dwelling densities, a subject periodically discussed by social reformers since the turn of the century (see review in Biderman et al., 1963), was again raised as a contributing source of abnormal personality development and family disorganization. In a widely read appraisal of urban life, *The Death and Life of Great American Cities*, Jane Jacobs reported that household crowding was a very significant aspect of urban decay and a contributory factor in increasing social disorganization (1961:205–8). The relationship between poor housing and family disorganization was later widely publicized as part of the Moynihan Report (cf. Rainwater and Yancey, 1967:366, 340), which suggested policies to alleviate the economic problems of urban blacks. The "culture of poverty debate," which concluded that poor people differed in values and life-styles from rich people, also discussed the relationship between inadequate household space, abnormal personality development, family problems, and social maladjustment. Crowding in the home has always been viewed as a stigma, and it was considered even more so as it was related to major social problems in the 1960s.

Concurrently, an awareness of worldwide overcrowding was arising: the so-called population explosion, with all its dreadful implications, had reached the public notice. Paul Ehrlich's writings, particularly *The Population Bomb* (1968), received wide attention because of his projections of increasingly unbearable world overcrowding and subsequent resource scarcity. This situation, if left unremedied, would create within the present population's lifetime too many people with too few resources (including habitable space and food). This was a terrifying notion to affluent Americans, and it produced continuing discussions of "zero population

growth," increased efforts for family planning, and various
public policies designed to defuse the population bomb. It
undoubtedly led to a greater sensitivity to present levels of
overcrowding and their consequences, along with more negative attitudes toward high densities (see discussion in Loo,
1975).

The "environmental movement" arose simultaneously
with concerns about overpopulation, leading to greater
awareness of several conditions: resource depletion, industrial growth, pollution, and the "unnaturalness" of the urban
environment. Though the movement's main concern was
with the preservation of the earth's beauty, it also developed a
critique of urban life-styles and land use, including dense
population concentration. The "back to nature" movement,
for example, can clearly be seen as a rejection of metropolitan
life. The slogans "No growth," "Managed growth," and
"Small is beautiful" were heard with greater frequency. This
led to new thinking for Americans raised on the concept of
the endless frontier: limiting the size of local and national
economies, so as not to destroy land and deplete natural resources further. Environmental impact statements were developed to institute or safeguard these new concerns, and
they typically included restrictions on the densities proposed
for new building sites. In some cases, municipalities (e.g.,
Petaluma, California) developed restrictive size and density
policies (see Law Week, 1975), which have led to heated debates among builders and residents on the limits of growth
and overcrowding.

The interest in the macro-environment led to a greater
awareness of the micro-environment—that is, the physical
settings that individuals inhabit and use in their daily lives.
This was particularly evident in the growth of environmental
psychology and various psychotherapies that stressed the
importance of "being in touch with" or more cognizant of
one's daily surroundings. Some individuals began to
examine, and even question, the wisdom of the designs and
densities of their environments. Later, this trend was encouraged by architects and urban designers seeking the public's

view as part of the decision-making process (see Heimsath, 1977). Architects also began to consider more carefully the social implications of the types of buildings and densities in their designs. Works such as Oscar Newman's widely noticed *Defensible Space* (1973) sought to provide recommendations for dense, but safe and communal, public housing projects.

Adding some apparent credence to the growing human interest story of urban life, overcrowding, and environmental stress were the theoretical and research developments in "sociobiology" or the interest in ethology (i.e., the biological basis of behavior). Best-sellers such as Desmond Morris's *The Naked Ape* (1967) and *The Human Zoo* (1969), which could be found on many drugstore book racks, made claims about humanity's innate tendencies toward violence and self-destruction, accompanied by passing references to urban life and modern social problems. The widely acclaimed naturalist Konrad Lorenz also excited world audiences with his best-seller *On Aggression* (1966). This work dealt with the genetic tendencies to use violence in human beings and other animals, otherwise referred to as the "killer instinct." Robert Ardrey's book *The Territorial Imperative* (1966) sought to examine people's reactions to, and propensity toward, territorial invasions. Again, the public was left with an image of a programmed individual in a most unnatural state (i.e., the metropolis) whose life centers on interpersonal violence, territorial defense, and spatial invasions. Given the enormous popularity of these books, it is obvious that the ethological notions were appealing. At the least, they reinforced existing "do nothing" anti-urban attitudes, offered easy explanations of present social problems (i.e., "people are born this way"), and increased the fears and biases associated with dense urban territories.

The most significant of these extrapolations from animals to humans, in terms of overcrowding, was an article published in *Scientific American* (Calhoun, 1962). After conducting a series of experiments on caged rats, John Calhoun claimed that overcrowding caused a long list of pathologies: poor nest building, homosexuality, high mortality rates, in-

creased aggression, psychological abnormalities. His terrifying description of crowded rats "going berserk" (1962:147)
quickly led to the inevitable analogies between mice and men
(Calhoun, 1962:148). Clearly, this indicated to some audiences
that, if it happened to rats in cages, crowded urbanites were
on the brink of disaster. Naturally, the discussions (and, in
some cases, the actual presence) of urban unrest, family disorganization, overpopulation, and environmental degradation made this cataclysmic view of crowded living all the
more convincing, and seemingly prophetic. It provided a
simple answer for the deterioration of urban centers and the
dissatisfaction with city life, while explaining high crime rates
and perceived breakdowns of the community and the family.
Crowding, which was reported as innately unbearable to
humans and animals alike, was the real public enemy number one.

Practical Interests

Several social policymakers and urban practitioners
have expressed concern with crowding, and they tend to use
measures of density both formally and informally in their
decision-making processes. Some approaches to describing
the ratio of people to space, along with their implicit connota-
tions for applied scientists, are the subjects of this section.

External Density

Urban planners, who are usually given responsibility for
overseeing land use, population growth, service delivery, and
housing construction in metropolitan areas, have always de-
pended heavily on the concept of density. Because of the
nature of their work, several kinds of density measures have
been developed to answer specific questions. For instance,
persons per square mile (i.e., gross density) allows one to
envision roughly the number of people per unit of land (often
census tracts) in an urban area. However, there is much error
in this measure, since large portions of the land may be unin-
habited (e.g., open space) or uninhabitable (e.g., under wa-
ter). The actual density of the residential section of a given

urban area may be higher than the gross measure indicates. Therefore, more sensitive measures are often needed, such as neighborhood density or residential density, which exclude various types of nonresidential land use, such as streets and commercial space, from the ratio of people to area (see Katz, 1961; Ronnigen, 1973; Wallace, 1952:24). Other measures, such as housing-unit density, involve land coverage, and in particular structures, rather than persons per area (though the two are related).[1] Depending on the issue or design problem, the term perceived to be "appropriate" is used. For example, in a central city tract with mixed land use one might want to know the residential density, while gross density may be useful for development plans in largely vacant suburban tracts.

Exactly what the density of an area tells a planner is a question of debate in this field, though the importance of this term is universally accepted. Some consider it a measure of the potential ability of an area to grow; presumably, less dense areas are ripe for further development (National Planning Data Corporation, 1974b:13). Others argue that density acts as a shorthand for planners, giving them an indication of the service and facility needs of a particular populated area.[2] More specifically, density is perceived to be correlated with the costs and use of human services. For example, planners expect problems of traffic congestion in dense areas, while at the same time knowing that such conditions make possible the existence (i.e., use and financing) of mass transit. Similarly, planners presume that dense areas without hospitals, schools, or mental health centers can support such services, since many people with varying needs would be within close range (i.e., accessible) to such services. Still others argue that density is an expression of the character of a neighborhood (e.g., good for middle-class families versus slums); as I describe in later chapters, low density areas in cities tend to be the sites of more expensive, single family homes, whereas high density areas are sometimes the sites of low rent apartments or areas for non-family-oriented households. Of course, the regulation of density in the political and legal process of zoning has made it an indication of disturbance of the status quo (e.g., planning for higher densities means change for an area, which must be prevented, or at least debated among those groups with influence). Some planners worry that zoning ordinances are often applied with little notion of the "meaning" of the particular density that has become legally sanctioned.[3] Once these decisions become law, they are difficult to alter for years to come.

There are also economic reasons for concern with the population size of a given area. Population density can be an indicator of the number of people in a particular region who seek sustenance (e.g., food, employment) and hence the potential for future economic growth. A dense area would be an asset for developing new consumer markets, depending on existing competition, since a potential buying population is both available and perhaps accessible through inexpensive advertising techniques. High density may also imply a good site for industrial or business concerns, since a sufficient supply of labor will be proximate.[4] Economic concerns with density are interwoven with the idea of *carrying capacity*, which is an indication of the ability of an area to support living organisms (Street, 1969). This term, often used by ecologists and anthropologists, is closely linked to the question of how dense an area has to be to exert overcrowding or "population pressure" on its constituents. In recent years, carrying capacity has been causally linked to situations of environmental degradation and decreased user satisfaction in national parks (cf. Wicker and Kirmeyer, 1977), and it could easily be extended to descriptions of the urban habitat. One last economic consideration has to do with the relation of land value to density. Any builder or realtor knows that the more dwelling units per given area, the greater the potential profit in many situations. Particularly if land costs are high and affordable rents are low, as they are in many downtown areas of major American metropolises, the only solution is to build at high densities (Straus, 1944:54). Thus, the importance of economic considerations in determining the density of a particular area seems evident (see also Osborn, 1956).

Various governmental agencies have expressed concern with the density of urban regions. After World War II, policymakers hired social scientists to consider the implications of high density public housing projects (see, e.g., Wallace, 1952). One issue was whether newly created dense neighborhoods would foster communality or social isolation. Of course, physical and mental health considerations were also important, since potentially high levels of interpersonal contact would increase the danger of contracting communicable diseases (see discussions in Cassel, 1971; Biderman et al., 1963). Implicit in these discussions is the idea that density (or congestion) may lead to too many interpersonal encounters, overstimulation, interpersonal thwartings, and a higher probability of exchanges with undesirable people (including the physically ill). Because these inquiries focused on public housing, no attempt was made to separate the conditions of poverty from the conditions of overcrowding. This blurred the discussions of density per se, though it did highlight a problem that I will discuss later: the interaction of low status and lack of space.

Internal Density

Architects are concerned with designing houses and buildings and are therefore more directly interested in the densities of small units of space (e.g., rooms) than they are with the densities of larger urban areas. Common concerns are with the number of rooms, square footage of the rooms, use of the rooms, and number and kinds of dwelling residents. The Census Bureau and many designers measure the overcrowding of a dwelling in terms of "too many persons per room" (usually 1.01 or more persons per room). Implicit in this measure is the need to limit contacts in the dwelling, separate activities in space, and optimize personal privacy through partitioning and doors. Missing, of course, is a consideration of the size of the rooms and the dwelling. Some have argued that this does not adequately describe the space needs of different age and sex combinations of dwelling inhabitants (Greenfield and Lewis, 1969), and they have called for empirical measures of the cultural norms related to privacy. For example, American culture would not consider a two-bedroom apartment inappropriately crowded if parents shared one bedroom and their two preadolescent boys shared the other; however, a family composed of two parents and a teenage son and daughter would be considered overcrowded in the same space. Others feel that the number of bedrooms per person (Wilner et al., 1962) is a better indication of familial crowding. Built into the use of this measure is obviously a concern with the need for individual space and the separation of certain kinds of activities (e.g., sleep and sexual intercourse) from others through the use of an area that is culturally defined as a private domain (i.e., the bedroom). With few exceptions (Chombart de Lauwe, 1961; Mitchell, 1971), the indicator of the average amount of actual space in the dwelling for each person, namely square feet per person, is not used. Admittedly, it is difficult to obtain this information through the census or surveys, even though it is an obvious part of the blueprint or design of the home. Anyway, the reservation that I raise in later chapters—that each person in the home may not have the same amount of space at his or her disposal due to status differences—seems to argue against taking this more exact measure too seriously. The design of buildings may also consider the amount of outdoor (recreational) space available for each dwelling or inhabitant, particularly in residential environments that include children. The architect often considers these factors when designing dwelling units, but usually not in a systematic or readily articulated fashion (see discussions in Riemer, 1943, 1945, 1947).

Housing standards for dwelling designers are equivalent to zoning regulations for urban planners. They set "acceptable" limits of space, design, and facility in the unit. Some of these standards are legal (see review by Mitchell, 1976), while some are merely recommended for particular populations (Blackshaw et al., 1959). They are most often concerned with safety and hygiene. While the social and psychological implications of these standards are sometimes discussed in terms of "livability" and satisfaction with the dwelling, they are not easily described to those outside the architectural profession. Sometimes they reflect "value statements" about privacy and how the home should be used; these judgments, generally by middle-class practitioners, have sometimes been criticized as ethnocentric policies (Mitchell, 1975, 1976).

Various government policymakers have also expressed concern over dwelling-unit densities and designs. The effects of crowded slum households on inhabitants' mental and physical well-being have been reviewed (see Schorr, 1966; Wilner et al., 1962; Chapin, 1951). The policymakers' interest is with the relationship between density and health—the potential effects on health of increased contacts and congestion and the psychological effects of the lack of privacy and greater personal interferences. Because of factors such as housing shortages during and after World War II, social scientists were consulted by government agencies about the effects of crowded home living on the family and the socialization process (Riemer, 1943, 1945, 1947; Plant, 1960; Merton, 1951). They attempted to examine the "fit" between the housing needs of individuals and the housing situations they might (or did) encounter: What was the possibility of adaptive adjustment, and what was the likelihood of social problems arising (see also Morris and Winter, 1975)? These issues reemerged during more recent discussions of the "culture of poverty" and the difficulties encountered by urban minorities, particularly in some of the assertions made by the Moynihan Report (e.g., about family size and household crowding—see Rainwater and Yancey, 1967:336, 340). Also, more general policy concerns with the high level of residential mobility in the United States led to examinations of household crowding as an explanation of why people move (Rossi, 1956).

Related to the general issue of household crowding, as discussed by those with applied interests, are several biases. For one, it is assumed that density is disliked and avoided when possible. Further, it is assumed that crowding may have various negative health, social, mental, and criminal consequences, because it creates a situation of too many contacts, too much stress, not enough privacy, too much stimulation, and too many interpersonal thwartings.

This section has shown that density is significant to planners, designers, and policymakers. Unfortunately, no clear model (or theory) of how density affects people in neighborhoods or houses has been expressed in discussions among these practitioners or in the literature aimed at the more popular interests, though many assumptions and assertions have been made. For answers to this question, I turn next to a review of several theoretical arguments on the effects of crowding on the family and community.

Academic Interests

Long ago, several social theorists expressed interest in the trend toward increased human population density. These turn-of-the-century writers were stating concern about the rapid urbanization of the western world and the social changes that they observed to result from modernization. Of particular interest to them was the fate of the "primitive" social bonds that glued society together, namely the community and the family. These issues reappeared in the works of succeeding generations of social scientists and even in some of the more recent crowding studies.

Past Theories

Herbert Spencer (1895), in asking a key sociological question concerning the causes of the division of labor, began an important investigation of population density. He believed that the revolutionary form of highly specialized social organization that took hold in the western world was a direct consequence of the increased population densities of certain societies. Using evidence and analogies from biological studies, particularly evolutionary theory in relation to plant ecology, Spencer argued that, in order for dense populations to survive, they must not compete for the same scarce resources in a given area. Rather, they must specialize and supply each other with various goods needed for survival, creating a pattern of interdependence in which each organism provides part of the whole needed for the group's existence. In this way, Spencer explained the development and functioning of modern social systems. Of course, on an interpersonal level this meant that individual actors within this new social form had little in common with each other, unlike the participants in earlier, less specialized, and more homogeneous social forms. This lack of community (or social solidarity) did not bother Spencer, since he believed that the only prerequisite demanded for a society to exist was contractual agreement among individuals to exchange the goods they each needed for survival.

Émile Durkheim carried on a great debate with Spencer on the causes and effects of the modern form of social organization. In *The Division of Labor in Society* (1893 [1964]), he argued that more than population density was responsible for the division of labor, though density was an integral part of the causal chain. Durkheim believed that an increased number of social contacts, made possible by preexisting normative similarities between different groups in a dense area, created a situation of intercommunication, interdependence, and specialization. Population density was thus only indirectly related to complex social organization, since dense but dissimilar aggregates of individuals must communicate to cooperate, which meant there had to be social and moral similarities underlying their contacts. Basically, while Spencer sought "biological" arguments that raised the importance of density, Durkheim examined social factors that facilitated the formation of complex organizations and the process of specialization.

These two scholars also differed in the effects they attributed to the division of labor. Durkheim, like other social theorists in that period (see discussions in Hawley, 1950:195–96, 208; Tonnies, 1887 [1957]), was concerned with the social and psychological dimensions of population growth and increased specialization. Again disagreeing with Spencer and the utilitarians, Durkheim did not believe that

modernization would increase "happiness." Rather, greater
satisfaction with life was found in simpler societies with
primary (i.e., all-purpose, informal) ties than in complex
societies composed of mostly secondary (i.e., functional,
specialized, formal) relations. Durkheim reasoned that socially and physically dense societies composed of "unlike"
individuals (what he called organic societies) were alienating,
since the socially intimate, primary ties among like-minded
individuals (what he called mechanical ties) were minimized,
and the remaining ties were functional and transitory. Thus,
with increased specialization and population density came
increased anomie and loneliness. This development was pre-
ceded by the decreasing effectiveness of primary ties (e.g.,
local community, family) as psychological buffers. So Durkheim, unlike Spencer, saw dangers in creating societies
composed of fleeting, economic exchanges and contractual
agreements among individuals who maintained segmented
roles.[5]

The fascination with the social and psychological effects
of population density was continued in the writings of Georg
Simmel, along with his followers in the Chicago School of
sociology. Simmel (1905 [1969]), in an essay entitled "The
Metropolis and Mental Life," was concerned with the
psychological consequences of the high number of potential
personal contacts (i.e., social density) associated with urban
life. He reasoned that the amount of social stimulation that
bombarded the urbanite was above a healthy level; in other
words, more social information was being received than
could be properly processed. In order to cope with this situation, individuals develop a strategy, or life-style, that protects
them from overstimulation. Simmel believed that urbanites
become "reserved" (1969:55) and socially withdrawn, adopt-
ing blasé attitudes toward their daily encounters. This adaptation, he felt, led to relations that he observed taking on the
character of "secondary" associations—a preponderance of
purposeful, functional, superficial, and transient ties.

Robert Park, who was greatly influenced by Simmel,
wrote an important essay on the sociological implications of

the urban environment. Though he did not directly address the issue of population density, he further clarified some of the points raised by Durkheim and Simmel. In "The City" (1915 [1969]), Park suggested ways to study the social and psychological effects of the ecological segmentation of urban society, which is directly attributable to population density. He also asked social scientists to examine the ecological separation of daily human activities (e.g., home from work), and the possible impact that this correlate of urban density had on local social ties, mental health, morality, and the range of social relations individuals may have. The social issues he explored greatly influenced the writings of his contemporaries in urban sociology, including Louis Wirth.

In perhaps the most important statement on urban life and the effects of density, Louis Wirth's "Urbanism as a Way of Life" (1938) attempted to merge the psychological "overstimulation" arguments of Simmel and the sociological "segmentation" arguments of Park. One of Wirth's major tasks was to define what made urban life unique. He decided that three factors—population size, population density, and heterogeneity—were what separated the city from the country. Given these attributes, he posited certain social and psychological consequences of great importance for the study of urbanism. Like his sociological predecessors, Wirth postulated that density led to diversification and role segmentation. He envisioned a highly differentiated social organization existing within an urban context of limited space and astronomical daily contacts (i.e., overstimulation). Wirth (1938:15) believed that the consequences of conducting dissimilar roles in an atmosphere of intrusion and interference (i.e., too many social contacts) were numerous. For example, such a situation created a high probability of conflict, exploitation, friction, frustration, and competition for scarce resources, including space. The high "role" densities and "social" densities were viewed as leading to a pattern of social relations best described as "abnormal," or superficial, functional, and transitory in contrast to personal, intimate, and communal ties. Wirth posited not only social consequences but also personality disorders (e.g., anomie, loneliness, social withdrawal), which in turn led to the further deterioration of interpersonal relations. The key to Wirth's thesis seems to be that *close proximity with no social ties* (cf. Wirth, 1938:14) is a dangerous, omnipresent trait of urban life. Given diverse role performances, scarce spatial resources, and great potential human contact, the logical effect of urban crowding is thus both social and psychological: mental stress and social conflict, leading to the disturbance of necessary and important (i.e., intimate) social relations (see reviews in Fischer, 1972, 1976).

Contemporary Theories

As interests grew in recent times, new theoretical works emerged on the effects of high population density. Some of these clearly represent continuities with issues raised by earlier generations of social theorists, while others take new directions or at the very least examine factors not considered before in detail. The new directions in particular raise questions about the applicability of general statements to particular kinds of residential environments. For example, I am concerned about what kinds of theoretical statements can clarify the impact of household crowding on families and what kinds of explanations are relevant to the urban context. However, I will hold most of my critical comments and contributions to the theoretical discussions for the summary section of this chapter, in the interest of providing an overview of recent influences that is an objective as possible.

Although research on crowded animals has played an important role in the study of crowding, it is not reviewed as a separate theoretical development for two reasons. First, I want to stress here interests that are more sociological and social psychological in emphasis. Second, to my knowledge no cogent statement has been developed that might be described as an ethological or biological approach to studying density. Rather, my impression is that the "popular" issues mentioned earlier led researchers to investigate whether or not crowding leads to "stress" without formulating a more complete theory.[6]

Continuities Stanley Milgram, in a widely noticed paper entitled "The Experience of Living in Cities" (1970), has extended and perhaps modernized the work of Wirth (1938) and Simmel (1905 [1969]). Using the language of systems theory (see Meier, 1962), Milgram argues that the excess of social stimulation in the crowded urban environment produces "overload," and this necessitates coping mechanisms (e.g., blocking or filtering social interactions). In agreement with earlier theorists, Milgram finds even successful adaptation troublesome, since the "cost" of alleviating overstimulation is the development of a life-style centered on aloofness, impersonality, dehumanization, superficiality, and segmented relations (see also Keyfitz, 1966).

This article by Milgram has not only encouraged other psychologists to seek physiological proof of stress-producing crowding (see Aiello et al., 1975) but also led others to investigate the concept of overload and reactions to overstimulation more carefully. For example, Cohen (1977) envisions high density as a condition that creates high attentional demand, and he thus argues that the so-called adaptations are actually mental exhaustion from responding to too many social cues rather than attempts to limit involvement. Altman (1975) has considered crowding as a problem related to regulating social contacts and conceives of an "optimal level" of social stimulation, somewhere between too many contacts (i.e., crowding or lack of privacy) and too few contacts (i.e., isolation or too much privacy). Milgram's work has also led to Sundstrom's (1975) theory that overload (i.e., unwanted intrusions and interferences) due to crowding may cause various stress reactions that in turn produce either positive or negative responses or both, depending on the situation. The aftereffects of inhabiting dense, overstimulating environments are also being reviewed (cf. Sherrod, 1974; Valins and Baum, 1973), and the possibility exists that the energy needed to cope with crowding may cause gradual decreases in subsequent performances (see also Lipowski, 1975; Evans and Eichelman, 1975).

In sociology, the social effects of the urban environment have come under increasing review despite disciplinary

biases against such investigations (see Michelson, 1976:3–32).
The debate "for and against" high density urban living can be
seen in two speeches by prominent sociologists. Philip
Hauser, in a presidential address to the American Sociological Association, entitled "The Chaotic Society" (1968), spoke
of the causes of urban social disorganization in terms of the
revolutionary trends toward population explosion (size),
population implosion (density), and population diversification (heterogeneity). Like Wirth (1938), Hauser sees these
three factors as leading to personal, social, and organizational
problems in modern urban society. The results of this "social
morphological revolution," according to Hauser (1968:8), can
be seen in the increased conflict among groups in American
society, the breakdown of the community and primary
groups as sources of moral direction, and the dehumanization and increasingly utilitarian nature of interpersonal relations. Hauser sees all these as determined at least partly by
the tremendous increases in population density in urban
America.

Amos Hawley, in his presidential address to the Population Association of America, entitled "Population Density
and the City" (1972), came to the defense of high densities in
an effort to counter the ideas of Wirth (1938) and Hauser
(1968) and the recent speculations on the effects of crowding.
Aside from the fact that he finds the relation between crowding and social pathology weak, Hawley argues that the densities of central cities have been steadily declining (1972:527)
while urban social problems have been on the increase. What
is more important, he believes that Americans should look at
the positive aspects of high density in conjunction with the
negative ones, in order to determine whether the costs out-
weigh the benefits. While not denying that social friction and
communication overload may exist, Hawley looks at the tremendous opportunities dense living conditions offer for
low-cost information exchange and interpersonal associations. In addition, density may provide speedy access to a
wide range of services and facilities (1972:525–26). Though
not discussed by Hawley, it is obvious that high density

environments may also conserve energy (e.g., in transportation), which is a major issue today. Density is thus viewed by Hawley as an "economizing factor," which has brought about all the blessings of modernization and industrialization (1972:523), though admittedly some of the curses as well. To Amos Hawley (1972, 1971:132–35), as to the well-known planner Jane Jacobs (1961:200–21), the opportunities created by high density living override the costs of urban crowding. In addition, they view the problems associated with population density as overrated and in some instances misrepresented.

New Directions   One of several factors not closely examined by past psychological and sociological statements on density is the role of *environmental design,* which I alluded to in the section on practical interests above. According to Mitchell (1974), the social effects attributed to density might actually be blamed on the intensity of space use (i.e., congestion), or the ways in which a particular sociospatial environment is designed. Others argue that if Americans would only design their high density environments correctly, they could alleviate the social and psychological problems associated with crowding and actually use high density to decrease social isolation and thus the prevalence of pathology. For example, Oscar Newman (1973) argues that crimes in high density apartment complexes can be prevented if buildings are designed to maximize feelings of "community" and thus increase participation in the surveillance of community property against outsiders.[7] This line of reasoning was also expressed by Jane Jacobs (1961), who believed that high density streets (e.g., Greenwich Village) are safe, since people in such neighborhoods survey them from ground floor and upper story apartments. Jonathan Freedman (1975), borrowing ideas from both Jacobs (1961) and Newman (1973), asserts that if architects design high density buildings so as to encourage and even force interaction among propinquitous individuals (e.g., provide lounges and soft drink machines), there will be friendliness and a sense of community. On the

whole it seems obvious to a number of practitioners and
academicians that design factors may *aggravate* existing space
shortages and that environmental manipulations may en-
hance inhabitants' abilities to interact with others and to conduct relations with less interference (see also Sommer, 1969).

Comparable to the concern for the physical environment
in which crowding takes place has been the attention paid to
cultural factors. In fact, there was little discussion of cultural
differences in experiences of or reactions to high population
densities in the sociological and psychological writings reviewed earlier. This raises questions about the generalizability and ethnocentricity of those arguments. Edward Hall, in
the *Hidden Dimension* (1966) and a number of other publications, provides one of the fullest accounts of how culture-
bound the use of space and reactions to spatial intrusions are
(see review by Baldassare and Feller, 1975). He argues that
different cultures socialize their members to expect certain
densities and interpersonal distances as "normal." Thus,
Latin Americans may like levels of density that North Americans find intolerable. In cities, where various cultures and
subcultures meet daily in dense settings, friction and misunderstandings are likely to occur, since varying definitions of
"appropriateness" cause disagreements and many groups are
competing for the use of limited space (Hall, 1966:165–68,
172, 173). Anderson (1972) has reviewed various aspects of
Chinese culture and family structure that seem to make possible high household densities with little social and
psychological stress. A recent review of several ethnographic
sources, including the classic work on family and housing by
Lewis Henry Morgan (1881), concludes that many societies
are able to live in what Americans would call high density
housing, largely because the social and economic structure
facilitates (or may even demand) the close living together of
community members (Mitchell, 1975). Thus, Mitchell considers many American housing standards and laws on density to
be culture-bound (1976). The moral of the "culture and density" notion is that the definition of overcrowding is relative
to the structural experiences of a specific culture. Further, the

social and economic characteristics of some cultures make them better suited to functioning at high population densities. Assertions that a particular level of density has a certain effect on all individuals would be unfounded given this perspective (see also Day and Day, 1973).

More recently concern has been raised that researchers do not pay close enough attention to the social situation in which crowding takes place. This would include a consideration of the purpose of the present gathering, the roles of each participant, and the rules that were brought into the setting or evolved through interaction. Social psychologists have argued that density may have negative effects only when it occurs in conjunction with other situational variables (cf. Zlutnick and Altman, 1972; Freedman, 1972a, 1975). For example, a crowded cocktail party may be an enjoyable environment for meeting new people, while a dense store may be a frustrating environment for accomplishing a limited but necessary task of living. Stokols (1972a, 1972b) believes that high density settings are not necessarily perceived as "crowded" and may not all have negative consequences. Individuals vary, for example, in their actual or perceived ability to control others' actions, to leave a setting, and to choose among actions they deem appropriate for their comfort (Proshansky et al., 1970; Stokols, 1976; Sherrod, 1974). The roles being performed in a crowded environment or the meaning a group attaches to a certain situation may either create opportunities for adapting to overcrowding or produce competition and conflict. These social situational arguments indicate, at the very least, that researchers should examine the social and psychological settings in which crowding occurs in order to understand the actions and reactions of individuals better. The number of interacting individuals (cf. Loo, 1973; Freedman, 1972a), their tasks (Desor, 1972), their relations to each other (Zlutnick and Altman, 1972; Mitchell, 1971), their psychological states (Stokols, 1972b; Zlutnick and Altman, 1972), the meanings they attach to a particular setting, and the importance of performing their roles in ongoing social interactions (cf. Wicker, 1974; Barker, 1968) should be

examined. The notion is that high density may be experienced more saliently at a given time and place than at
another.

As researchers consider different social situations, a distinction between crowding in the two types of residential
settings that are studied here develops: neighborhoods,
which are large public settings, and homes, which are
bounded, small, and private environments. This is important, because too often people have assumed that household
crowding is equivalent (in effects and responses) to urban
crowding. This could result (and in my opinion has resulted)
in the testing of hypotheses that are too general or inappropriate. In fact, very few theorists have tried to develop an
understanding of crowding in the home, which has been a
detriment to development of the area.

Stokols (1976) has helped to clarify the differences between perceived crowding in primary environments (e.g., the
dwelling) and its occurrence in secondary environments (e.g.,
neighborhood street, supermarket, train station). His work
remains one of the few discussions to guide researchers. The
distinction is between a setting in which a person performs
important activities in the presence of intimates (i.e., primary), and one that an individual inhabits briefly to participate in marginally significant activities in the presence of
others known more superficially (i.e., secondary). Drawing on
attribution theory, Stokols argues that crowding in primary
environments will more likely lead to stress and conflict,
followed by reactions by those able to usurp the space needed
to conduct important activities. To summarize, without fully
explicating Stokols's rather complex model, inhabitants of
crowded primary settings, as opposed to dense secondary
settings, take each others' actions more "personally" and are
more likely to react negatively to any thwartings, since the
goals they are pursuing in these environments are crucial
ones. Crowding in intimate environments is thus potentially
more troublesome for the individuals involved than is crowding in public settings.

In another article considering crowding among intimates, Dorothy Smith (1971) argues that houses with in-

adequate space create social strains among family members, because actors are attempting to enact roles and perform needed activities in a situation with uncontrollable intrusions and interferences. Competition for household space thus not only causes friction among family members but also sometimes leads to authoritarian mechanisms for controlling access to and use of this scarce resource (see Smith, 1971:65; Lewis, 1961).

Some social scientists have pondered the impact of household crowding on children. It is argued that overcrowding in the home increases the probability that children will lack the privacy they need to develop healthy personalities and will allow children access to and view of adult actions (e.g., sex, nudity) that they may not be mature enough to comprehend (cf. Merton, 1951; Plant, 1960). Others have expressed interest in assessing the strategies families adopt to overcome the negative consequences of limited dwelling space (Riemer, 1943; Morris and Winter, 1975). Making alterations in the dwelling, ordering activities in time and space, and readjusting family norms are all frequently mentioned options. The success of these adaptations in decreasing conflicts due to inadequate space and their consequences for particular individuals have yet to be fully explored.

At this writing, social psychologists involved in the study of crowding have indicated great interest in the concept of "control." Indications are that this development may have important implications for studies of high densities in general and household crowding in particular. For example, Cohen (1977) has conceptualized high density as a situation in which an individual perceives a lack of control over the environment. Supporting this perspective, Rodin (1976) found that children who experienced chronic household crowding developed "learned helplessness" or a general pattern of not attempting mastery over the environment (e.g., completion of complex tasks). Other works from this perspective suggest that people can overcome psychological difficulties associated with crowding if they believe that they have some level of control over their crowded surroundings (Sherrod and Cohen, 1977; Sherrod, 1974). Further evidence and more com-

plete explanations of this process are yet to come, in addition
to discussions of collective attempts to control situations and
the consequences of individual differences in ability to implement control.

All these theoretical discussions clearly indicate that
academic interests in density are keen. They are also developing a greater sophistication as the field emerges and more
explicitly defines problem areas and intervening or moderating variables. Gaps do exist in the logic and context of these
discussions, however, and throughout this book I will discuss
what is needed to better understand the characteristics and
impacts of household crowding and the dense neighborhood
environment.

Summary and Conclusions

The introduction to the study of crowding that I have
presented has focused on issues and concepts that have surfaced in public debates, practical fields, and academic circles.
The purpose was to extract some major themes from these
broad concerns. Further, my intention was to develop an understanding or a general orientation that can guide subsequent research on the human consequences of residential
crowding.

Since the present study is primarily designed to
examine social patterns and personal attitudes, discussions
were often directed to the impacts of household and
neighborhood crowding on the quality of family and community life. For instance, a concern voiced by many was that
urban crowding may result in a variety of problems related to
the livability of localities: difficulties in conducting meaningful personal relations; lessening of physical and psychological
well-being; weaker "attachments to place"; and more dissatisfactions with the residential setting. Household crowding was sometimes raised as a separate issue, particularly
when it was seen as a cause of problems involving members
of the family unit: increased hostility and friction among residents; adverse effects on children's personality developments
and relations with parents; deficiencies in mental and physi-

cal well-being; increased pressures on individuals to relocate; and decreased satisfactions with the residential environment.

The issues and problems sorted out of the above discussions motivate a search for theories to guide the development of hypotheses and later analyses. The orientations found in this chapter are presented here, along with my interpretations, revisions, and criticisms. More detailed discussions follow in later chapters; the intention here is to reject (or present as untestable) certain approaches, while abstracting and revising others for the specific purposes of this study.

First comes the issue of the *ethological determinism* of crowding effects, which has caught the attention of the public and has left its mark on many recent human crowding studies, as I demonstrate in later chapters. Rather than conduct a debate with ethologists on territoriality and related concepts, as others have chosen to do (see, e.g., Suttles, 1972), I will ignore that framework as much as possible. While the genetic tendencies of human populations may set the range of possible behaviors, my basic premise is that most explanations of social life should be dealt with in terms of sociological and psychological models. A long and rich history of such theories was documented in the section on academic interests above. Instead of viewing urbanites as beings subjected to the whims of overcrowding, like rats in crowded cages who are acting instinctively, I see most human beings as problem solvers who are *conscious* of the constraints that certain situations create (e.g., crowded residences) and who attempt to devise a *rational adaptation*, using the resources available to them. In later chapters I will further specify this notion. For now, suffice it to say that I reject ethological determinism in favor of an "exchange theory" approach (cf. Thibaut and Kelley, 1959; Blau, 1964; Homans, 1974), which posits that people rationally attempt to maximize rewards and minimize costs in their social lives.

The *cultural determinism* of crowding effects, correctly identified by the pioneers in the "personal space" field (cf. Hall, 1966; Sommer, 1969), is probably an important and valid approach, though one that needs further elaboration (see

Baldassare, 1978). Unfortunately, it calls for more complex theories and research approaches, along with more extensive data collection, and thus is beyond the scope of the research reported here. Cross-national comparisons of population densities and personal and social reactions to overcrowding are sorely needed in this field. However, because the survey data used in the present research are from the United States, and because cultural factors may influence crowding effects, the discussions, conclusions, and policy implications drawn from this book cannot be generalized beyond American society in the 1970s. I am actually assuming a certain degree of cultural homogeneity within the United States regarding values about and responses to residential crowding, and I am thus ignoring subcultural differences. Some evidence suggests that such differences exist, and thus my materials do run the risk of oversimplifying the American case. However, to do otherwise would be impossible, given the limitations of the survey data being used and the present lack of knowledge concerning subcultural spatial preferences in the United States (see Baldassare and Feller, 1975).

The strict environmental or *design determinism* of crowding effects, largely raised by practitioners and designers, seems overstated in my view. Certain spatial configurations may help facilitate interaction under special circumstances (e.g., in very homogeneous groups), or may dilute certain problems associated with high density (e.g., congestion). However, I have not been convinced by either the logical arguments or the data that design can create positive or communal associations or reduce the impact of high densities to insignificance. For example, I have taken issue elsewhere with Oscar Newman's (1973) assertion that high density in conjunction with good design can create community spirit, leading to large scale surveillance of property and thus decreased crime (Baldassare, 1975c). There are a number of other mediating factors in this chain of reasoning that could just as easily determine the end result; for example, a design that would make a potential criminal perceive that he was in view might reduce stealing or mugging without actually increasing communality and surveillance. In addition, I question some statements by Jonathan Freedman (1975) to the effect that, if high density buildings force social contact through design, greater neighboring and togetherness will develop. Overload theories and consideration of the social characteristics of the potential interactants would have to be carefully considered before such conclusions could be made. In this work, design factors are not considered significant elements that can explain away the effects of crowding, nor are they viewed as active agents in determining social behaviors and attitudes. Within certain limits, design can improve or worsen conditions that are associated with overcrowding, though on the whole I do not see design as a major factor to contend with in this analysis. Rather, in the remainder of this discussion and in the analysis that follows, I place primary emphasis on sociological and social psychological explanations of the human social behavior and personal attitudes that result from exposure to high densities.

One social psychological concept that seemed to be raised by a number of sources was that urban crowding can be characterized as "overstimulating" the individual—that it confronts people with more social contacts than they can properly respond to in their daily lives. The consequences are reported to be a lessened ability to conduct meaningful (i.e., nonsuperficial, intimate, frequent) relationships with others, a greater risk of psychological withdrawal, and a greater risk of poor mental health. I assume that the possibility of overload actually exists, and that individuals must adapt to overcome this condition. However, past accounts tend to exaggerate the facts and underestimate the abilities of most people to devise more rewarding alternatives. The prevailing idea has been that urban crowding affects individuals' abilities to conduct relations with others, since they must filter, block, and rechannel their social contacts to avoid overload. While overcrowding may cause overload, individuals need not suffer from the experience over time, nor do all of their relationships have to be affected. Urbanites can learn, through experience, to avoid social stimuli or decrease their receptivity to encounters and thus not suffer from mental fatigue. Further, they can choose to concentrate their time and energy on certain relationships and keep other associations at a minimum when their social capacities are being taxed. The notion I add is that they do so on the basis of the value or pleasure certain relations give them. As I discuss in greater detail later on, crowded urbanites in situations of potential overload decide, on the basis of costs and rewards, which social contacts deserve their full attention, which deserve less involvement, and which should be avoided totally or severely curtailed. Therefore, important and intimate ties are probably unaffected by urban crowding, while less rewarding and potentially costly contacts may suffer. This, in fact, may be why visitors to big cities feel that residents are unfriendly, while the crowded city dwellers may have as active and fulfilling social lives as others.

Sociological theorizing about urban density tends to emphasize that this factor is associated with increasing social complexity and role diversity. Popular and practical writings alike argue that high density neighborhoods are qualitatively different from low density neighborhoods. Some have argued that high density is good, creating diversity and opportunities, while others say it is bad, creating congestion, conflict, and ugliness. I argue that the quality of life in more dense urban neighborhoods, measured by resident satisfaction with various aspects of the environment, cannot be characterized simply as a favorable or unfavorable setting. Other things being equal, higher levels of neighborhood crowding probably imply both a wider range of services and activities and more congestion, competition, and environmental degradation. The issue of satisfaction with the neighborhood environment thus cannot be understood without examining the life-style sought by residents and the values these residents place on factors such as excitement and diversity versus regularity and predictability. At the very least, this indicates that people perceive both the costs and the benefits of their settings. Though crowded inhabitants might be less satisfied overall with their neighborhoods, the opportunities present may make these neighborhoods satisfying enough to induce the residents to remain. Then again, those who are forced to stay in high density neighborhoods because of economic necessity may also account for general comments concerning dissatisfaction.

It has been argued throughout that crowding has different impacts on individuals, as their activities, social situations, and social positions vary. For this reason, it is essential to distinguish between household crowding and neighborhood crowding. Surprisingly, past discussions of density did not typically draw a strong distinction between these two residential settings in terms of crowding effects. One obvious difference is that it is difficult to think of benefits associated with household crowding, or to think of any reasons why people would prefer overcrowded homes. There are not, for example, increased services to offset too many contacts, as there are in a high density neighborhood. In addition, while people can conceivably escape or avoid outdoor neighborhood scenes, how can they avoid contact in a setting filled with familiar people or shrug off intrusions and interferences when they occur in what is the most intimate and private environment (i.e., the home)? A different kind of adaptation emerges in high density homes, one that allows the family unit to function adequately using its own power structure (see figure 1). In other words, I am arguing that family members with power can determine how space should be used and who should use space at what time, thus limiting (through their legitimate abilities to make and enforce decisions) potential conflicts and interferences. Consequently there is an increased likelihood that residents will either be controlled or control others as space per person decreases. Since there are obvious discrepancies in power, some family members (e.g., children) may be more likely to suffer constrained social relations and reduced privacy from overcrowding, while others with more authority (e.g., adults) may be considerably less affected by household crowding.

It also becomes necessary to examine subjective and objective household crowding indices separately. According to

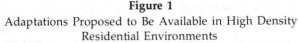

Figure 1
Adaptations Proposed to Be Available in High Density
Residential Environments

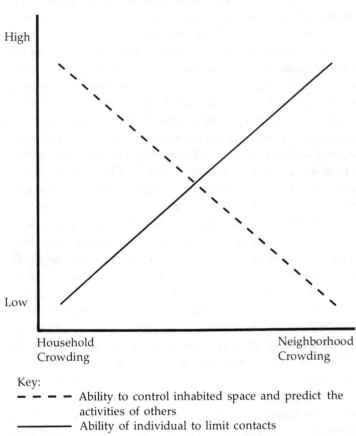

some authors, high density situations vary in the degree to which they are perceived as crowded and thus in the degree to which they have negative impacts on individuals. It is my position that this distinction is important, though for the study of residential crowding it is overstated. Certain conditions may make household densities more salient, and, in addition, perceived crowding may in itself be related to various kinds of environmental, social, and personal dissatisfactions. However, the nature of high densities (e.g., scarce space for many activities, overstimulation, social adaptations) are independently related to the social and attitudinal patterns discussed above and are not explained away by perceptual factors.

Finally, a position must be taken on the crucial topic of residential crowding and well-being (i.e., happiness, mental health, physical health, satisfaction with life). The orientation that guides my analysis has two parts: that adaptations to household and neighborhood crowding prevent severe stress in many or most cases, and that the present status of public health and sanitation in the United States (especially in urban areas) makes disease due to "contagion and crowding" less likely than would be expected by crowding researchers. In general, I have the notion that social position and economic status are more significant determinants of well-being than household or neighborhood crowding. While these statements hold for the general populace, those who experience crowding and lack control over space, or do not have the competence to adapt, or lack the desire to avoid overstimulation—perhaps children, or the mentally disturbed, or the poor and powerless—may experience greater deficits in well-being, since they may not benefit from the maneuvers others use to overcome high densities and overabundant contacts.

These are the basic topics I review in detail later and the ideas that guide my analyses of the national surveys. The general theoretical framework, sketched in this section, provides a launching point for the selection of data, substantive problems, and methodological approaches that follow.

2. Research on the Effects of Crowding: Design of the Study and Alternative Approaches

In addition to the variety of ideas about the effects of crowding reviewed in chapter 1, there are several techniques for studying those effects. Methods for seeking evidence of the impact of high densities are reviewed in this chapter. After evaluating the pros and cons of various research strategies, given the issues concerning residential crowding that were highlighted in chapter 1, I present the design of this study.

A comprehensive review of research findings will not be reported here. I considered such an approach inappropriate for several reasons. First the results of crowding studies take on more meaning as they are presented in the context of substantive issues, since these studies are typically narrow in scope. Therefore more complete discussions of empirical findings are given in later chapters that examine specific problems related to density. In addition, many reports have not been sufficiently concerned with residential crowding and thus their relevance to the present investigation is dubious or limited. Finally, review of a broad spectrum of the crowding literature would repeat the endeavors of several already in existence (see Altman, 1975; Sundstrom, 1977; Freedman, 1973; Lawrence, 1974; Fischer et al., 1975; Baldassare, 1978; Stokols, 1978).

The major task of this chapter, instead, is to examine critically the methods used in crowding research.[1] In particular, given the crucial questions raised about the impacts of residential crowding, which of the available techniques, data, and variables are appropriate for the present study? The issue of the relevance of data collected in different kinds of settings using various strategies thus takes on special importance, since the primary task of this book is to assess social patterns and personal attitudes in natural settings (i.e., neighborhoods and households).

Out of this fairly critical assessment of past techniques, I select an approach to conducting research on crowding that has hardly ever been used in the past. It combines information on residential environments with the self reports of attitudes and behaviors of those occupying the specific settings. I argue that this method is well adapted to addressing the major issues mentioned previously and that it is considerably more effective than the other approaches that are reviewed. Though the "contextual" method described here has numerous positive aspects, there are also limitations and problems with the way the approach is operationalized in the present study, and these are made visible. A review of the data sources, major variables, analytical methods, and hypotheses is then presented as preparation for or an overview of the empirically oriented chapters that follow.

Techniques Used to Study Crowding

In this section, I review in a very general way six research methods: nonhuman research, laboratory experiments, field studies, housing surveys, areal comparisons, and contextual studies. Some methods have provided very sound and useful information on specific crowding issues, while their ability to answer other kinds of questions is more limited. I am most concerned here with attempts to generalize from certain kinds of data and research settings to urban and household environments. Unwarranted generalization has been an unfortunate and all-too-common problem in the literature to date. If there is a bias in my account, thus, it is in the direction of overcriticizing techniques. This is because others have sometimes not seen how ill-suited some methods were to examining the complexities of human behavior and attitudes under conditions of residential crowding.

Nonhuman Studies

Some investigators who have expressed concern with human crowding have conducted research on animal populations. Others have used results from nonhuman studies to build models of human reactions to space shortages or even as general evidence of the effects of crowded living conditions. Nonhuman crowding studies have been conducted with captive animals in laboratories (Calhoun, 1962) and with animals in their natural habitats (Christian et al., 1960). They usually involve formal and informal observations of health and behavior over extended periods of time.

Although such crowding studies may provide valid information about the reactions of a specific group of animals in the study setting, statements about urban populations based on such data seem unjustified. However, a variety of factors account for the trend of making such statements. Animal researchers who are often confronted with challenges about the human relevance of their studies may present a very general picture of the similarities between humans and nonhumans, without fully considering the implications of human logic, mobility, and social structure. This view may lead to unsound statements concerning the similarity of crowding responses in humans and animals. Also, because of difficulties in the use of human subjects, researchers often use animals to gauge responses to extreme and chronic crowding. The unfortunate result may be an association drawn between animals in a very unusual setting and humans in their homes and natural neighborhoods. The most obvious reason that studies of animals have attracted widespread attention is probably the appeal of "ethology" in both scientific circles and among the general public. The ideas of ethology have led many to believe that humans share with other animals certain innate tendencies, including adverse reactions to territorial invasions and overcrowding. I do not profess to be an expert on animals, so I cannot discuss the relevance of such research to biological and medical research. However, as a social scientist I am disturbed by attempts to relate the human condition to crowding in the animal kingdom. Thus, the topic is given some critical exploration here (see also Fischer and Baldassare, 1975; Fischer et al., 1975).

First of all, no imaginable human habitats approximate the conditions under which crowded animals have been observed. Since the settings inhabited respectively by humans and animals differ in so many respects, any attempt to compare behaviors across species would be improper. Second, generalizations about innate crowding responses across *all* species seem dubious because few genetic traits (especially behavioral ones) are found in precisely the same form in all animals. If genetic predispositions to react to crowding are not found in all species, then it is uncertain which animals share responses with others. For example, do rats and humans have similar innate behavioral tendencies? Obviously, this is an assumption that calls for careful cross-species testing, not extrapolations from one mammal to another in greatly varying situations. In addition, evidence from our closest "relatives," nonhuman primates, suggests that they exhibit varying responses to high densities, depending on environmental and social conditions, and do not all seem to react in a specific pathological way (Baldwin and Baldwin, 1973a, 1973b). Finally, animal studies provide poor guidance for human crowding researchers because the ability to develop complex strategies and adapt to difficult environmental circumstances, which separates humans from nonhumans, is underrepresented in their extrapolations from nonhuman subjects to urbanites. Decision-making capabilities and sociocultural factors preclude the possibility of considering only the programmed aspects of human behavior, even in crowded settings.

The major reason for not accepting this strategy thus is simple: It ignores sociological and psychological concerns that appear to have much relevance to the impact of residential crowding on social patterns and personal attitudes. If animal crowding studies were based on social psychological theories, which to my knowledge they have not been, perhaps they might point to processes worthy of investigation at the human level. Animal research that did consider sociological and psychological theories, however, would still demand carefully conducted replications at the human level before one could make accurate cross-species generalizations. In brief, people must be studied directly in order to determine the effects of residential crowding on them.

Laboratory Experiments

One method that avoids some of the criticisms leveled at animal studies is the "crowding experiment." In essence, psychologists who searched for the pathological reactions cited by Calhoun (1962) and others, could actually herd humans into small rooms and carefully observe them under controlled laboratory conditions (see, e.g., Freedman et al., 1971, 1972; Griffitt and Veitch, 1971; Ross et al., 1973; Aiello et al., 1975). Not all experiments were influenced by the assertions made in animal research, since some had a narrower and more practical focus, such as the amount of space and size of groups needed for healthy and successful space travel (e.g., Smith and Haythorn, 1972). The studies that concern me the most are those that attempted to replicate animal crowding studies and, in some cases, apply their findings to urban environments. Too often, such research lacked an appreciation for the limits of the particular method (i.e., experimental) and data. Therefore, I will pay particular attention to the ability of this approach to provide dependable information about some of the major issues in the debate about residential crowding.

An objection that I have often voiced about crowding experiments is that they have been obsessed with the results and factors measured in animal studies. In other words, they have attended more to replicating Calhoun's (1962) findings than to developing a separate set of concerns about human crowding. For example, experimenters would place groups of the same size in small and large rooms (or groups of different sizes in the same amount of space) and then measure the amount of stress (e.g., galvanic skin response) or hostility (e.g., reported affect, competition during games, facial expressions). Rarely (though with greater frequency in recent studies) did experimenters consider group adaptations, the social positions of participants, or the influence of social situational perceptions. This approach has led to a series of studies that tell little about human responses to crowding and much about the present influence of "pop ethology" on experimental social psychology. Ironically, most laboratory studies have not even shed light on the replicability of Calhoun's findings, since for various ethical and practical reasons the conditions in which they have been performed and the data that were collected are in no way comparable to the original animal studies.

Because experimental research was often influenced by descriptions of crowded animals, some of the work clearly has an atheoretical flavor. With few exceptions (see Sherrod, 1974; Stokols et al., 1973), experimenters have not tested the kinds of theories that were discussed in the first chapter. This is unfortunate, since the controlled laboratory experiment could be a means of examining some of the assumptions underlying sociological and psychological theories of residential crowding (see also Baldassare and Fischer, 1977).

Added to the lack of theoretical guidance is the more common complaint of experimental research: that the extreme artificiality of the laboratory makes generalizations to the "real world" in most cases difficult. For example, experiments typically involve individuals who are not representative of the general public and who are often alike in age and background (i.e., college students). Subjects are also supposed to be complete strangers, and they interact for a very short period of time (e.g., a few hours). They are often forced to "behave" in extremely contrived settings (e.g., playing games) under the surveillance of others who are evaluating their actions (i.e., experimenters). For the researcher interested in residential crowding, these conditions raise questions of relevance. For instance, how can one say that inhabiting a crowded laboratory room for a short amount of time is similar to living in a crowded house or neighborhood? Further, can the actions of a homogeneous group of strangers in a laboratory—actions that are not very private in nature—be related to behavior in a crowded family or among neighborhood acquaintances? The answers range from a resounding no to a very conditional maybe.

Clearly, there should be more direct ways to test theories dealing with residential crowding. Because of both the unusual circumstances surrounding the laboratory experiment and the inadequate specification of theories relevant to urban conditions, this approach has in the past failed to elucidate the social and psychological processes at work in dense residential settings. Though experimenters have sometimes made the leap from results in the laboratory to life in the city, I will take a more cautious approach and judge this method inappropriate for the present purposes.

Field Studies

Some social psychologists, disillusioned with the artificiality of experimental settings, have observed people in "real" crowded environments (cf. Loo, 1972; Hutt and Vaizey, 1966; Ittleson et al., 1970). These so-called field studies occurred in settings such as schools, hospitals, prisons, dormitories, and urban public places. In some instances, the researcher manipulated aspects of the environment (e.g., room or group size), while in other cases no experimental manipulations were made before systematic data collection. Though this approach was suggested in order to avoid the problems associated with experiments, it instead generated several new methodological dilemmas.

Field studies conducted on the effects of crowding were also heavily influenced by animal studies. In fact, the method itself approaches that used by ethologists. Unfortunately, this also meant that investigators sometimes went into the "real world" with a checklist of pathologies that closely approximated the factors measured in nonhuman studies. Because of this influence, with few exceptions until the present (Stokols et al., 1977; Rodin, 1976; Cohen and Spacapan, 1977), this work as a whole has shown little concern with theoretical development. Though data from field studies may be collected under less contrived conditions than experimental data, the theoretical concerns addressed in most of these studies were still far removed from humans operating within their habitats.

In addition to their similarities in shortcomings with other approaches, field studies create some unique problems as presently practiced. First, it is difficult if not impossible to get permission to observe "normal" people in their everyday settings. Thus, populations with unusual characteristics (e.g., criminals, mental patients, institutionalized individuals) often become the subjects of field studies, and this has not aided knowledge about the reactions of the majority of people to crowded settings.[2] Second, even when it is possible to obtain representative samples, it is difficult to get individuals (particularly adults) to "be themselves" as they are observed and evaluated by social researchers. Third, observational studies present serious questions about the generalizability of findings. Usually, observational studies very thoroughly examine one or possibly a few settings. Unlike social surveys and experiments, which ask for responses from subjects, field studies often force the investigators to wait for the behaviors that are being coded to occur. Thus, in observing a crowded environment, the researcher may learn a lot about how people react to social overload and spatial constraints in a particular social situation. What, if anything, though, can be said about the relations of those findings to crowding in other groups and settings? Obviously, a narrow sample of subjects and settings would limit the researcher to discussing only social processes in the observed social environment or others very similar to it. Unfortunately, some have assumed that field studies are naturally addressing larger urban issues, a factor that I am afraid adds further confusion to the study of residential crowding.

Field studies of crowding have a distinct advantage in their "in vivo" character. They also might be the best approach for carefully studying reactions to crowding in specific settings. Observations, or ideally field experiments, might thus be best suited to detailed analyses, exploratory research, or specific policy questions concerning an intervention in a particular crowded environment. This method should be encouraged for those purposes. However, such studies also have an important set of disadvantages, most notably a lack of control over extraneous factors. In addition, it may be difficult to extend their findings to other settings and groups. For properly testing general propositions about residential crowding, thus, I find field studies often too narrow in scope, too uncontrolled to be reliable, and too unrepresentative to reveal valid and generalizable data.

Housing Surveys

Despite evidence that I have thus far presented to the contrary, social scientists have in fact studied individuals in residential settings that vary in space per person. For example, one strategy is to examine the attitudes and reported behaviors of individuals and then associate these data with in-dwelling densities (cf. Mitchell, 1971; Gasparini, 1973; Chombart de Lauwe, 1961; Wilner et al., 1962). Another approach is to look for relationships between building densities and the social behaviors and attitudes of the inhabitants of those structures (see Bickman et al., 1973; Newman, 1973; Valins and Baum, 1973).

Most studies of this sort depend on interviewing or questionnaires, since direct observations or experimental interventions are usually not feasible. This research is thus based on people's verbalized accounts of their relationships, their environmental conditions, and their well-being, rather than their actual behaviors or environments. Further, in the case of the family, one individual usually acts as a spokesperson for the beliefs and actions of the entire household. Despite the known unreliability, for example, of parents' reports of children's behavior (cf. Yarrow, 1963, 1968), no attempts to date have been made to interview whole households in crowding studies.

Housing surveys have given us some of the best evidence we have thus far about the effects of the *immediate* residential environment on social behavior. For example, through this method, researchers have documented preferences to move and familial difficulties in a large number of randomly selected overcrowded homes. Unfortunately, so many household surveys concerned with crowding have been conducted outside the United States that an assessment of the research findings may result in cultural misinterpretations, or perhaps the data are not relevant to the American situation. The surveys were sometimes more exploratory in nature and possessed only vague theoretical rationales. Thus, they may lack an appreciation for the special nature of the home environment or may not be sensitive to searching for special kinds of adaptations or types of people who may be more vulnerable to the effects of crowding. The information compiled to date thus provides only clues and not answers to many of the issues that have been raised about household crowding.

In reviewing the benefits and limitations of this approach, it should be noted that housing surveys by nature ignore the setting outside the immediate residential environment. Studies of residential crowding must also consider the neighborhoods in which dwellings are located. In other words, while housing studies provide useful information about the effects of in-dwelling densities, they do not address sociological and psychological issues concerning the densities of urban areas or the combined effects of household and neighborhood crowding on attitudes and social patterns.

Areal Comparisons

Several social scientists have stressed the study of urban crowding rather than examining the impact of household densities on individuals (cf. Factor and Waldron, 1973; Levy and Herzog, 1974; Galle et al., 1972; Schmitt, 1957, 1963, 1966; Freedman, 1972b). They have done so by using an approach made popular decades ago by urban sociologists at the University of Chicago. The "ecological approach," as it is often called, usually compares several areas (e.g., census tracts) within one city, with regard to their social characteristics, living conditions, and ratings on various social and psychological factors.[3] Urban crowding studies have often compared neighborhoods of varying population densities (e.g., persons per square mile, percentages of overcrowded homes) in relation to the levels of social pathology they possess (e.g., crime, fertility, mortality, mental admissions). In the end, the research points to an association (or causal link) between urban crowding and social or personal disorganization. In other words, a search is made to see if crowded neighborhoods can be defined as more pathological in character.

The major problem with much of this research is that, with few exceptions (see Winsborough, 1965), these social scientists have also bypassed sociological and psychological explanations of residential crowding. Instead, they too have searched for a black plague common to mice and men. Like studies using other approaches, then, this work also tells little about crucial issues and much about popular assertions about the effects of crowding. For example, while few theories I reviewed earlier are concerned with the effects of urban crowding on fertility rates, tuberculosis rates, mortality, or the size of welfare rolls, ecological studies of crowding have measured such factors.

Serious complaints can be lodged against the areal comparison per se as a strategy for examining crowding issues. First, there is the inherent problem associated with the use of ecological data: the individual is ignored, since the data are in an aggregate form (i.e., a group statistic, such as tract median income). Statements about individuals living in crowded neighborhoods cannot, or shall I say should not, be made when using such information (see Robinson, 1950; Clausen and Kohn, 1954). Since almost all the issues concerning household and neighborhood crowding involve its effects on individuals and personal adaptations, this method seems to approach the problem from the wrong angle.[4] Highly aggregated data also tend to obscure individual differences in responses that may be caused by variations in social position, life-style, or attitudes.

Another problem with this approach is the reliability of the data used to measure "pathology." Deviance rates are not usually collected with equal zest in all parts of a metropolitan area, nor are they easily accessible and visible in all neighborhoods. Certain characteristics of an area, perhaps even the population density (Beasley and Antunes, 1974), may make it more likely for crimes to be seen and reported. It is also well known that poor people with mental health problems are commonly admitted to public institutions, while wealthier individuals with those problems may choose private hospitals or psychiatrists (Hollingshead and Redlich, 1958). The former become statistics, while the latter are unrecorded instances of "pathology." This fact becomes particularly salient in light of the fact that residential crowding may correlate with low economic resources. The issue of self selection of residences also presents doubts about the ability of the areal approach to provide reliable answers. Differences among urban areas may exist merely because of the kinds of people who choose to live in particular settings, and not because of the effects of residential environments (e.g., neighborhood crowding) on individuals.

Overall, my assessment of the areal comparison approach is less than enthusiastic. While the independent variable that interests me (i.e., neighborhood crowding) is used, certain aspects of the dependent measures are not satisfactory for my purposes. The data are highly aggregated, sometimes unreliable, and often irrelevant to sociological and psychological concerns about crowding. Though areal comparisons are relatively easy to collect and interpret, they tell precious little about the direct effects of residential crowding on an individual's family relations, psychological states, environmental preferences, and social patterns.

Contextual Analyses

Recently, a promising union of ecological and survey data has occurred—one that offers special relief from many of the shortcomings of past crowding studies. Spurred by the lack of attention to individuals in ecological studies and the lack of concern for the urban milieu in housing surveys, a new method has emerged to bridge the micro and macro levels of analysis.[5] The basic "contextual approach" is to conduct interviews on social patterns and attitudes (e.g., family life, residential satisfaction, friendships, reported well-being) in various parts of the metropolis, while including objective information about the neighborhood environment (e.g., census tract data) as part of the data collected on individuals. Thus, a few crowding researchers have actually been able to talk about the direct effects of *dense urban environments* on *the social behavior and attitudes of individuals* (cf. Kasarda and Janowitz, 1974; Baldassare, 1977, 1975a, 1975b; Booth, 1976; Michelson and Garland, 1974; Davis, 1975; Lansing et al., 1970).

My belief is that this approach is most appropriate for studying the effects of residential crowding. Data on the individual and the urban environment are directly examined, and this process helps avoid the pitfalls of indirect and inferential arguments from micro-environments to macro-environments. Since sociological and psychological theories on crowding are concerned with human beings' actions and adaptations to the settings they live in, it seems best to use contextual analysis. Such an approach is also needed when crowding in the home and crowding in the neighborhood are jointly assessed (see Booth, 1976; Michelson and Garland, 1974).

There are a number of problems associated with contextual analyses of crowding effects, however. First, most studies have been in only one metropolitan area (e.g., Detroit, Toronto).[6] The difficulty with this is that the particular history of a given metropolitan area may dictate certain land use patterns and thus a particular range of densities. For example, a southwestern metropolis such as Los Angeles is characterized by relatively low density and sprawl, while a northeastern metropolis such as New York contains many more high density neighborhoods. Thus, the distribution of neighborhood densities in any specific metropolis may not be wide enough unless researchers take great care in choosing the urban area to be studied, which they usually do not. Contextual studies may substantially misrepresent associations between residential crowding and other factors due to these sampling problems. Besides, if some social scientists are correct in assuming that each city has its own "culture" and life-style (see Feller and Baldassare, 1975), then there is a need to examine not only one city, but several, in order to reduce this possible confounding effect.

Another problem involves the issue of self selection of residences, which was also raised in relation to areal studies. To reiterate, studies that use ecological data must recognize that effects apparently due to urban areas may actually reflect the kinds of people who choose (or are forced) to live in certain places. Thus, a crowding study that finds an association between population density and lack of community ties must consider the hypothesis that certain kinds of individuals (e.g., poor, young, or uneducated) who may have the reported social pattern irrespective of residence may also be more likely to inhabit crowded neighborhoods. Few studies have properly dealt with this issue in conceptual and statistical ways. Indeed, it may be difficult to fully factor out the effects of self selection.

An issue that has been relatively ignored by contextual analysis thus far has been the study of both household and neighborhood crowding. As I discussed in the first chapter, the issues that I am most concerned with are the effects of residential crowding on the community (i.e., neighborhood) and on the family unit (i.e., household). In order for this study to address many of the relevant questions properly, the density of both residential settings must be ascertained and examined. This can be done by gathering both census data and objective information about the physical characteristics of the dwelling during the interview. Some investigators may want to consider separately the effects of household and neighborhood crowding, as I do, while others may be concerned with interaction or joint effects, since crowding in one environment may limit opportunities or possibilities for escaping the effects of crowding in the other.

A practical problem that limits the use of contextual analysis is cost. In order to obtain an adequate distribution of neighborhoods and households, a large geographic area (perhaps even the whole country) must be sampled. Further, a large number of households and neighborhoods must be sampled to obtain the demographic variability among places and respondents that will allow the researcher to control for extraneous factors (e.g., income, length of residence, race, stage of the life cycle). The very nature of survey research also requires great technical expertise in sample selection, a tremendous effort in interview and interviewer preparation, machinelike precision in coding responses, and considerable work to transform the collected data into computerized form. All of these, along with the extra task of adding census or neighborhood data (collected from books or in the field) in contextual studies, produce a very expensive and time-consuming process. It is thus not surprising that so few studies of this sort have been conducted. My impression, though, is that the contextual approach is well worth the effort, particularly since it is the most satisfactory—perhaps the only satisfactory—method for studying residential crowding.

Thus, the best "fit" between residential crowding issues and methods seems to entail contextual analyses to study individuals' social patterns and attitudes. Surveys of households provide a representative sampling of individuals and allow the researcher to examine their reported behaviors and feelings. Ecological or objective data on residential conditions inform the researcher of the residential settings, including the levels of crowding, in which these actions occur. Assuming, then, that the *total residence* is considered and properly measured (i.e., neighborhood and household), along with information on the *total range* of activities and attitudes salient to the investigator's theoretical and practical concerns with residential settings, and that an *adequate sampling* of densities and individuals has occurred, this strategy is highly sensitive to answering a variety of questions about residential crowding.

Design of the Present Study

In chapter 1, I placed considerable emphasis on reviewing the orientations and concepts that guide interests in residential crowding. After sorting through a good deal of varied information, key issues were found, such as the impact of residential crowding on residential satisfaction, well-being, family life, and social relations. A theoretical bias was introduced that stressed (1) the ability of most individuals to choose environments that fit their needs; (2) a number of adaptations to overcrowding that should be available to many people; (3) important distinctions between household and neighborhood crowding that relate to the type of environment; and (4) relations among residents in these two settings. This chapter, on the other hand, searched among the available methods to find an adequate approach for studying the phenomena outlined earlier. After close scrutiny, I decided that a contextual analysis would best suit the present needs.

The task now is to present the specific data sources that were chosen from among the alternatives and to discuss why these surveys were selected. Then the variables, analytic (i.e., statistical) strategies, and specific hypotheses that flow from the available data are presented.

Data Sources

A search was made for secondary surveys that met certain criteria.[7] I needed, first of all, recent (i.e., post-1970) surveys in order to provide the most up-to-date account of Americans' experiences with overcrowding. For various reasons, national surveys seemed most appropriate for my purposes. Their samples are broad enough in composition and large enough in size to control for extraneous factors as needed. Data collected from a variety of metropolitan areas would also be more likely to provide a substantial range of urban densities and residential conditions. Information about the respondents' residential locales also had to be traceable. Data that could be used to provide information on in-dwelling densities (i.e., number of persons, number of rooms) had to be present in the interview schedule, and the survey research organizations had to have knowledge of respondents' 1970 census tract locations (and a willingness to provide such data). Also the survey items had to reflect interests similar to my substantive concerns with the effects of crowding: attitudes toward residential environments; the quality and quantity of social ties; familial relationships; and reported well-being. Very few surveys met all of these conditions. Most were too general or too specific, dealing with the investigator's issues rather than concerns with crowding that some future investigator might have.

One survey that met these specifications was the Quality of Life study conducted by social scientists at the University of Michigan Institute for Social Research (see Campbell et al., 1976). The interviews were administered during the summer of 1971, and involved a national sample of 2,164 individuals. Persons who were eighteen years old and over, living in households within the United States (excluding Alaska and Hawaii), were chosen through a multistage probability sampling procedure.[8] This included individuals living in a large number of Standard Metropolitan Statistical Areas. That group of respondents will be considered exclusively in this analysis, since neighborhood level data were not available for rural dwellers. The residential locations (i.e., census tracts) of the metropolitan respondents were obtained, in order to determine residential densities and various other neighborhood factors reviewed later.

The characteristics of this interview that make it useful for present purposes also present certain frustrations and disappointments. The items ascertain data on a wide range of life circumstances in a rather general fashion. Particular sections of the questionnaire are devoted to topics of interest to this study: the city and the neighborhood; housing; organizations; friends and family; satisfaction with life and well-being. Thus, while the Quality of Life survey dealt with most of the issues I regarded as crucial to the study of crowding, it did so in a fairly undetailed manner.

I therefore searched for another recent national survey. Preferably, the instrument would address these same issues, though in greater detail, keeping in mind the need to both validate and expand on the general items found in the Quality of Life survey. The Continuous National Survey conducted by the National Opinion Research Center, under a special arrangement with several federal agencies, was chosen. Actually, twelve separate national surveys (called cycles) were conducted beginning April 1973 and ending May 1974. Each cycle involved on the average about 660 respondents. Some questionnaire items were included in each cycle and others were added and deleted from month to month. In all, a national sample of 7,954 individuals was obtained, though the number of responses varied drastically (i.e., from 610 to 7,954) from one item to another because of the cycle approach. The sample was based on a selection of households and individuals using the National Opinion Research Center's multistage, stratified probability sampling of all persons eighteen years old and over in the United States (excluding Hawaii and Alaska).[9] This survey contained interviews conducted in a great variety of Standard Metropolitan Statistical Areas, some of which were not involved in the Quality of Life study. The rural residents of the Continuous National Survey are eliminated from the analysis here, for the reasons cited above. The survey's sampling points, or the residential locations (i.e., census tracts) of the respondents, were also obtained.

The Continuous National Survey has many items useful to my purposes in four of its cycles (3, 4, 11, 12). Some concerned respondents' general and specific attitudes toward their neighborhoods and were specifically requested by the Department of Housing and Urban Development, while a number of questions about housing conditions and psychological well-being were included by the National Opinion Research Center itself. These add depth and believability to the findings discussed in conjunction with the Quality of Life study.

Before I proceed with a description of the variables used and the rationale for using them, a few critical words about these national surveys are in order. First, as stated earlier, the questions are not as directly related to problems associated with crowding as I would prefer. In fact, some subtle issues, such as parent–child relations are not explored in a satisfactory manner for the present purpose. Also the samples were chosen with the individual in mind, and normal distributions of densities are not obtained, as might be possible with a specially designed sample. That particular skewing problem requires additional statistical tests, which are discussed in subsequent chapters. Though more skewed than I would optimally desire, the density distributions cover a wide range of residential crowding conditions, which is after all what I needed to study the main effects of household and neighborhood crowding. This problem, however, severely disrupted attempts to study "interaction effects." Despite these shortcomings, the national surveys chosen are very useful instruments for an intensive study of various aspects of residential crowding.

The Crucial Variables

The independent variables, the three categories of dependent variables, and the several control variables needed for the analyses are now introduced. The items selected from the present data sources reflect the theoretical concerns with density outlined earlier.

One of the two *independent variables* used here is the measure of household crowding available in both national surveys, namely persons per room. More accurate measures of the area in the dwelling, such as square feet per person, may have been more desirable. However, such data were not found in any of the existing surveys conducted in the United States. Some have criticized the persons-per-room measure and have suggested that household density should be corrected (or adjusted) for such factors as the age and sex combinations of children or the employment status of the adults (see Greenfield and Lewis, 1969). The decision to add these dimensions, in my opinion, is the result of cultural or normative assumptions. For example, is there certain knowledge that body size, opposite sex siblings, or daytime hours spent out of the home affect the problems associated with overcrowding? No. Thus these factors should be studied separately before they are incorporated into objective measures.

An additional issue is that persons per room does not

typically include the number of bathrooms, and some have argued that exclusion of this area of the home is not wise. While bathrooms may be an interesting place to study the effects of crowding and social interference, it would be necessary to separate one-bathroom dwelling units from multiple-bathroom dwelling units if such rooms are as important as some assert. Alternatively, I would suggest separate studies considering specifically the number of "persons per bathroom" as a fully researchable issue. For present purposes the number of persons per room is used, since it provides a universal index of spatial constraints in the home, and it includes large portions of the home in which a good deal of the social stimulation seems to occur. However crude, the measure chosen provides a comparable assessment of space in each person's home, while limiting possible biases and unsubstantiated assumptions.

The other independent variable is neighborhood density, operationalized as persons per residential acre within 1970 census tract areas. These data were obtained for both national surveys, after the research organizations provided the tract of residence for each metropolitan respondent. Neighborhood densities were calculated through very precise procedures by the National Planning Data Corporation.[10] Using census maps, staff members calculated the areas of tracts with an electronic planimeter, a very sensitive measuring device used by planners and geographers, which is much more accurate than the hand calculations more often used by researchers. Using detailed land use maps provided by localities, they then eliminated nonresidential lands from their calculations of the residential acreage within the tract. This excluded such land uses as industrial buildings, institutions, highways, and large open or unused areas. Then the numerators (i.e., number of persons within the tracts) were coded from the 1970 tract data provided by the United States Bureau of the Census. The ratio of persons to residential acreage within the 1970 census tracts, or what will be referred to as *neighborhood density*, was calculated. While this ratio is more exact than many other measures, it does not reveal, for example, respondents' experiences in their more immediate neighborhood environments as a block level measure of density would. In the final analysis, I decided that a block measure involved too small an area, since "neighborhoods" seemed to be conceptualized as an area of several blocks or miles, both as an independent variable (theoretically) and as a dependent variable in the national surveys. Besides, block data consider only the people on one block and do not account for people living across the street (i.e., the fact that blocks face each other). I also rejected a measure of neighborhood density based on dwellings rather than people, since the present theoretical orientation stresses social contacts rather than land use patterns. Finally, it must be mentioned that neighborhood density is most accurately described as a measure of nighttime density, since it involves only residents and does not account for those who may visit or leave the tract during the day. Of course, given the theoretical emphasis on potential contacts, a more accurate measure (e.g., average daily neighborhood density) would be desirable, though it would require considerable effort. In using neighborhood density I am making two assumptions: that the residents of a given area comprise a substantial part of what the individual considers the number of potential contacts in the neighborhood; and that nighttime densities of areas are to a considerable degree good predictors of relative differences in average daytime densities among areas. In all, the neighborhood density measure I have chosen seems to be a fairly dependable indicator, particularly when considered against gross density (persons per square mile), which in no way accounts for variations in land use within a tract.

Another comment must be made about the measures of household crowding and neighborhood density. They are mainly considered as interval variables, rather than ordinal or nominal, since the analysis here does not attempt to define overcrowding. Instead, my concern, rather, is with the significance for social patterns and attitudes of experiencing more or less density. At times, though, I collapse variables into categories for special purposes, doing so cautiously and with full explanations of the procedures. Also, this study considers only metropolitan respondents; since my interest in neighborhood density could be pursued only where tract data were available, those respondents living in rural households had to be excluded for the sake of comparability. Nonmetropolitan areal data below the county level of analysis are not readily available; in addition, they are delineated as "minor civil divisions" (i.e., political in nature) and are thus not comparable to tracts.

The *dependent variables* are grouped into three broad categories, reflecting substantive issues of residential crowding. First are the perceptions and reported levels of satisfaction with the residential environment. For various theoretical and practical reasons further explicated later, the perception of crowding (e.g., overcrowding, congestion) is an essential factor, since it not only reflects the individual's experience of crowding but may also temper subsequent responses. Reports of satisfaction with the dwelling (desire to move, dwelling satisfaction) and the neighborhood (location, condition, safety, transportation, services) are used because they contribute substantially to the debate on the costs and benefits of high density living. A second kind of dependent variable is concerned with quantitative and qualitative aspects of individuals' social relations. Questions concerning the frequency and intimacy of social contacts with individuals not living within the same dwelling (e.g., friends, neighbors, relatives, strangers) provide needed data on the effects of overload created by neighborhood density and household crowding. In order to examine the effects of limited space in the home on the role performances and uses of power among intimates, items reporting the relations between spouses (e.g., arguments, companionship, understanding) and among parents and children (e.g., problems, satisfaction) are also examined. Finally, dependent variables that measure reported well-being have been chosen for this analysis. Fortunately, items on this topic were plentiful, allowing for careful consideration of this issue of primary importance. Good measures of well-being are available in both surveys, though especially in the Quality of Life study (e.g., nervousness, happiness, general life satisfaction, loneliness).

Residential crowding, as one might guess, often occurs in conjunction with other social factors (e.g., poverty, ethnicity, youth),[11] and certain attitudes and social patterns are more common among some kinds of people or places than others. A well-designed crowding study must partially solve this sort of problem by using carefully selected *control variables* to account for extraneous factors through multivariate statistics. Since I am specifically dealing with both the actions of individuals and the characteristics of urban areas, both kinds of "noise" in the data had to be considered. Examples of individual and ecological control variables are: median tract income; percentage of black population within the tract; renter versus homeowner status; individual's stage of the life cycle and length of residence at the current address; individual's income; and individual's education.[12] The choice of control variables is determined by the particular substantive issues that are analyzed. The basic strategy, however, is to eliminate factors that may distort associations between crowding and the dependent measures.

The Basic Analytic Scheme

The significance and size of the relationships between the substantive items and the measures of residential crowding are assessed through statistical procedures that I have tested and developed in previous research on neighborhood density (see Baldassare, 1975a, 1975b, 1977). The present study involves several different dependent variables and both household crowding and neighborhood density, and thus it requires a description of the somewhat complex statistical approach.[13]

The process begins with bivariate analysis, or more specifically the examination of zero-order correlations and their significance levels. Observing the associations between

the density, dependent, and control variables provides preliminary evidence for hypotheses and helps to sort out the
items that demand further scrutiny. For the most important
items discussed in relation to the three substantive issues, the
correlational analyses are supplemented by cross-tabular
techniques. This is done to search for possible curvilinear
relationships or for possible "threshold effects" that would
not be visible otherwise.

The research next takes on a multivariate character,
relying substantially on various regression techniques. Extraneous factors are accounted for by examining the partial
correlations between the density variables and the dependent
variables. The remaining significant relations undergo "con-
servative tests" through a series of stepwise regressions
meant to assure, as much as possible, that the findings are due
to density per se and not other factors. For example, a series
of control variables are entered into the regression equation
before the density variable. Also, in subsequent equations
the numerators and denominators of the density variables
(e.g., persons, residential acreage) are included in the regression equation before entry of the density ratios (e.g.,
tract residential density) to ensure that the effects of density
are not "explained away" by the number of persons or the
amount of space alone. The logarithms of neighborhood density and household crowding replaced the actual residential
crowding measures in subsequent equations, so as to ensure
that the findings were not distorted by the skew of the independent variables. In discussing these crucial tests, I will
highlight the findings by referring to the percentages of
explained variance, the beta weights, and the significance
levels of the independent and control variables in the regression equations. These data provide dependable indications of
effects of density on social patterns and attitudes, and they
allow comparisons of the strength of density with the
strength of important social and physical factors in the respondent's world. In essence, though, the major purpose is
to assess the unique effects of density by eliminating as much

of the "noise" created from other factors as possible. This is a problem that has not always received careful attention in crowding research.

The Guiding Hypotheses

These general hypotheses, which will be tested in the following chapters, evolve from the orientations presented as a "guide" in chapter 1 and the data on hand as reviewed in this chapter. They are introduced here in order to give the reader an overview of the study that will follow. In the substantive chapters, the rationale for these hypotheses will be explored in detail before they are tested with the national survey data. At the end of the book, I evaluate the success of the approach taken here. The hypotheses involve the three major categories discussed earlier: the residential environment; social relations; and well-being.

Environmental satisfactions and perceptions concern attitudes toward the dwelling and the neighborhood. The ideas I have presented on the effects of neighborhood density on residential satisfaction are guided by sociological discussions of the structural changes produced by increased crowding. The hypothesis I present is that *neighborhood crowding is perceived by residents as having both positive and negative aspects*. For example, the services available to residents of more dense neighborhoods may be more diverse, accessible, and plentiful, yet the neighborhood environment itself is probably heavily used and thus less pleasing aesthetically, keener in competition for services, and less attractive as a place of residence. This irony of modern urban life, I postulate, is readily perceived by residents of crowded neighborhoods.

Discussions of household crowding highlight the difficulties faced by intimates who are forced to perform important activities in limited space. *Household crowding is thus perceived by most people and labeled as dissatisfying* due to the presence of social strains and personal annoyances. Since crowding in the home probably has few redeeming qualities for anyone, though it is probably worse for those who lack equal access to space because of their low social status, *it can be a major reason why people prefer to change residence.* These negative attitudes are not "explained away" by the perception of being crowded. In this analysis, higher levels of household crowding are considered more unbearable and undesirable in and of themselves, since overcrowding produces too many social contacts and the need for spatial and social regulations (i.e., a loss of freedom for some or all in the home).

The topic of *social relations* has produced a concern that potential contacts, including unwanted or uncontrollable encounters, increase with more residential crowding. The coping response to this overload, according to past arguments, was a "turning off" and "tuning down" of all relations. I propose that reactions to potential overload are more specific, rather than global effects on the quantity and quality of interpersonal relations. In other words, *individuals maintain their important relations* (e.g., friendships, kinships, voluntary groups) *under conditions in which they cannot respond to all contacts, such as high neighborhood density.* Therefore, if social energies must be curtailed to protect the individual from overload, this will occur largely in the realm of superficial and transient contacts. *Potentially less rewarding contacts* (e.g., encounters with strangers, neighbors, new people) *are thus subject to less input from individuals faced with the necessity of limiting social stimuli in crowded situations.* The assumption is that the effects of neighborhood densities cannot be successfully avoided without social adaptations and that coping mechanisms have consequences that go beyond the neighborhood and influence behavior in specific kinds of encounters in a variety of settings.

Household crowding is a special kind of social situation and therefore one cannot expect it to produce effects similar to neighborhood density. The key to adapting to the home condition is for the individual to obtain and use space for personal needs. Such an ability is related to the power the individual has over others in that setting or how likely one person is to usurp space in a highly competitive situation and limit the movement and activities of others. In the home, for cultural and situational reasons, parents can legitimately use force or coercion against children to do just that. The result is that *adults obtain the household space needed to conduct social relations "as usual" even in crowded dwellings.* Perhaps children's relations with siblings and peers may be affected by household crowding, though unfortunately the present data do not allow an adequate test of that idea. In addition, while perceived crowding may be associated with dissatisfying interpersonal encounters, it will be difficult to point to the independent impact of that survey item, since a respondent's complaints about one domain in life may lead to complaints about another, in a blanket (i.e., response set) fashion.

Relations among family members are of substantial concern in this book, since they are primary in nature and occur within the dwelling. First, I assume that *neighborhood density has no impact on family life.* Individuals protect these relations from the effects of social overload at the cost of others, because these relations are most essential. Therefore, my attention is turned toward the effects of household crowding on family members or intimates. A shortage of household space could conceivably lead to two states of affairs: intrusion on and interference with important role performances, or the ordering of space use and activities by the use of power within the dwelling. In either case, *the result of household crowding is conflict and strain on spousal and parental relations. The quality of spousal relations will thus be affected by crowding,* since adults must either exert efforts to control "traffic" within the dwelling or experience a loss of privacy. This effect is not strong, however, due to the abilities of most adults to adapt at least temporarily. *Children will probably be more affected than adults by shortages of dwelling space,* however, because of their weak social position and their general inability to thwart their parents' demands on them. As a result, *a larger percentage of parent–child interactions within the crowded home are authoritarian, because of the need to maintain "order." This situation probably makes family life less enjoyable for all.*

The hypothesis concerning the effects of residential crowding on the health and mental health of individuals is most straightforward: *Since most adults develop strategies and use their power to overcome the condition of social overload in the home and neighborhood, their well-being is largely unaffected by the objective and subjective densities of their household and neighborhood settings.* Certain subgroups may be marginally affected by residential crowding (e.g., children, the grossly inept, those who feel powerless), but since the major concern here is with the general population, it is argued that as a whole other social factors are more important determinants of well-being than is density.

Summary and Conclusions

This chapter has examined the methods used to study the effects of overcrowding. Several of the existing strategies have inadequacies that make them ineffective tools for the present purpose. In addition, I have argued that some research designs were guided by the wrong issues. Others considered a variety of important issues related to residential crowding, but the strategies used to collect data created methodological problems that leave me with a nagging sense that the conclusions may be irrelevant to humans in their residential settings. For methodological and conceptual reasons, I concluded that research findings of the past rarely provided satisfactory answers to the major issues in residential crowding.

Though "contextual analysis" is not free of criticism, my general conclusion is that it is the only direct way to study the impact of density on individuals' attitudes and social behaviors in residential settings. Using some past contextual studies as a guide, I devised a strategy to investigate carefully the important issues in discussions of crowding. The data chosen were gathered in recent, large-scale national surveys. Use of these sources helps to avoid the pitfalls of studying single metropolitan areas subject to unique land use patterns and densities. This study uses measures of both household crowding and neighborhood density, and further contains information on both the individual and the neighborhood. This allows for an account of the two levels of density in residential environments, while also controlling for the various neighborhood and respondent characteristics that may cloud the view of crowding effects. The data analyzed include environmental perceptions and attitudes, social behaviors, and psychological well-being. Since more than one national survey with these measures is used, the research findings are replicated and extended by the different data sources. Finally, the research is guided by hypotheses derived from sociological and psychological theories that have provided basic propositions concerning the effects of residential crowding.

This method and thus the research do have shortcomings. These have been referred to in various sections of this chapter and will be noted throughout the book. The method is, however, well suited to responsibly answering many of the key questions that have been raised concerning the general impact of residential crowding.

Part II—The Housing Environment and Family Relations

3. Cramped Quarters and Housing Discontent

The household is both a major arena for important personal activities and a physical setting in which a good portion of the day is spent.

Some "time budget" studies provide evidence of the large amount of time individuals spend in their homes. A recent national survey of metropolitan residents found that on weekdays Americans spend almost half of their time awake in the home (estimated from Chapin, 1974:102). Thus, about two-thirds of an average day for the average American takes place in the home. Of course, on weekends even more time is spent in the dwelling. While the number of hours at home varies with the age, employment status, sex, and income of the individual (see, e.g., Brail and Chapin, 1973), there is still little doubt that the home is occupied extensively by its inhabitants. This differentiates the dwelling from most settings, which are used transiently in the course of a day, by comparison. This also delineates the home as an important place in which to examine the impact of crowding on various aspects of housing satisfaction and perceptions.

In addition to the significance of the home in terms of time spent there, consider the importance of the activities done there, both in American society and in most other cultures. The household is where the individual seeks privacy from unwanted contacts, participates in important social activities, eats, sleeps, makes love, relaxes, and trains younger generations for adulthood. Appreciating the importance of this setting, Robert Merton (1951:181) stated: "With all the apposite observations, there still remains an important area for investigating systematically the social psychological consequences of [household] overcrowding." Starting with the empirical investigation of reported dissatisfaction with the dwelling, I hope to examine in the next two chapters some of the social and attitudinal consequences of high density in the home.

I begin with an overview of the national averages and historical trends in household crowding in the United States. This should not only set the stage for studying the effects of crowding in the nation's metropolises but also allow a comparison of the levels of household density found in the two national surveys described in chapter 2 with recent distributions of national crowding reported by the United States Bureau of the Census. Along with this validity check, I will carefully compare the rates and frequencies of household density found in the two surveys, in order to ensure that there is a statistical basis for discussing the replicability of findings. The next task is to examine, through a variety of statistical techniques, the correlates of household crowding. In other words, the important social, physical, and ecological characteristics associated with higher household densities are determined, and some statements are made about the relative importance of these variables and their combined abilities to predict persons per room.

After this empirical introduction to the variable *household crowding*, support for various propositions raised in the last section of chapter 2 will be examined. The major effort is to determine if, as expected, higher persons-per-room ratios are associated with more discontent with the dwelling and a greater desire to move. The place of residents' perceptions of household spatial inadequacies will also be examined in this context, even as an explanatory factor of dissatisfaction in its own right. Data from both the national surveys and earlier studies on smaller samples will provide the evidence for and against the effects of density.

National Levels of Household Crowding

A variety of misunderstandings seem to plague all discussions of overcrowding, even about a seemingly straightforward topic such as historical and empirical trends in national levels of household crowding. Admittedly, part of the problem lies in the existence of evidence that seems to evade common sense. For example, a widely read historical study, *Time on the Cross*, reported that the "typical" slave cabin in the South was more spacious than workers' dwellings in New York City at the turn of the century (Fogel and Engerman, 1974:116)! In order to ensure that readers do not bring misconceptions about household crowding in modern America with them through this analysis, I now review some available census materials on this topic.

The first task is to look at crowding in American households in historical perspective. Despite the recent concerns with overcrowding, some of which were reviewed in chapter 1, the number of American homes defined by the Census Bureau as overcrowded (i.e., 1.01 or more persons per room) has steadily *declined* for several decades. While one in five occupied dwellings was overcrowded in 1940, only one in twelve housing units was found in this condition in 1970 (see Carnahan et al., 1974; U.S. Department of Housing and Urban Development, 1974:166). Very dramatic changes occurred even in the period between 1960 and 1970; nearly 900,000 *fewer* individuals were overcrowded, a 3-percent decrease nationally (Taeuber et al., 1972:13). Several factors presumably accounted for this improvement, most notably a decrease in the number of persons per household, or the size of families, and an increase in availability and quality of affordable (particularly suburban single family) housing after World War II.

Yet I do not agree with those who complain about the emphasis that has been given to household crowding, especially those who point to the relatively small number of housing units that are overcrowded and the historical decline. After all, almost three and a half million of the approximately forty-four million metropolitan housing units are overcrowded (U.S. Bureau of the Census, 1972:54). By the best estimates I could find, the National Institute of Mental Health Demographic Profile (see Windle et al., 1975), approximately one-sixth of the American population experiences household crowding. When one considers further that a substantial portion of that population is children, it seems shortsighted to ignore this factor, particularly if there are theoretical reasons for believing that density in the home may have significant impacts on all or certain people. Further, I do not assume, particularly as a witness of skyrocketing housing costs in the 1970s, that the problem of household crowding will continue to disappear. It may, in fact, become more prevalent in the future.

Another fallacy that should be dispelled once and for all is that the metropolis, where the land density is highest, is also where household crowding is most frequently found. First, a close observation of urban ecology would probably reveal that high urban densities are not due to overcrowded homes but to increased land coverage and the greater number of multiple family dwellings found in metropolitan areas (see also chapter 5). Even if this misconception was based solely on the stereotype that metropolitan households are more often overcrowded than nonmetropolitan units, this clearly is contradicted by available census data. With historical consistency, a *larger* percentage of rural dwellings have been overcrowded than either total metropolitan, central city, or suburban households (Carnahan et al., 1974). While about 8.2 percent of the nation's housing stock was reportedly "overcrowded" in 1970, nearly 9.3 percent of the nonmetropolitan dwellings were classified as overcrowded, as opposed to only 7.8 percent of the units within Standard Metropolitan Statistical Areas (U.S. Bureau of the Census, 1971:16).

Since the analysis of the national surveys reported in this book deals solely with residents of United States Standard Metropolitan Statistical Areas circa 1970, a comparison of the housing densities of metropolitan America with those of the survey respondents is necessary. Table 1 presents the percentage of housing units in four levels of household density, both for the census and for the two national surveys. Note that the data from only cycles 11 and 12 of the Continuous National Survey (NORC) are used, since only the items from that time sequence are relevant to the interests in this chapter.[1] We can see that the median persons-per-room ratio

Table 1
Percentage of Metropolitan Housing Units at Different
Persons-per-room Densities:
Census Data and National Surveys

Persons per Room	1970 Census of U.S. Housing[a]	1971 ISR Quality of Life (N = 1,360)	1974 NORC Continuous National Survey (N = 852)
.50 or less	49.0%	49.0%	45.5%
.51–.75	23.5	24.8	28.9
.76–1.00	19.8	19.3	19.2
1.01 or more ("overcrowded")	7.8	6.9	6.4

[a]Figures derived from U.S. Bureau of Census (1972:54). Persons-per-room categories are those used by the census.

for the census and the Quality of Life (ISR) metropolitan housing units is very close to the lower category of .50 persons per room, while the median for the Continuous National Survey is somewhat higher.[2] While the basic comparisons between the national metropolitan surveys and the census data seem reasonably close, particularly in the case of the Quality of Life study, both groups of survey respondents underrepresent overcrowded dwellings. Several possibilities may account for this discrepancy. First, because both of the national samples were of individuals eighteen and over, the household crowding experienced by the entire American populace may have been underestimated (e.g., the unsampled segment of the population, those under eighteen, may live in more crowded quarters). A plausible argument could also be made that these figures represent the continuing decrease in the percentage of overcrowded households, though one would probably need to await the 1980 census for conclusive evidence.[3] A less interesting, but equally plausible argument could be made that differences are due to "sampling variability" in the national surveys, "corrections" on the basis of calculated "error" by the Census Bureau, or "missing data" from either source. Fortunately, though, the national surveys and the census figures appear similar enough to assume a fairly representative sample of American dwelling-unit densities.

Next, to go beyond the favorable percentages reported in table 1, the similarity between the distributions of household crowding in the Quality of Life study and the Continuous National Survey should be more carefully examined. This is because I place a good deal of emphasis on replicating and expanding findings through the data from both surveys. Table 2 indicates that the statistical properties have a substantial amount of similarity in a number of ways. An exception is the difference in the highest reported number of persons per room. This, however, represents the placement of a few outlying cases rather than an important difference in the distributions. It is also a factor that can easily be accounted for by conducting separate tests using the logarithm of persons per room rather than the actual ratio. Apparently, as noted in chapter 2, the similarities in timing and sampling techniques created a close comparability in the degree of encountered household crowding. It can thus be said with considerable confidence that the distributional properties of persons per room in these surveys do not hinder attempts to replicate results or compare and extend findings by using both data sources.[4]

Table 2
Statistical Distributions of Persons Per Room
for Metropolitan Respondents

Persons per Room	1971 ISR Quality of Life (N = 1,360)	1974 NORC Continuous National Survey (N = 852)
Lowest ratio	.10	.08
Mode	.50	.50
Mean	.62	.63
Median	.57	.60
Highest ratio	4.00	2.33
Standard deviation	.33	.31
Percentage "overcrowded" (1.01 or more)	6.9 %	6.4 %

Properties Associated with Metropolitan
Household Crowding

There have been very few empirical analyses of the factors associated with higher persons-per-room ratios. Earlier, I noted the lack of support for the notion that urban living and household crowding are integrally linked. Now I examine the validity of another popular stereotype: that poverty is the greatest determinant of crowding in the home. To begin with, an analysis of 1970 census data shows that the lower third of the income distribution in the United States does not have a higher proportion of overcrowded dwellings than the national average (U.S. Department of Housing and Urban Development, 1974:173). However, this subject is of greater complexity than it seems at first glance and deserves closer attention. I review findings from another study along with the data from the national surveys.

In the context of research on the effects of urban crowding in Toronto, Alan Booth and his associates investigated the determinants of persons per room (Johnson et al., 1975). They examined the predictive powers of occupational status, residential mobility, age, and nationality, using multiple regression techniques. They concluded that age was the best predictor of persons per room, not occupational status (all four of their measures together explained a little more than one-quarter of the variance). Adding the size of the household membership to the four-variable regression equation doubled the explained variance (i.e., to over 50 percent). This indicated that life cycle or family stage (i.e., age of adults and the number of family members living at home) may actually be the best predictor of household crowding.

I used the national survey data to compare the influence of socioeconomic factors (i.e., education, income, dwelling ownership) and life cycle (i.e., age, years in the dwelling). In addition, the explanatory powers of the number of dwelling rooms and number of household members were also reviewed. The latter two items (i.e., the numerator and denominator of household crowding) were used because number of persons seemed to represent another family stage measure (i.e., in most cases, families with several of their children living at home) and number of rooms was another indicator of socioeconomic status (i.e., the ability to pay for more household space). The statistical procedure used here was first to examine the simple (zero-order) correlations between persons per room and these seven factors and then to enter these factors into regression equations in prescribed ways.

Table 3 shows that the number of persons in the dwelling has the highest correlation with persons per room and alone explains about half of the variance. The life-cycle variables (i.e., age, years in the dwelling) are next in their strength of association with the number of persons per room. These factors explain little additional variance, though, when entered into the regression equation after the size measure. Indicators of socioeconomic position (i.e., income, dwelling ownership, and education) are, on the whole, weakly associated with household crowding. This analysis adds little credence to the belief that household crowding usually occurs among the poorest people. Clearly, the number of dwelling inhabitants and related indicators of life cycle appear to be the

Table 3
Factors Associated with Persons Per Room:
Zero-order Correlations and Explained Variance

	ISR (N = 1,360)	NORC (N = 852)
Zero orders		
1. Number of persons	.76	.70
2. Number of rooms	−.16	−.31
3. Age of respondent	−.40	−.28
4. Years in dwelling	−.26	−.22
5. Ownership of dwelling	.13	.22
6. Family income	.06	.01
7. Education of respondent	−.01	.13
Percentage of persons-per-room variance explained by factors		
Factor 1	57.7%	48.4%
Factors 3–7	19.6%	17.4%

major determinants of household crowding. These findings were in agreement with Booth's results.

Though poverty per se does not appear to be associated with overcrowding in the home, except for perhaps more extreme cases, the association between relative affluence and persons per room is somewhat clouded by analyses of the general population for several reasons. Family income is positively associated with number of household members, and it is this relationship that suppresses the association between persons per room and income (since household size is strongly related to overcrowding in the home).[5] The above-mentioned positive association is, to a good extent, explained by the very low incomes that some single person households (e.g., the elderly, the young and unemployed—see note 16 below in this chapter) experience in the United States. For example, if one were to consider only households with parents and children, as is done in a section of chapter 4, the relationship between high household density and low income is three times as high as it is for the general population. Further, while large, overcrowded families may not have total incomes that much lower than others, it must be remembered that their economic resources are spread thinner (e.g., they have more mouths to feed and need more rooms in their homes). Thus, to ignore the impact of income entirely would be a hasty, inappropriate judgment.

Along with the factors reported in table 3, I used the Quality of Life (ISR) data to see if any major macro-level factors were strongly associated with household crowding. These added little to the ability to predict the number of persons per room. For instance, measures of urbanicity (i.e., size and type of community) and tract-level data (i.e., income, race, and neighborhood density) explained little more than 1 percent of the variance when entered separately into a regression equation. Dwelling and building type were also weak predictors. In all, aggregate-level data were insignificant in comparison to individual-level factors.

Why do family size and life cycle seem to contribute so much to household crowding? First, I examined this relationship more closely through the ISR data. The fact that there were children present in the dwelling was found to be correlated at .90 with the number of persons in the household. Thus, I decided that the actual age of children or the period of family growth or formation may account for a high ratio of persons to rooms. A specific family stage variable in the ISR survey reported the respondent's marital status and the ages of the children in the dwelling.[6] These data indicated that more than one-half of those living in "overcrowded" homes (i.e., homes with 1.01 or more persons per room) were married, between thirty-one and forty-five years of age, and had children living at home. Most of the so-called overcrowded homes reportedly had children under five years of age present in the dwelling. The least dense homes were largely inhabited by older married people with no children living at home (i.e., they had never had children or their children had grown up and left). Naturally, persons living alone also accounted for a good number of the low density households.

Further, almost one-fourth of the young families who were surveyed (i.e., the respondent was married, was between thirty-one and forty-five years old, and had a child under five years old) experienced overcrowding. In summary, higher household densities should be viewed as determined largely by life-cycle position. Household crowding is usually brought on by the addition of children during the early years of marriage. When childbearing is completed, the family may find itself at its peak density. The degree of crowding then begins to diminish as children leave the home and as deaths occur in the family (e.g., widowhood). Of course, individuals may adjust their housing densities by moving to roomier quarters. The desire for mobility could be a factor that is facilitated by household crowding, but I would argue that actual mobility is constrained by life-cycle and economic factors. Young families often contain one or more adults in the early stages of career development, and thus they may not have the resources on hand to meet all their needs immediately. Obtaining appropriate household space may have to await salary increases, which come with greater occupational experience, or additional capital, which may accumulate through savings over time. The ability to change residence may be further constrained by a desire to keep children in local schools or by attachment to the neighborhood because of children's friendships. It may be some time, if ever, before the young family can meet its housing needs. Of course, if a satisfactory move never is made, relief from overcrowding occurs naturally with changes in the life cycle. Three events may facilitate this in the later middle years: adults may achieve greater financial capabilities as they acquire occupational experience; children become adults and leave the home; and children eventually become less dependent on their parents for financial support. This leaves most adults at the end of child rearing with more space and greater opportunities for residential mobility.

While the data do not allow a conclusive settlement of this issue, it appears that higher household densities are brought about by *life-cycle* factors. Particularly important factors are the age of parents and the number and ages of children in the family (see also Rossi, 1956:178). The economic resources of the family, though, seem to indicate this relationship in important ways, not so much in terms of poverty versus nonpoverty status, but in terms of some ratio of family income to family size. A more complete analysis of this problem would demand longitudinal studies that follow the "fit" between family resources, housing choices, and family size and composition over time. For now, I offer this finding and my interpretations so that, when significant relationships are found between household crowding and some dependent variable, the reader can keep in mind the kinds of people who are likely to be involved in the statistics.

Satisfaction with the Dwelling

Living in cramped quarters indeed seems less comfortable for individuals than living in a spacious home. Since people spend a great amount of time in their homes and engage in important activities that demand space and privacy there, a decline in dwelling satisfaction with increased household crowding was hypothesized in chapter 2. The strains and annoyances of competing for the use of space to engage in preferred activities, it was argued, limits the degree of positiveness a person will attribute to the residential environment. Whether individuals operating in cramped quarters "win" or "lose" in their attempts to obtain the space they need, the additional frictions, discomforts, conflicts, and frustrations caused by a struggle for space would make homes with high densities less liked than homes with fewer persons per room. For that reason, the adults in the sample who experience higher densities should report significantly more housing complaints.

The link between household density and residential satisfaction is, in fact, perhaps one of the best documented in the literature. Svend Riemer found this effect in research he conducted in the 1940s on housing adjustments and maladjustments. In a survey of Seattle residents, he found that "maladjustment" was strongly related to the number of persons per room in the dwelling. More powerfully than other factors (e.g., family size, income), household crowding accounted for a variety of dissatisfactions with the home (e.g., space, design or plan, and activities). From the data analysis, Riemer (1945) concluded that crowding is the *major* determinant of complaints about the home.

A study that examined the effects of improved housing conditions among a test group of former slum dwellers, and then compared their responses to those of a control group still in poorer housing, also provides evidence on this subject. Daniel Wilner and his associates reported that the Baltimore slum residents who moved to better, more spacious dwellings (i.e., the test group) reported less discomfort and dissatisfaction than did the control group. Furthermore, the safety from accidents apparently increased, as did the degree of individual privacy with more room in the household (Wilner et al., 1962). The problem with this study, of course, is that many other housing factors varied along with less crowding (e.g., newness, better design), making it difficult to determine the importance of the differences in household density in reducing dissatisfaction. However, because other housing studies reported elsewhere (cf. Chapin, 1951:166) conclude that dwelling-unit density is a significant indicator of expressed happiness with the home, one can probably assume that more space contributed significantly to the former slum dwellers' positive sentiments. Some evidence to the contrary has been reported (Schorr, 1970:323–24), but such reports are rare.

Other studies have used a precise measure of crowding, namely floor space (i.e., square feet) per person. Chombart de Lauwe's (1961:36) study of Paris households (which Americans should examine cautiously, since it was conducted in another culture) indicated a "threshold level" at which satisfaction with the dwelling declined rapidly. In fact, he tentatively specifies a point at which density begins to have a strong effect. For present purposes, the important finding is a significant relationship between space shortages in the home and discontent. Eoyang (1974) studied American university students living in trailers. The size and layout were the same for all these homes, so that variations in the number of household members accounted for differences in number of square feet per person. Again, negative ratings of the living space and general dissatisfaction with the dwelling were strongly associated with the higher levels of household crowding.

In addition, a few residential mobility studies have addressed the supposed link between household crowding, residential satisfaction, and moving (see the conceptual model provided by Morris and Winter, 1975). In the process, both Speare (1974) and Rossi (1956:79–80) have shown empirical evidence for the association between greater amounts of household space and higher levels of satisfaction with the home. The latter attitudinal variable is considered an intervening factor in determining mobility, a link that is irrelevant for present interests. Before turning to the national survey data, therefore, I can conclude that the evidence reported to date supports the existence of an association between household crowding and housing dissatisfaction.

The ISR survey contains several questions concerning the dwelling unit, while the NORC survey has only a few items on this topic. One item from each survey concerning satisfaction with the dwelling is examined here, basing the selection on similarity of tone and wording. The ISR question was: "Considering all the things we have talked about, how satisfied or dissatisfied are you with this house/apartment?" and the ranking was from one (completely satisfied) to seven (completely dissatisfied). The NORC question was: "All in all, how satisfied are you with living in this house/apartment?" and the ranking was from four (completely satisfied) to zero (completely dissatisfied). The NORC item was recoded for this study to order the ISR and NORC values similarly. Approximately half of the people who checked the "most dissatisfied" category lived at household densities greater than .75 persons per room; about 20 percent of the high complaints were from individuals living in overcrowded homes (i.e., 1.01 or more persons per room). For the ISR survey, the zero-order correlation between persons per room and the chosen household satisfaction measure was .25 (p < .001), while for the NORC survey it was .24 (p < .001). This provides a solid indication of the strength and reliability of this association.[7]

In order to assess the strength of this association carefully, certain extraneous factors were taken into account through the use of regression techniques (see table 4). The variables chosen represented items found in both surveys that could account for socioeconomic and life-cycle conditions: age, years in the dwelling, home ownership, education, and family income.[8] The five factors were entered in the first step, followed by household crowding on the second step. These controls did not significantly alter the size of the relationships (NORC: beta weight = .17; ISR: beta weight = .16), nor did they change the significance levels (p < .001 for both surveys).

The ISR survey had several other items that measured the degree of satisfaction a respondent felt about the dwelling. One question asked people how "good" their house or apartment was as a place for themselves (and their families),

Table 4

Beta Weights for Housing Discontent Regression Equations: NORC and ISR Comparisons[a]

	Household Crowding	Age	Home Ownership	Years in Dwelling	Education	Income
Dissatisfaction						
ISR—with dwelling	.16c	-.17c	-.19c	.02	-.02	-.02
NORC—with dwelling	.17c	-.15c	-.27c	-.13c	.04	-.09
ISR—with leisure	.05	-.10b	-.06	-.01	.07	-.08
NORC—with leisure	.08	-.06	-.06	-.01	.03	.01
Residential Mobility						
ISR—move	.12c	-.18c	-.24c	.06	-.03	.01
NORC—live elsewhere	-.01	-.23c	-.01	.04	.08	-.02
Perceived Crowding						
ISR—small rooms	.18c	-.11b	.01	-.03	-.01	.02
NORC—not enough rooms	.34c	-.12b	-.07	-.06	.01	-.04

[a] Beta weights and significance levels reported are for the final multiple regression equations.
[b] p < .01.
[c] p < .001.

ascertained on a scale of one (very good) to five (not good at all). While almost half the respondents rated their dwellings as "very good," only one-quarter of those at 1.01 or more persons per room did so. Two-thirds of the poorest ratings were in homes of .75 or more persons per room. Again, the relationship with household crowding was strong ($r = .28$, $p < .001$), even after controlling for the five extraneous factors mentioned earlier (beta weight = .21, $p < .001$). Toward the end of this interview, individuals were asked to sum up their feelings about the subjects on which queries had been made, including their present housing conditions. The item that asked how much satisfaction they received from this area of life (i.e., house or apartment) had a zero-order correlation with household crowding of .20 ($p < .01$), and an item that asked the respondents to assess the degree of dissatisfaction they received from the present dwelling was correlated with persons per room at .18 ($p < .001$) (both items were scaled from one to seven for high to low degrees of satisfaction). For the latter item, only 4 percent of those at 1.01 or more persons per room reported "no" dissatisfaction (19 percent for the total sample), while 24 percent reported at least "quite a bit" (12 percent for the total sample). The control variables had little effect on these associations and had no impact on the significance levels. An item in a nearby section of the interview, asking "how important is it to have a house or apartment that you like to live in," however, was unrelated ($r = .002$) to the household crowding measure (this dependent measure was scaled one to five, from "extremely important" to "not at all important"). The latter item may not really represent attitudes toward the present dwelling.[9]

The NORC and ISR surveys asked similar questions concerning satisfaction with leisure time. Since such a good deal of leisure time is spent within the dwelling, this was viewed as an indirect indicator of household satisfaction (see table 4). There were not very strong zero-order correlations between household crowding and leisure satisfaction (ISR: $r = .09$; NORC: $r = .11$) and these associations fell below acceptable significance levels for samples of large sizes ($p > .02$, when controlling for the five life-cycle and socioeconomic characteristics). Satisfaction with leisure time thus did not seem to be significantly related to internal dwelling-unit densities. In examining yet another ISR item concerned with activities at home, females did not appear to report disliking of housework more frequently as household density increased ($r = .02$).[10]

It is apparent from the analysis of the two national surveys that satisfaction with the housing environment declines as the number of persons per room increases (and neither transforming nor decomposing the crowding variable altered these conclusions).[11] However, there is no indication that household crowding has an impact on leisure satisfaction, housework, or general attitudes about the importance of housing. These latter items reflect more than the constraints caused by the physical environment, since they encompass deeper (or perhaps vaguer) psychological attitudes and may even reflect adaptations to overcrowding. While individuals report that high household densities provide less satisfactory housing, the extent to which crowding in the home is indicative of greater distress or disruption is yet to be determined. Perhaps an examination of preference for moving will indicate the importance of crowding discomfort and the strength of the desire to escape high density environments.

The Desire to Move

A preference to leave one's present dwelling is perhaps the strongest statement of housing discontent. Given the findings concerning the association between residential satisfaction and household crowding, it is crucial to determine if density in the home is so disliked that individuals would prefer to leave their current residences.

Several social scientists have previously made the conceptual link between household crowding and residential mobility (see, e.g., Morris and Winter, 1975; Sabagh et al., 1969; Simmons, 1968).

Of course, positing a relationship between household density and mobility usually assumes that a change has occurred in the ratio of people to space that requires a reassessment of the dwelling's adequacy. Since housing units do not typically shrink in size, it is evident that growth of the family in various sections of the life course (e.g., early marriage) creates the need for space. Rossi (1956) was one of the earliest researchers to examine the relationships between life cycle, household crowding, and mobility. A more recent study has also shown that the addition of children in the early stages of marital life creates a need for more household space and thus the likelihood of mobility (Chevan, 1971).

Before I proceed, it is useful to distinguish between two basic types of mobility: long-distance and short-distance moves. There is wide consensus that intracommunity moves are largely attempts to improve one's housing conditions, while long-distance moves are more often for job-related purposes (U.S. Bureau of the Census, 1966; Abu-Lughod and Foley, 1960; Simmons, 1968).[12] Short-distance moves, which are the most common, should thus be at least partially determined by attempts to improve the ratio of persons to household space. In fact, convincing evidence exists for the association between residential mobility and household crowding (Rossi, 1956; Chevan, 1971; Clark and Cadwallader, 1973; Speare, 1974; Michelson et al., 1973), especially in the less dramatic short-range moves.

This section examines only the preference to move, which is a separate entity from actual mobility. As an attitude, it does not always predict the occurrence of changes in residence (cf. Lansing and Ladd, 1964), since it tends to underrepresent the real-life constraints against actual mobility (Long, 1972; Foote et al., 1960). It is considered here the "ultimate complaint" about the dwelling (short of leaving). The basic proposition is that high density households should elicit this attitudinal response more frequently. The social frictions and various problems associated with managing activities within a crowded space will make remaining within the high density dwelling less appealing. Thus, the desire to move would reflect an interest in obtaining a lower density, with fewer annoyances, than the presently unfavorable ratio of persons per room. Empirical evidence for this assumption already exists (Stueve et al., 1977; Clark and Cadwallader, 1973; Speare, 1974).

One item from each of the national surveys concerned the desire to move from the present location. An ISR question asked: "At the present time, are you satisfied to stay here, or would you like to move to another house or apartment?" and was coded either "stay" or "move." The NORC item was worded considerably differently; it asked: "If you could live anywhere in the United States that you wanted right now, would you rather live in this (city/town/county) or somewhere else?" and was coded "here" or "somewhere else." The variation in these items can be reduced to the basic distinction between long-distance and short-distance moves. The NORC item is pointed more toward migratory preferences than moves to adjust housing inadequacies. Since the ISR question refers, though somewhat ambiguously, to a preference to move based on present housing discontent, this mobility item should be associated more with household crowding than the NORC item, which refers somewhat to the preference for moving to an area of the country for nonhousing reasons (e.g., climate, jobs, cost of living, recreation). Because of its emphasis on long-distance moves, the NORC item should thus not be associated with household crowding.

At densities of 1.01 person per room or more, half the ISR respondents wanted to stay and half wanted to move, while two-thirds of all ISR respondents wanted to remain at their present residences. Proportions of individuals wanting to live "here" versus "elsewhere" did not seem to vary with level of density for the NORC survey. The zero-order correlations indicate a significant association between dwelling-unit density and the desire to move for the ISR item ($r = .21$; $p < .001$) but not for the NORC question ($r = .05$; $p > .05$). The five control variables mentioned in the previous section were again entered into the regression equation before household crowding. In the final equation, the beta weight of persons per room for the ISR item is .12 (p < .001), while for the NORC question the beta weight is .01 (p > .05).

The prediction that the expressed preference to move was an indicator of dissatisfaction with housing density was thus confirmed, provided one accepts the conclusion that the NORC item was tailored to a special form of mobility with non-housing-related implications. Neither transforming nor decomposing the crowding variables altered these conclusions.[13] Perhaps questions addressed more directly to preferences for local moves due to housing factors would have been even more strongly related to the present dwelling densities. What remains unsubstantiated in this analysis is the causal role that household crowding plays in actual mobility. The answer to this issue could not be ascertained from the national survey data.

The Perception of Household Crowding

Another task of this chapter is to determine the degree of awareness individuals have of their present housing densities. It seems evident that people are able to perceive spatial inadequacies, but to what extent are spatial perceptions associated with persons per room? Do other factors play a significant role in defining a residence as too crowded? Later the independent effects of crowding perceptions on housing dissatisfaction are also explored. A continuing concern here is the degree to which subjective measures "explain away" relations between objective crowding and environmental attitudes.

"Subjective" crowding has attracted attention from several environmental psychologists (see especially Stokols, 1972a, 1972b, 1976, 1978; Stokols et al., 1973, 1977). Such studies commonly rely upon posttest attitude questionnaires in the laboratory. The argument has been made that it is subjective crowding (brought about by physical, social, and psychological circumstances) that determines behavioral responses and attitudes to dense conditions: high density is thus a necessary but not a sufficient cause of problems that are associated with overcrowding (Stokols, 1972a, 1972b).

In contrast, my view is that the objective measure of household crowding is the central explanation of dissatisfaction with the dwelling. This is because the actual number of persons per room creates an atmosphere of too many activities in too little space, causing friction and, for some, frustration. I assume, however, that people do perceive dense housing situations as "crowded," since these situations contain a less-than-ideal ratio of persons to available space. I am also in agreement with those who argue that other (social, psychological, physical) factors lead people to define a situation as overcrowded. I am skeptical, though, of the ability of current methods to enable a researcher to obtain a subjective crowding measure that is uncontaminated by other attitudinal dissatisfactions. In other words, the validity of some of these measures should be questioned. Perceptions are seen here as other expressions of housing discomfort rather than factors that explain away the effects of high density. Objective measures remain at the heart of the analysis, since they create certain physical and social constraints, not cognitions or evaluations, that lead to attitudinal and social adjustments. First, the little evidence available on perceptual household crowding is reviewed, and then the national surveys are examined.

Riemer's (1945) previously mentioned housing survey had several items ascertaining the adequacy of household space for various social and personal functions (e.g., sleeping, leisure, housework). Higher persons-per-room ratios were related to more complaints about the amount of household space. Compared to factors such as income, family size, and dwelling attributes, household crowding had the strongest impact on the perceptual variables. Recent non-American studies, one conducted in Hong Kong and the other in Toronto, also reported an increase in complaints about the availability of space in the dwelling in higher-density households (Booth and Edwards, 1976; Mitchell, 1971). The mobility study by Rossi (1956) that was reviewed earlier found associations between the amount of space per person in the dwelling and subjective crowding. Actually,

Rossi (1956:78–80) concluded that mobility was predicted better by the subjective indices than by objective housing conditions, placing his data in agreement with some of the ideas expressed by environmental psychologists.

The analysis of the national surveys depends on two items, one drawn from each survey, that differ somewhat in their format. The NORC question was worded: "Does this (house/apartment) have enough rooms to meet your household needs?" and required merely a yes or no answer. The ISR item stated: "Would you say that, in general, the rooms in this (house/apartment) are too large [1], too small [5], or are they about the right size [3]?" and was recoded as indicated in the brackets. Thus, one item refers to a shortage of rooms, while the other refers more to a shortage of space within the rooms themselves. Both, however, allude to spatial inadequacies in the dwelling and thus to the respondent's perception of household crowding. The number of individuals registering complaints about the lack of space should thus increase with density for either item. The "enough rooms" item (NORC) will probably be a better indicator, though, since the independent variable includes rooms. The "room size" item (ISR) would have been better suited if square footage had been used as the spatial measure.

The NORC item was correlated with household crowding at .37 (p < .001). A little over half of those living in homes of 1.01 or more persons per room reported that there were not enough rooms, while only about one in seven respondents reported this complaint. This relationship was basically unaffected by adding the five control variables to the regression equation before persons per room was added (beta weight = .34, p < .001).

The ISR item was associated at .24 (p < .001). Three-quarters of all respondents felt that the rooms were the right size, but only about half of those at 1.01 or more persons per room reported this. It also continued to be a strong relationship after controls were instituted through stepwise regression (beta weight = .18; p < .001). Predictably, though, the relationship was weaker than with the "enough rooms" question (see also table 4). In sum, a relationship between perceived crowding and objective household crowding has been confirmed using the two national surveys. Thus, another link between household density and discontent has been uncovered (and neither transforming nor decomposing the crowding variables altered these conclusions).[14]

It is obvious from the size of the correlations that other factors contribute significantly to the perception of spatial inadequacies. For the ISR item, persons per room explained only 6 percent of the variance, while for the NORC item the objective crowding measure explained 12 percent of the variance. Consideration of the five control variables in addition to persons per room still accounted for only about 7 percent of the variance for the ISR item and 16 percent for the NORC item. The additional explanatory power of those factors was mostly the result of family stage variables such as age and number of persons, which of course ultimately represent the presence of children in the dwelling (for the ISR data, the number of children in the home correlated with subjective crowding at about .2). The number of rooms in the dwelling was only weakly correlated with perceptual crowding in the ISR study (−.1) and, because of the difference in wording, was more strongly related to subjective crowding in the NORC study (−.2). I examined the relationships between perceived crowding and the "family relations" measures used in chapter 4, and the "psychological well-being" measures mentioned in chapter 7. Many of the zero-order correlations were around .1, and none was above .15 (i.e., they showed weak associations between subjective crowding and detriments in mental health and family life). In all, only the items concerning satisfaction with the dwelling were as strongly related to subjective crowding as persons per room, and those variables raise questions about causal interpretation and validity. Though subjective crowding is obviously linked to other factors, these factors may be idiosyncratic to the setting or poorly measured through these surveys, since other factors do not seem to have the predictive capacities of persons per room.

Next, does perceived crowding really account for dwelling discontent, which has thus far been attributed to objective crowding? The basic procedure was to take the dependent variables listed in table 4 and to use stepwise regression techniques. The five control variables were added first, followed by household crowding and subjective crowding. This was performed in order to determine whether the results attributed to the objective crowding measure would be explained away by accounting for the perceptual crowding item. The subjective crowding expressed by the respondents did not negate any results previously attributed to persons per room reported in table 4: the significant and insignificant findings remained in effect in every case. However, the thrust of this analysis does not lead me to minimize the importance of subjective crowding. This attitudinal measure was significantly related to dwelling discontent—in fact, more so than was objective household crowding in most cases. In addition, the measure of subjective crowding enhanced the ability to predict housing dissatisfaction when considered along with objective crowding and the control factors (i.e., it increased the percentage of explained variance in the final regression equations).

There is an explanation, which I alluded to before, that could account for the unexpected strength of effect for subjective crowding. Unfortunately it is only conjecture and cannot really be empirically tested. Since the perceptual crowding item is one of many questions concerned with housing attitudes, perhaps there is a "response set" effect. People tend to be consistent in their responses to survey items, and it is possible that those expressing displeasure with the dwelling or family relations also felt obliged to report dissatisfaction with its spatial aspects. The objective measure, since it is unconnected to attitudes and feelings, is not subject to this sort of bias. Thus, the greater predictability of the subjective measure could be spurious or merely an indication that it was one of many interconnected items concerning satisfaction with the dwelling and home life.

However, if subjective crowding measures are assumed to be somewhat dependable, several important propositions emerge. Since objective measures of crowding do not explain away the effects of subjective indices, it appears that perceived spatial inadequacies operate to some extent independently. Individuals thus respond to feelings of crowdedness due to social situational and psychological pressures, in addition to purely physical circumstances. In fact, stable attitudes about spatial inadequacy may be even more powerful indicators of dissatisfaction than persons per room. Further, the inclusion of both subjective and objective measures (i.e., physical, social, and psychological factors) in the examination of housing discontent added predictive power to the analysis. Apparently this allowed a partial analysis of the social situational and attitudinal factors that confound the existing implications of high density households. In other words, subjective crowding indirectly taps personal adjustments and maladjustments to crowding and social coping mechanisms that have succeeded or failed. This might explain why even those at the highest densities disagree on the adequacy of their spatial resources; it would also explain why subjective crowding is a stronger predictor of residential dissatisfaction.

In any case, it was shown that the impact of objective household crowding remains, despite a consideration of subjective or perceptual assessments of dwelling-unit density. The strain on activities in the dwelling that is brought about by more persons per room seems to create dissatisfaction for most residents. A high persons-per-room ratio means that individuals actually experience or fear breaches of privacy and social interference and must compete for limited resources. If they do not experience such discomforts, then they must develop strategies that allow them to coordinate their actions in time and space. In many cases this may mean restrictions and rules, which also limit the pleasure of inhabiting a particular residential setting. Theoretically and empirically, high density and an awareness of spatial inadequacies thus seem highly related to housing discontent.

Some Evidence for the Impact of Social Position

I argued in Part I and in previous works (Baldassare, 1977, 1978), that certain social positions may allow some individuals to have more control over scarce spatial resources and social overload than others. Those who lack the power to make and enforce decisions in the home, such as children, thus appear to be more vulnerable to the effects of household overcrowding than others. Unfortunately, this proposition could not be tested with the available surveys of adults. However, it might also be argued that the female suffers more from household overcrowding due to the position of women in society and the demands placed on the mother or wife in the home. In a recent study, Gove et al. (1977) provided a theoretical argument and data indicating that the "role position" of mother and wife places significant demands on women's privacy and creates high levels of social interference in overcrowded homes. Women in a crowded home would, according to this line of reasoning, suffer greater psychological and social deficits than would men. This section reanalyzes the data reviewed in this chapter to search for evidence of the impact of social position.

My approach was to examine all of the ISR items pertaining to attitudes about the housing environment, duplicating the earlier analysis but splitting the metropolitan sample into subgroups: husbands versus wives and males versus females. On the whole, differences among subgroups in the size of the zero-order correlations or the beta weights (i.e., in final regression equations with household crowding, age, length of residence, education, income, home ownership) were not very large for any item. Also, male–female differences were quite similar to husband–wife differences. The main findings, and in particular any suggestion of variations due to social position, are highlighted below.

The core item on dwelling satisfaction (i.e., the one reported in table 4) showed no noticeable variations by subgroup, nor did the item pertaining to "how good the dwelling is as a place to live." Surprisingly, the items that asked respondents how much satisfaction and dissatisfaction the dwelling gave them (i.e., the questions that were asked toward the end of the interview and involved various domains of life) showed some of the largest subgroup discrepancies, though not at all in the expected direction. Husbands had stronger correlations between dissatisfaction and persons per room (beta weight = −.24 versus beta weight = −.11 for wives) along with a somewhat stronger association between low satisfaction and high levels of household density (beta weight = .17 versus beta weight = .13). Perhaps this finding reflects a greater likelihood of males to complain while interviewed than females, or it may indicate greater willingness among males to face up to the fact that the dwelling has less than satisfactory impacts. Alternatively, it may reflect some internal dynamics of family life that neither Gove's model nor my own has accounted for thus far.

While no differences were found among subgroups in preferences to move, there were some minimal differences, in the expected direction, for both perceived crowding and leisure satisfaction. Wives at higher densities tended to complain somewhat more about spatial inadequacies than did husbands (beta weight = .16 versus beta weight = .11). Though the difference is small, it could reflect variations in social position: women may notice the lack of space more because they experience more social overload, thwarting, and loss of control over space; women may have greater demands placed on them to make do with existing space and to allocate spatial resources (e.g., among their children) because of their societal role, their weaker power in the family, and the greater amount of time they spend at home. In addition, though the effects of household crowding on leisure were insignificant for the total sample, wives tended to complain slightly more about the way their spare time was spent than did husbands (beta weight = .10 versus beta weight = .07). The size of these associations and the difference between the subgroups may be too small to matter; on the other hand, the differences can be viewed as some evidence to substantiate the claim that greater demands are placed on women as household density increases, due to both their role in the family and the weakness of their social position in relation to men.

In all, there is some support for the notion that social position, in this case husbands versus wives (or alternatively gender), has an effect on residential satisfaction. Evidence of substantial differences, though, was not found, and there were some indications that husbands actually reported receiving more dissatisfaction from living in an overcrowded home than did wives. The overall trends reported here do not, in my opinion, refute my earlier claims. Pertaining to the control of space and interactions, I would expect large differences in the impact of crowding between children and adults, while relatively smaller differences would arise between husbands and wives. In other words, the variations in social position that make the major difference between being able to escape social overload and to usurp household space and being unable to do so are along the parent–child dimension; the husband–wife differences are not as powerful.

Summary and Conclusions

This chapter began by stressing the importance of the household setting for the family and the individual. Viewed in terms of time spent in the dwelling and the importance of activities performed in the dwelling, the home is obviously of major significance. The importance of positive attitudes toward this setting and minimal complaints was thus stressed.

Some researchers have studied the effects of cramped quarters on housing discontent, though few have provided theories or examined in detail the process by which density impinged on enjoyment of one's home surroundings.[15] I argued that high density means that space is in short supply and high demand, and thus it could be asserted that household crowding leads to more competition, social conflict, and attempts to control space for important activities. Even if the family managed and organized the crowded dwelling (i.e., developed the best possible coping mechanisms), the control over space and activities that would be necessitated would cause that home to be less pleasurable than a low density home. So, whether or not adaptation occurs and whether a person has more or less power matters little here: living in crowded homes was assumed to be disliked and preferably avoided by all.[16]

The first empirical task was to examine trends and determinants of household crowding in metropolitan America. It was found that household crowding has been decreasing for decades and is not a particularly urban phenomenon, nor is it really an indicator of poverty. Rather, crowding is best described as a factor facilitated by certain stages of the life cycle, most notably the years of rapid family growth. Attention then focused on dwelling discontent, and the data showed with good consistency that the persons-per-room ratio correlates with dissatisfaction with housing. Using both the NORC and the ISR surveys, the persons-per-room ratio was associated with increased complaints about housing, the desire for short-distance mobility, and the perception of household crowding.[17] These relationships stood up under stringent controls (see table 4), even when considering subjective crowding. There was some evidence of greater reactions to crowding among wives than husbands; the proposition that children (i.e., household members with a low social position) would complain more could not be tested because of sampling limitations.

While various kinds of dissatisfaction with the residential environment itself were expressed, no impressive effects on housework and leisure were reported. Since adults were interviewed, and since they are more likely to obtain household space for their activities than their children, this may be why they reported no more "activity" dissatisfaction with increased household crowding. When it comes to displeasure with the environment per se, though, these adults expressed complaints more often at high densities. This indicates the presence of costs—even if not measured in terms of impairment of the ability to perform important functions satisfactorily—of living in a household with less space per person.[18]

4. Family Relations in High Density Homes

Because one primary concern of this book is social patterns—in particular, intimate relations—it is crucial to examine family life under dense housing conditions.[1] Social relations in dense neighborhoods are examined later, in chapter 6.

In this chapter the ISR national survey is used to assess two aspects of family life.[2] First, the effects of household crowding on spousal relations are examined, using the subsample of presently married individuals (N = 906). The concern here is with the effects of household crowding on behavior among intimates and attitudes about the "quality" of the marriage. Next, parenting activities in the dwelling are reviewed among respondents who have children under eighteen years of age living at home (N = 634). Here, patterns of parent–child relationships and attitudes about the quality of family life are assessed in a search for deficits among individuals with less household space per person than others.

Some of the limitations inherent in the present examination should be discussed. First, the data rely on information from only *one* individual per household. Basing an investigation of a collectivity on one member's word is always a risky proposition, and, as many small group researchers have noted, one with questionable validity. The respondent's assessment of dyadic or multiple exchanges (e.g., spousal, parent–child) may thus be far from an adequate and truthful characterization of familial relations. The other shortcoming involves the sampling of only *adult* household members in this survey. This is a particularly serious problem since I argue that some residents in the home (those with lower social positions, such as children) have a more difficult time adjusting to overcrowding than others, and most of the former were not sampled. This severely limits the ability to test specific hypotheses that seem quite reasonable and important. The items used may also be methodologically unsound. The researcher here is forced to rely on parents' unverified evaluations of their children and their own parenting behavior (see Yarrow, 1968).

These problems are not serious enough to warrant abandoning the present study of family interactions in dense homes, however. They serve as reminders of unresolved difficulties in collecting and analyzing dependable data on intradwelling relations in most studies, including this one. The shortcomings of survey data used by most crowding researchers become even more significant when, in the next section of this chapter, a theoretical model of family relations and household space is developed. Past empirical studies are reviewed for evidence favoring the interpretation presented here. The data from the ISR national survey are then used to test the proposition that family relations in crowded homes can be differentiated from behavior among intimates in less dense households. The proposition that weak social position entails more problems associated with crowding is partially tested by examining the responses of husbands and wives. Finally, the analysis raises a number of questions that are presented as suggestions for future research directions.

Crowding and Intrafamilial Relations: Searching for a Theory

In Part I, a rich collection of theories concerning the effects of urban density on individuals and communities was reviewed. Theoretical work on the effects of household crowding and family life has developed at a slower pace. In fact, this topic has rarely been explored in explicit detail by sociologists. I now discuss some past and contemporary thoughts on household crowding and the family unit. Later a framework for understanding family adaptations and the effects of household crowding on specific social positions emerges. The perspective stresses the importance of family social structure.

Several authors posit a direct link between household crowding and various kinds of pathology, though largely for poorly specified reasons. Jane Jacobs, in *The Death and Life of Great American Cities* (1961), defends high neighborhood densities, while claiming that urban social problems are really caused by household crowding. Aside from the claim that "everybody hates [household] overcrowding" (Jacobs, 1961:208), she offers no explanation to substantiate this powerful and controversial assertion. Of course, the supposed link between neighborhood and household crowding (an essential ingredient in her argument) rests on false assumptions (see chapter 3). Many condemnations of household crowding are also based more on common sense than theory. However, some social scientists have more carefully considered relations among family members within the crowded dwelling.

Robert Merton (1951) sensitized sociologists to the importance of household crowding, noting in particular that the home is where important family interactions related to socialization take place. Svend Riemer (1943, 1945) and F. Stuart Chapin (1951) provided some substance to discussions of the impact of household crowding on family life. They expressed concerns that family members come into contact with each other too often in crowded homes, and they assumed that this "overstimulation" would create (or increase) social frictions. Actually it is not contacts but unwanted contacts (i.e., intrusions and interferences into activities of an intimate nature) that seem likely to heighten feelings of interpersonal hostility and decrease positive sentiments among family members. These rather exploratory discussions did not examine any differential effects on individuals due to position within the family group but rather described an overall decline in the quality of family life.

James Plant (1960) studied crowded slum housing during the Depression and developed a keen interest in the unique effects of dense dwellings on childhood personality development. After studying youths from poor backgrounds who exhibited "pathologies," he concluded that overcrowding had long-term effects on children. Household crowding,

for example, increased the likelihood that children would observe adults in a variety of private activities (e.g., sex) that
they should be sheltered from at an early age, according to
Plant. Thus, the likelihood of being exposed to social stimuli
with which one could not yet maturely cope (i.e., a kind of
undesirable contact) was thought to result in abnormal personality development. Further, Plant argued that crowded
children were not always able to obtain the space and privacy
they needed for healthy ego development and as a consequence did not develop a strong sense of individuality.
Despite the questions one could raise about the limitations of
the case studies on which Plant based some of these views, he
should be credited for appreciating the impact of household
crowding on familial interaction patterns, and particularly for
his attention to the spatial needs of different individuals
within the family.

Recent discussions of crowding have paid limited attention to relations among intimates in the home. Daniel
Stokols's (1976) theory of primary and secondary environments is relevant to this discussion. His model clearly differentiates settings such as the home from less significant
environments in terms of individuals' ongoing performances
and their consequences. In the process, Stokols develops
several ideas that are potentially important for the study of
household crowding.[3] He labels settings such as the home
"primary environments," based on the significance of the activities that occur in them and the intimate nature of relations
among inhabitants. These are distinguished from settings
that are used transiently for specific and often unimportant
purposes, usually involving low levels of interaction and intimacy (i.e., secondary environments). Based upon Stokols's
analysis, some fundamental predictions can be made about
the character of interpersonal relations in a home defined as
"overcrowded": Individuals will perceive the actions of
others more personally (i.e., with more attributes of inten-
tionality) and will be more inclined to defend themselves
against attempts to thwart the important activities they are
engaged in at any particular time. Given a greater likelihood

of intrusions and interferences in the crowded home, and considering the special nature of activities and social relations there, more strain and perhaps even violence can be expected among crowded family members.

Dorothy Smith's (1971) analysis places a strong emphasis on "role performances" in the home. Though her approach is different from Stokols's (1976), she makes very similar predictions about the effects of household crowding on the family. Smith assumes that less household space leads to greater difficulties in performing important roles and preferred in-dwelling activities. These personal discomforts inevitably lead to interpersonal hostility among family members, even though Smith alludes to the fact that strategies are used to manage activities and reduce conflict in the crowded household. She considers the means available for reducing overall tension in the crowded home and refers to the "authoritarian father figure" (relying on data from Oscar Lewis, 1961) as a role that could substantially determine disputed claims for space and role performances (Smith, 1971:65). A theoretical paper on familial adaptations to residential discomforts (Morris and Winter, 1975) agrees with this interpretation, arguing that behavioral adaptations in the family must occur to counter spatial incongruities, unless residential mobility, reductions in personal expectations, or rearrangements of the household facilities are possible.

Two studies of Chinese households contain data on coping strategies used by families to overcome the effects of overcrowding. Anderson (1972), in an ethnographic investigation of Chinese families, found that households were capable of minimizing the disruptive effects of crowding through culturally specific adaptations or certain institutionalized values. The Chinese seem to have very formal rules for determining who uses household space, for what purpose, and for how long. Though their concern with budgeting this scarce resource seems explicit, Anderson makes little note of the procedure used to ensure adherence to restrictions on space use and activities. There is some discussion of the role of family members with power, namely the more senior males, as enforcers of household rules. Similar to the Latin family under dense housing conditions described by Lewis, the crowded Chinese family seems to follow a formalized system of space use, enforced by a culturally determined legitimate power structure within the family. Robert E. Mitchell's (1971) survey of Hong Kong residents can be viewed as indirect evidence of the success of these mechanisms, since he basically found no relationship between serious psychological stress and high levels of household crowding. Most methods seemed to have minimized the degree of social friction that could take place in the dwelling. Important exceptions noted by Mitchell (1971:27) were households comprised of both relatives and nonrelatives, since forced interactions in these settings seemed to have an impact on emotional stress (Mitchell, 1971:23–24). Perhaps, one could conjecture, the authority structure that normally controls the use of space in crowded Chinese homes cannot work effectively in these dwellings. When doubling up with nonrelatives occurs, there may be less agreement about who possesses the legitimate power to make spatial decisions and to control the flow of household activities (or what a fair solution would be). Given the lack of a clear-cut hierarchy, two problems could result: more arguments about the control of space at any given moment and increased social friction due to invasions of privacy and unwanted contacts. In addition, a social situation in which it is difficult to predict the duration and impact of role performances, as it is when living with strangers, may aggravate the effects of household crowding. Mitchell thus points out the special circumstances under which the so-called Chinese adaptation to household crowding may not operate.

During these and earlier discussions of household crowding and family life, a variety of explanations and predictions, ranging from "gut" feelings about the negative impact of household density to more systematic notions, have been raised. In the discussion that follows, I synthesize and expand on these various arguments. This synthesis involves a discussion of four interrelated events that I believe take place at some time or another in overcrowded homes: social frictions due to overstimulation; intrusions into highly personal activities by intimates; differential access to space and control over contacts due to intrafamilial position; and the use of power to control other people's activities and to obtain household space. Following this, I offer hypotheses that will be tested using the ISR survey and evidence from past research.

My model of crowding among family members begins with the same notion used in discussions of the urban density literature: that crowding within residential settings is a problem, since it can result in social overload. The special problem of too much contact within the home needs to be clarified, but I can begin with the simple fact that the number of daily encounters in this setting may be above "tolerable" levels. Dense dwelling units, when not alleviated by sociocultural adaptations (such as those presented by Anderson, 1972, and Mitchell, 1971), are thus potentially capable of creating the same problems as dense urban environments (e.g., the neighborhood): psychic overload, social friction, frustration, and interpersonal hostility.

To make matters even more difficult, the home is a social setting that does not allow the kinds of coping mechanisms available in larger urban settings (see chapter 6). Within the crowded home, people are not exposed to others of either "primary" or "secondary" importance to them. Rather, all individuals in the house may, in one sense or another, be considered "intimates." Because there are no casual encounters that can be turned off in favor of more rewarding relationships, the strategy of specialized withdrawal (see chapter 6) is not likely to be a rewarding one in the dense dwelling. There is another reason why this coping mechanism is unrealistic in this setting, and it has been alluded to in earlier discussions (Stokols, 1976; Smith, 1971). Because of potential and real costs, people cannot turn off their relationships with others in a crowded home: inattention to others may lead to intrusions into the individual's ongoing role performances and prevent the completion of important activities. There is thus little sense in ignoring encounters with household members, since these other individuals could still have a harmful impact on a person's preferred actions. In summary, specialized withdrawal is not a useful strategy against crowding (or social density) in the home: all of the relationships are of a primary nature, and there is a need to attend to potential social interference. This means that other methods must be available in order to control access to the self, obtain needed space, alleviate friction, and reduce personal frustration.

An important distinction between the urban world and the household environment, in my opinion, best explains how family groups can adjust to crowded dwellings. Within most homes, an ancient and important social system is in operation, namely the family. The activities of family members in the dwelling are thus at least partially determined by social control mechanisms. Not all family members have the same likelihood of being controlled or of controlling others, since status differences exist within the group. Typically, the power to influence outcomes (including decision making and the use of force) is in the hands of adults, rather than children, and perhaps fathers somewhat more than mothers. Two ideas have very special implications for the study of crowding within the home: that the family unit often has a legitimate structure for making and enforcing decisions, and that inequalities of an enduring and predictable nature exist among group members.[4]

The core concept guiding my understanding of crowded family life is that overload, or a high level of unwanted contacts in the home, is reduced by the ability of some members of the family with power to control contacts and allocate space. They do so under the conditions of high density, which is one time when such control seems most necessary, in order to ensure that the family as a collectivity can continue to function successfully. Earlier theoretical discussions (Mitchell, 1971; Anderson, 1972) support the assumption that, under conditions of spatial scarcity, it is parents (and perhaps other elders) who determine the allocation of this important resource in the home. The management of space and activities, along with the enforcement of home rules, is possible as long as there is some agreement that social control is fair or legitimate. When consensus does not occur, perhaps in homes inhabited by short-term residents and unrelated individuals (Mitchell, 1971), conflict over the use and allocation of space is more serious. Not only are social frictions that arise from inadequate spatial management more numerous, but also resolutions of disputes in the absence of a stable social system are more difficult.

Other aspects of living in a stable, intimate social system such as the family also make household crowding more tolerable than one might expect. Activities of others are not only controllable, but also somewhat predictable. A good knowledge of other people's schedules allows the individual to plan to engage in behaviors that demand space and privacy when the home is not at a peak density; it may also make it easier to predict what kinds of interruptions to expect at what time intervals. There may be greater willingness to tolerate inconveniences in the home if, as is often so, there is a good amount of trust in, respect for, and belief in the long-range benefits of the intimate relationship (this seems to reduce social strains especially if the family members believe that the crowded housing conditions are only temporary). Still, it seems most likely that, as the amount of space per person in the home decreases, in most cases some control of space and activities within the home must increase, to ensure acceptable levels of social stimulation and friction.

Of course, like most coping mechanisms, the use of power and control in crowded homes is not without negative consequences. For example, unequal power can lead to unequal spatial allocations, and an unjust distribution of activity curtailments. Adults (who hold most of the power) can decide to limit space use on the basis of what *they* consider to be too much activity, or worse yet they may decide to control others more than themselves. Some indirect (and albeit weak) evidence for this can be found in chapter 6, in that adults' social lives suffered little from household crowding per se, presumably because they were able to obtain the space they needed. The consequences for children (who have less power), however, could be less favorable, though I have no way of knowing for sure, since they were not sampled in these surveys.

More probable statements can be made about the consequences for family relationships. If it is possible to manage roles and activities in order to minimize personal annoyances due to crowding, such a strategy would have an unfavorable impact on the quality and kinds of interactions that are prevalent. There would, for example, be a greater number of attempts to control others (particularly by parents toward their children). Adults (usually husbands and wives) would need to spend more time "policing" space use and activities within the home, which affects not only their relationships with the children but also the quality and quantity of their own encounters. Besides, whenever spouses need to make decisions concerning the use of scarce resources—whether time, money, or space—there is an increased likelihood of conflict or disagreement.

With this in mind, the following hypotheses are tested using the data in the ISR survey and whatever evidence can be found among the results of past studies. First, since families develop mechanisms to alleviate unbearable levels of social stimulation, severely abnormal family interaction patterns do not usually occur. The result of crowding in the home can thus be best measured in terms of the quality of spousal and parental relations. Thus, one could expect adults in more dense homes to show somewhat less satisfaction with aspects of parenthood and marriage than those in less dense dwellings. However, no serious signs of the degeneration of the family will be found, since the family structure works to reduce stress. The presence of less satisfying family relationships can be expected both because the strategies may not be fully effective or used by all families and because the changes in family interaction patterns that such adaptations entail produce somewhat less rewarding interpersonal encounters in higher household densities (i.e., greater social control).

Unfortunately, only portions of the model I have developed in this section can be tested, because of limitations in the available data sources. The analysis is thus much more suggestive than definitive, and it raises as many questions as it answers. Most notably, although I have measures of household density and family relations, I can only infer that "social control" in the home explains the association between these two variables (i.e., the outcome), since no measures of familial control or decision-making capacities were available. I readily admit that the statements made on the basis of such information are weak, but I would also argue that the findings provide encouragement for a more thorough testing of this model. In addition, I cannot fully verify the idea that an individual's lower social position in the home results in a lessened ability to control the environment and thus produces more serious impacts of household crowding on that individual. Ideally, if the data were explicit and the sample appropriate, I would test this proposition by examining separately the responses of parents and children. Since, in reality, children are not sampled and the parent–child items asked of adults are fairly general, at best I can examine the responses of husbands versus wives. Because gender status distinctions are less extreme, I would expect females to report only slightly more dissatisfaction with family life.

The analysis is divided into two sections: relations between spouses and parent–child relations. At the end of this chapter, I provide some suggestions for future research on this complex but extremely important topic of family life in crowded homes.

Marital Relations: An Empirical Analysis

Does evidence exist for the hypothesized association between household crowding and a decline in the quality of spousal relationships? It is important to begin by noting that this topic has received only sparse study despite the strong interest in residential crowding documented earlier.

Two studies conducted outside of North America dealt with marital satisfaction and housing conditions, but they should be interpreted with caution because of their cultural contexts. Alberto Gasparini (1973) surveyed one thousand families in Modena, Italy, to try to ascertain the relationship between household space and family interaction. He found that crowding within the home (measured in persons per room and square meters per person) led to more reported quarreling among couples. This association remained significant even after the author accounted for a variety of possible intervening variables, such as family structure, social class, and education. Gasparini (1973:347) also found that reported quarreling increased as husbands and wives perceived their dwellings as spatially inadequate, providing evidence for the effects of "subjective" crowding. The other survey, mentioned earlier, was a study of Hong Kong households conducted by Robert Mitchell (1971). He did find some marginal effects of household density on specific aspects of family life or under special conditions, and these are discussed later. There was little evidence, though, that in general the quality of husband–wife interactions was significantly related to the amount of household space per person. This statement was particularly substantiated after accounting for the effects of socioeconomic position.

A recent survey conducted in North America asked residents of Toronto some very specific questions about the effects of crowding. In the process, it examined a variety of factors related to family life. A rather brief and preliminary report on the differential effects of household crowding and neighborhood density found no evidence that a higher persons-per-room ratio led to either more spousal arguments or threatened marital dissolution (Michelson and Garland, 1974). However, an "interaction effect" from combined high household and high neighborhood density emerged: individuals experiencing both kinds of densities argued with their spouses significantly more than others residing in different combinations of dwelling and neighborhood densities (Michelson and Garland, 1974:19). Perhaps this finding can be explained by the combined overload in these settings or a lessened ability to escape crowding. On the other hand, there may be something special about the kind of people who live in crowded homes in the most crowded areas of the city.

Michelson and Garland also reported an unusual finding (with no explanation provided) that is beyond most people's speculative abilities: high neighborhood densities led to more threatened marital breakups! A more thorough analysis of this survey's contribution to the study of dense family life is reported by Booth and Edwards (1976). They found that objective measures of household crowding[5] had no impact on various measures of the quality of husband–wife relations. There was some evidence that subjective indices of household crowding were related to behavioral deficits in the husband–wife relationship (e.g., number of arguments, "love decrement" scale).

A recent survey conducted in the United States by Galle and Gove (1974) pertains largely to the effects of household crowding on family life and well-being (see also Gove et al., 1977).[6] The study involved households in Chicago that were sampled in an effort to obtain an adequate distribution of dwelling-unit densities. At the present writing, only preliminary results are available, though this research will probably soon become one of the most significant contributions to the literature. Of particular relevance to my interest in marriage, they report that household overcrowding was related to more recollections of "negative" spousal experiences in the past few weeks and fewer recollections of "positive" husband–wife interactions in the recent past (Galle and Gove, 1974:21). The results concerning positive marital relations stood up under more stringent statistical controls, while the negative scale did not. New analyses of these data also point to the importance of subjective crowding for family relations (Gove et al., 1977).

With the exception of the Gove and Galle study, whose full findings are awaited, most past studies indicate a less than thorough, systematic analysis of this topic in the United States. The results thus merely suggest avenues for further exploration. For example, two studies give evidence of the influence of subjective crowding, which points to the need at least to account for its importance in the present analysis. The importance of carefully selecting control variables was accentuated by studies that reported the disappearance of effects when socioeconomic factors were considered. Finally, a wide variety of variables seems to be needed to measure the quality of the husband–wife experience. Mere indicators of traumatic experiences (e.g., divorce, wife-beating) may not suffice, since household crowding (if it is mitigated by the adaptations suggested earlier) may be associated with a decrease in the "good" experiences of marriage rather than an increase in extremely unpleasant experiences.

The examination of the national survey data is limited to one section of the ISR survey that asks a number of questions about family life. The items concerning marital relations varied significantly, ranging from questions about the prevalence of serious marital disorders to indications of overall satisfaction with marriage. In this respect, it serves the purpose of testing my model very well. This survey, of course, also includes a subjective household crowding measure and the necessary control variables.

Table 5 summarizes the analysis of family life and household crowding for the 906 respondents who comprise the married members of the metropolitan sample. Approximately 7 percent of these individuals lived in overcrowded households.[7] The zero-order correlations between persons per room and the indicators of husband–wife relations provide varied evidence: some indicate moderate associations, while others are insignificant.[8] Most striking is the association between household crowding and the index of "poor marital relations." This correlation remained significant after a variety of controls. The marital relations index contained items of the following nature: how well the husband understood the wife and how well the wife understood the husband (both as perceived by the respondent); how much time the couple shared; and how much the couple argued about such things as money.[9] Another indication of a small but significant decline in the quality of the marriage with greater household crowding can be seen in responses to the "overall marital satisfaction" item. For that question, individuals were asked to assess their marriage "all things considered" from seven

Table 5

Household Crowding and Marital Relations: Zero-order
Correlations and Beta Weights
from Three Regression Equations[a]
(N = 906; ISR *metropolitan data*)

	Zero Orders	Regression Equations		
		1	2	3
Poor marital relations (index)	.23	.16[c]	.12[b]	.15[c]
Overall marital satisfaction	−.14	−.13[c]	−.14[b]	−.12[c]
Satisfaction from marriage	−.09	−.09[b]	−.10	−.09[b]
Dissatisfaction from marriage	.12	.08	−.01	.07
Importance of marital happiness	.09	.07	.10	.08
Frequence of contemplation of divorce	.10	.06	−.00	.05
Unhappy with choice of spouse	.08	.03	−.02	.03

[a]Equation 1: Household crowding, age, education, family income, years in the dwelling, home ownership. Equation 2: equation 1 plus the number of children in the dwelling. Equation 3: equation 1 plus respondent's perception of room size. Beta weights reported are from the final multiple regression equations.
[b]$p < .01$ in final equation.
[c]$p < .001$ in final equation.

(completely satisfied) to one (completely dissatisfied). Though the size of the relationship is smaller than in the case of the marital index, it remained very stable throughout a variety of fairly stringent controls. About one-third of the respondents in overcrowded homes were completely satisfied with their marriages, while over one-half of all respondents reported this highest degree of satisfaction. The next three items asked people to evaluate the importance, satisfactions, and dissatisfactions associated with one aspect of their lives, namely marriage.[10] As indicated in the zero-order correlations and beta weights, there is little evidence of greater dissatisfaction from marriage or a lesser importance of marital happiness with increased household crowding. There is a weak association between the density variable and satisfaction obtained from marriage, which parallels the findings for overall marital satisfaction. Finally, two items involving serious marital disorders, contemplation of divorce and whether the respondents "wished they had married someone else," both scaled from five (often) to one (never), were not significantly associated with household crowding after controlling for the extraneous factors listed in table 5.[11]

The evidence that these findings support the hypotheses is discussed shortly, but first I will complete the review of the analyses regarding spousal relationships. The addition of the "presence of children" or the "number of children" into the regression equations, though obviously strongly associated with persons per room (see chapter 3), did not significantly change the results reported earlier. However, these variables did show an independent effect: the presence and number of children had a negative impact on marital satisfaction.

As table 5 indicates, subjective crowding had no impact on the associations between persons per room and the three significant dependent variables. When other factors were accounted for, perceived crowding was independently related to one item, the index of poor marital relations. Even in that case, the beta weight was smaller than that of the objective crowding measure, however. Despite the problems alluded to earlier with this attitudinal measure (see chapter 3), which work in favor of producing strong associations among satisfaction items and perceptual crowding, evidence for the notion that subjective crowding is a predictor of marital problems was not strong.[12]

The analysis of family life under crowded conditions can be summarized by stating that some support for the hypotheses was found. Using the ISR data, evidence did not suggest that household densities caused widespread or severe marital problems. There were not, for example, more frequent thoughts of divorce or more frequent complaints about the choice of spouse as the persons-per-room ratio increased. In addition, the amount of dissatisfaction associated with marriage and statements concerning the importance of marital

happiness were not significantly related to household crowding. Perhaps this indicates that the high level of social overload, which one would expect in overcrowded homes to
result in marital disruption, is avoided. If so, this is probably
because the family as a group is able to limit or order space
use and activities in the dwelling. More specifically, I would
argue that those with power in the home, namely the adults
or spouses studied here, make great efforts to limit overstimulation and interference in order to protect their primary
relations from severe disruptions.

However, no strategies for coping are without cost, and
as a whole the adjustments necessitated by high densities
make certain aspects of life less pleasurable than they might
be at lower densities. Although serious marital problems
were not more likely to occur, there were indications that the
quality of husband–wife interactions declined with greater
household densities. An index accounting for marital understanding, companionship, and arguments showed a decided
negative impact of household crowding. Two items assessing
satisfaction obtained from marriage (as opposed to dissatisfaction) indicated a lessened pleasure from marriage with
more persons per room. These findings remained substantial
even after controlling for life cycle, socioeconomic factors,
and family size. Strategies for minimizing conflict within
crowded homes, and perhaps also the inadequacies of such
methods or the inability of some families to adopt them, appear to bring a decline in the "good things" associated with
marriage (see also Galle and Gove, 1974; Gove et al., 1977;
Gasparini, 1973).

Parent–Child Relations: An Empirical Analysis

This section is limited to a discussion of parents' relations with their children. No studies, including the present
one, have obtained detailed and highly dependable information on sibling relations under conditions of high density, in
my opinion, so, I unfortunately had to rule out this potentially important area of investigation. In addition, as stated
previously, the sampling of adults only in these national sur-

veys provides a one-dimensional and unverified view of family relations. Thus, another limiting factor is that discussions of parental actions, child misbehavior, and satisfaction with family life reflect merely the parent's point of view.

The empirical investigation of parent–child interactions in crowded homes begins by reviewing studies conducted outside North America. The early studies of Chombart de Lauwe (1961), conducted in Paris, indicated that too little floor space per person was likely to create more family discord. In one of the few reviews in English of these important studies, he reports that household crowding was associated with "tensions" between mothers and children, along with more frequent reports of child misbehavior by parents (Chombart de Lauwe, 1961:36). Robert Mitchell's (1971) study of Hong Kong households also touched on the possible strains that crowding placed on parenthood. He found that parents in dense homes were less likely to know where their children were at any given moment and had less control over their children's outdoor activities. Some would view these as clear deficits in parenting and breakdowns in familial ties. Mitchell (1971:26) has argued that giving children more freedom to leave the home at will probably allows the remaining family members to have some relief from overcrowding. The absence of parental supervision and surveillance, of course, also is assumed to have negative consequences for the children involved.[13] Whether children are forced to leave the dwelling by their parents or whether they do so in an attempt to find space to conduct activities they value was unfortunately not ascertained.

Two recent North American studies review the issue of parent–child relations under conditions of household crowding. The Galle and Gove (1974) Chicago-based survey indicated that density in the home is associated with parental reporting of more problems with their children (see also Gove et al., 1977). They found, as did Mitchell (1971), that parents had a greater likelihood of not knowing where their children were, as household crowding increased. The analysis by Booth and Edwards (1976) of the Toronto crowding survey also explored some areas of parent–child interactions. There was on the whole very little evidence of severe familial disruption. For example, they found no relationship between household crowding and parents' play time with children. However, they did report a small relationship between crowding and the frequency of parents striking their children.[14] This study suffers from a methodological problem that surveys of parental reports about their children probably often contain. No attempt was made to direct the entire inquiry toward relations with one particular child. Instead, the questions were vaguely worded about "children." Therefore, increased parental aggression in crowded homes could be a spurious relationship, merely indicating that there are more children present and thus greater activity of various sorts (since household crowding and the number of children in the home are highly related—see chapter 3). Similarly, the decreases in parental attention toward each child, which might be expected under crowded conditions, may be suppressed because vaguely worded questions lead respondents to answer about the total time they spend with all their children. It is clear that poor instrument construction and choice of controls limit the ability of the previous data to properly test relationships between parent–child interactions and household density.

The ISR data involved a sample of metropolitan residents who were parents of children presently living at home (N = 634). Approximately 12 percent of these respondents lived in homes with 1.01 or more persons per room. For the selected sample, three questions on parent–child relations and several items concerning satisfaction with family life were analyzed. Because of the general nature of these questions, the best that I could do was to search for any effects of crowding on parenting and family life. Presumably these would be caused by both the strains of living in a crowded home and the types of adaptations high density family life might entail (i.e., more attempts to control space and activities, particularly in relation to children). Of course, it was expected that most of the statistical relationships would be rather small, given the kinds of discontent that these items were tapping and for the reasons outlined in the previous section on marital life.

The analysis is summarized in table 6.[15] The first three questions were asked of all surveyed parents, and the subsample of those with children in the residence were selected for present purposes. The first item asked, "Compared to most children, would you say your children have given you a lot of problems [5], quite a few [4], some [3], only a few [2], or haven't they given you any problems at all [1]?" and was coded as indicated in the brackets. This item was unrelated to household crowding both before and after a series of controls. The next question asked if "in your case, being a (father/

Table 6
Household Crowding and Parent-Child Relations: Zero-order
Correlations and Beta Weights
from Three Regression Equations[a]
($N = 634$; ISR *metropolitan data*)

| | Zero Orders | Regression Equations | | |
		1	2	3
Children frequently a problem	.04	.03	−.03	.03
Children frequently enjoyable	−.16	−.17[c]	−.10	−.16[c]
Desire freedom from parenthood	.11	.11[b]	.06	.10
Overall familial satisfaction	−.09	−.09	−.06	−.08[b]
Satisfaction from family life	−.05	−.04	−.01	−.03
Dissatisfaction from family life	.03	.01	−.10	−.002
Importance of a good family life	.04	.06	.06	.07

[a]Equation 1: Household crowding, age, education, family income, years in the dwelling, home ownership. Equation 2: equation 1 plus the number of children in the dwelling. Equation 3: equation 1 plus the respondent's perception of room size. Beta weights reported are from the final multiple regression equations.
[b]$p < .01$ in final equation.
[c]$p < .001$ in final equation.

mother) has been enjoyable," and was scaled from one
(hardly ever) to five (always). This item had the strongest
zero-order correlation of any of the dependent measures,
even after controlling for life cycle and socioeconomic factors.
However, entering the number of children living in the
dwelling unit in a later regression equation resulted in
only a weak and insignificant relationship between household crowding and the enjoyment of parenthood. The last
item asked the respondent if "you ever wished that you could
be free from parenthood," and was coded often (five), sometimes (three), or no (one). Again, this relationship was significant after the first series of control variables, but the effects attributed to household crowding were "explained
away" by the number of children within the dwelling.

A careful examination of these parent–child items and
the findings from them reported above indicates that they are
far from perfect for present purposes. Since the items ask
about attitudes toward "the children," they are more indicative of family size differences than of qualitative changes in
relations between a specific parent and child. The ability of
these items to explore the impact of overload and coping
strategies used by adult family members to overcome household crowding is thus very questionable. The mere number of
children in the dwelling, which is highly related to household
crowding in this subsample ($r = .6$), is more powerfully associated with the parent–child items, since they are actually
worded to be more sensitive to family size effects.[16]

The next four items used dealt with attitudes toward
"family life." These items were also riddled with problems
that inhibit a satisfactory appraisal of family life within the
dwelling. Specifically, almost all the respondents in this survey answered these family items, whether they were living
alone, were married, or were parents.[17] This indicates that
expressed attitudes toward family life encompassed more
than intradwelling relations, thus blurring actual parent–
child relations within crowded homes. With this defect in
mind, I again selected only those respondents with children
living at home, in the event that these items would at least tap

some of the less satisfying aspects of family life within dense dwellings. The first such item stated, "All things considered, how satisfied are you with your family life?" and was scored from very satisfied (seven) to very dissatisfied (one.) This item was not strongly related to household crowding, either before or after controls. The other three items were taken from a section of the questionnaire that asked individuals to assess the satisfaction, dissatisfaction, and importance of this and other life domains (see the previous section on marriage for the format of these items). As is obvious from table 6, there were no meaningful relationships with the persons-per-room variable.[18] The beta weights for the number of children variable, not reported in the table here, indicate higher associations with familial satisfaction items than are reported for persons per room. In many cases, the number of children in the home was actually significantly related to dis-satisfaction with intradwelling relationships even after con-trols were instituted.

As table 6 also indicates, the subjective household crowding measure did not play a major role in disturbing the relationships discussed in this analysis. Considering it as a factor in its own right, in only one instance was perceived crowding associated with a family life item. That was in the case of overall familial satisfaction ($r = .12$). This association remained about the same size when considering all the variables present in regression equation 3 in table 6 (beta weight $= .10$; $p < .01$). Still, this relationship was not very strong, nor was it free from the "response set" problems raised in chapter 3. In addition, the causal ordering of these variables appears to be unclear: does familial dissatisfaction precede perceived crowding, or does perceived crowding help to cause familial problems?

I must conclude this section by stating that there was very little information to support a relationship between problems with family ties and household crowding. How-ever, in this study, like previous ones, this particular issue was not fully examined in a satisfactory manner. Reliance on parents' reports is extremely limiting, and questions concerning "the children" reflect family size variations more than differences in household density. Finally, the items on family relations were global and lacked specificity. The search for qualitative variations in intradwelling dynamics that may not have been very large to begin with was further hampered by using data on satisfaction with family members who might not be living at home. Until the proper questions are asked and directed toward all family members in the dwelling, I cannot fully accept or reject the original hypotheses concerning household crowding and parent–child relations. The present analysis, along with its predecessors, proved an unfair test. For this reason, a separate section of this chapter addresses issues and approaches for future studies. First, though, I examine the evidence available for variations in reported family relations in crowded homes that may be due to social position.

Some Evidence on the Impact of Social Position

I reviewed the items on marital, familial, and parent–child relations and attitudes to determine if social position within the family causes crowding to be more of a problem for those with low status than for those with high status. Ideally, this analysis would include examinations of two subgroups, namely parents and children. Since the data do not allow that sort of study, husbands' responses are compared to wives' responses. There is some evidence that women in the home, due to their role position or social status, have more demands placed on them and have less ability to control contacts and allocate space than men do (see Gove et al., 1977). While this may be true, I do not expect sex differences to be very large or perhaps even consistently in one direction, as I noted in chapter 3. I consider the variations in power among adults in the home to be less consequential than those between parents and children. Further, power may be allocated between a husband and a wife so that one has considerable influence in certain domains and little in others. Thus, the effects of crowding may be felt in certain ways by fathers and in other ways by mothers, depending on their specific responsibilities and jurisdictions.

The procedure was to redo the analyses outlined in this chapter for husbands and wives and then for mothers and fathers. The regression equations summarized in tables 5 and 6 were used for these subgroups. In examining the major findings of this separate analysis, the reader should note that the same qualifications I raised about these items earlier apply here.

Differences between husbands and wives concerning attitudes toward the marriage were significant, but not in the expected direction. For most of the items listed in table 5, the correlations with household crowding were almost twice as large for husbands as they were for wives. This finding remained intact after stringent controls were introduced. An explanation of this result is not obvious. It may simply reflect varying styles of responding to surveys between the sexes. However, I will offer one tentative explanation that is related to variations in social position, though more indirectly than the model presented earlier. Perhaps husbands have a greater ability to escape the effects of a crowded home, yet in the process they may have to reduce contact with (i.e., feel isolation from) their wives, who are more directly involved in the moment-to-moment management of household space and activities (e.g., their children). Wives, on the other hand, may not feel this isolation (or marital dissatisfaction) as much, since their social capacities are more taxed by their roles and because they may have a harder time separating marriage from familial functions and attitudes. Again, this is obviously only a suggested interpretation, and more detailed analyses are needed before any solid conclusions can be made about the impact of social position on marital relations in crowded homes.

Items related to parental attitudes toward their children reflected sex differences in the expected direction. For the first three items mentioned in table 6, as household density increased, mothers tended to complain more about the burdens of parenthood than did fathers. The zero-order correlations were about twice as large for the former group as for the latter, and this finding seemed only marginally affected by the controls outlined earlier (the number of children did, however, diminish these relationships). The remaining familial items listed in table 6 did not indicate any consistent differences, and in some cases (e.g., dissatisfaction from family life) there were not significant relationships for either group. The relationships reported for this set of questions may merely indicate the inadequacies I mentioned above in these family attitude items, and they should thus not be used as definitive evidence against the social position hypothesis. In all, with some hesitation, I think the findings reported here give some support for the notion that household crowding has a greater impact on those who have more social demands placed upon them, are allowed less privacy and "personal" space, and are given greater responsibilities for managing a situation with limited space. In many instances, this social position may better describe the role of the mother than that of the father.

An interesting finding emerged for the differential impact of subjective crowding, which reflects back on some of the sex differences reported in chapter 3. I reported earlier that females tended to notice spatial inadequacies (or complain about them) slightly more than males. In the analysis conducted here, dissatisfaction with available space was, in most cases, significantly associated with complaints about familial life (i.e., marriage, family, parenthood) for females but not for males. Further, the differences in the correlations between these two groups was fairly dramatic (i.e., a negligible association for males and an association of about .2 for females). Perhaps the stronger feelings females have about spatial constraints (because they spend more time in the home or are more involved with managing inadequate space in the dwelling) create more feelings of frustration and hostility about relations in the dwelling. On the other hand, it is again difficult to order these factors causally, since negative feelings about relationships may result in attributions about the dwelling. Nevertheless, variations between those in different social positions were found in the expected direction, adding some support for the proposed model of crowding in the home.

This analysis, though limited by the available data and sample, raises some interesting thoughts about the differential impacts of household crowding on specific members of the family. It points to the potential rewards of examining the role of social position more systematically. It also reveals the need to define what a social position entails in terms not only of relative power or influence over people and other factors but also of responsibilities delegated in the crowded home.

Needed Research on Household Crowding and Family Life

Because the present model of the effects of household crowding on family life is more complicated than past approaches, the more common survey methods and items were found to be less appropriate. I would like to outline some directions for future work on this topic, in the hope that it will further stimulate thought and research on family relations in the home. Most of these comments could also be applied to extending the analyses of housing discontent in the previous chapter.

The most obvious need noted throughout is for a more complete sampling of family members. Either there should be an attempt to select members of the household on a more random basis and thus include observations of children, or, preferably, the research design should call for questioning all members of the household. The latter approach would allow the researcher to develop, for example, a "group adjustment score," while also determining the effects of overcrowding on specific individuals who vary in social position and on households that vary in structural characteristics (e.g., whether they contain nonrelated individuals, extended kin, stepparents and stepchildren).

A more tailored sample could provide astounding contributions, but only if careful thought went into the questions asked during the interview. Throughout this chapter I have been forced to infer that the findings could be explained by specific kinds of adaptations in crowded homes, such as control over the use of space and control over the timing of ac-

tivities, which presumably are results of decision making and
rule enforcement within the family. Items should directly ask
if these adaptations occur, and responses should be ascertained from each household member. More substantial
statements could thus be made about the need for control to
reduce the effects of household crowding (i.e., it should occur
with greater frequency at higher densities) and the differential constraints placed on family members (e.g., children may
report more difficulties in obtaining space than adults). It
would also be important to obtain information on the
strength and visibility of family hierarchies, since this would
indicate whether crowded homes have more highly developed power structures (i.e., for decisions and rule enforcement) or whether the lack of a legitimate power structure
(or a weak structure) in a crowded home results in more
familial conflict and less effective adaptations. By collecting
data on actual control and controlling forces in the home, the
researcher would be able to determine whether the weak association between familial satisfaction and household crowding occurs because of the existence of families within the
sample who cannot cope or cannot completely implement
adjustment schemes, or whether it is more of a residual "cost
of coping" experienced by the families who can implement
the needed adjustments. A more detailed examination of social and spatial dynamics may reveal that specific attributions
about family members (e.g., trust, respect, an appreciation
of children's needs) influence the effects of household
crowding.

I suspect that even these suggestions will lead only so
far toward understanding the impact of household crowding
on family life, and in the near future even more complex
theories and methods need to be developed. A one-
dimensional view of persons per room, for example, is hardly
adequate for housing policy. Design factors including number
of bathrooms, number of bedrooms, traffic patterns, and
areas of congestion for crowded families of specific composi-
tions need to be considered. Similarly, the parameters that
cultures set for possible adjustments need to be examined

through more detailed studies of the values in this and other cultures. For example, North American culture may be less able to tolerate the loss of individual privacy or the imposition of authoritarian family rule than others, and this has definite implications for the effects of household crowding and the success of adaptations to high density situations. Finally, studies conducted at a specific time must give way to longitudinal research designs. Not only would this inform researchers of the process through which the family attempts to achieve "environmental optimalization" (see Stokols, 1977), but it may also have implications for policymakers and practitioners who want to develop intervention strategies for reducing the personal and social costs of household crowding.

I have presented some ambitious proposals for future research. The importance of this topic and the shortcomings of past attempts, though, indicate that the definitive study of household crowding and family life needs to be done and that it will require a substantial effort.

Summary and Conclusions

This chapter began by discussing the critical nature of the effects of household crowding on family life. A review of the literature indicated considerable deficiencies in theory and research.

The first section analyzed the significance of household crowding for intimate ties and the importance of considering the family unit as a source of possible coping mechanisms. Since the number of unwanted contacts could be considerable at high persons-per-room ratios, crowding in the home (like crowding in any other setting) can potentially be a source of social overload that could result in disturbed relationships. The special nature of the home seems to prevent adaptations under high density conditions and aggravate spatial shortages. The amount of time spent in the home is unsurpassed, and the roles and activities performed there are of great importance. Unwanted contacts and the lack of adequate space should thus create a high potential for intradwelling conflict and interpersonal frustration. In addition, strategies that serve to limit the individual's attention to others (e.g., "specialized withdrawal"—see chapters 2 and 6) may not be useful methods of coping with crowding in this setting. Selectively limiting contacts in the home is a difficult strategy to implement, given the primary nature of relationships there and the problems that arise from "turning off" potentially disruptive contacts.

The costs of crowded family environments and the coping strategies available in such settings should thus be viewed in a special manner, since the home is unlike any other dense situation. Of primary importance is a consideration of the power structure within which the household operates. Since the family possesses a status hierarchy that is used for decision-making purposes, under conditions of spatial scarcity it can determine the use of space and control the flow of activities within the home. Such a strategy would be used to minimize friction and interference among family members, thus alleviating the threat of serious household disruption. There probably are, however, some residual effects from this coping mechanism. To name a few: the family members whose actions are controlled to a greater extent may not find this very satisfying; the strategy may be the best available yet inadequate to meet the severe lack of space; the burden of control may be felt unequally by members due to their status differences. Though the effects are far from "pathological," in most cases higher levels of household density would probably result in less satisfying spousal and parent–child relations. It was thus predicted that respondents' assessments of marriage and parenthood would reflect less satisfaction in these life domains, though not to a very strong degree.

This hypothesis was partially supported by an analysis of married individuals in the ISR survey. Though reports of marital breakdown were not related to household crowding, there was a tendency, even after a series of stringent controls, for household crowding to be associated with a less positive marital experience. These findings were replicated in a recent study conducted, as this one was, within the United States (Galle and Gove, 1974; Gove et al., 1977). However, general-

izations from these findings should be made cautiously because of the limited scope of the empirical analyses.

While limited support for the hypothesis was available
in the reports of marital satisfaction, no such confirmation
existed for the items concerning parent–child relations. There
was no overall decline in the enjoyment of parenthood, nor
did parental problems and responsibilities seem to increase
with higher densities. Some evidence of differences related to
social position was found (i.e., husbands versus wives,
mothers versus fathers), which pointed toward the useful-
ness of this distinction. Not satisfied with the scope and format of the questionnaire items, though, I concluded that the
effects of crowding on family life need to be explored with
more detailed data. Some proposals for future research were
outlined.

Part III—The Neighborhood Environment and Social Relations

5. Neighborhood Density and Residential Satisfaction

There is no shortage of opinions concerning the quality of life in high density neighborhoods. Public feelings on this subject are strong and, more often than not, negative. Social philosophers continue to debate the costs and benefits of crowded residential environments. Government officials throughout the world, faced with the growing dilemma of populations competing for limited space, have also questioned the "environmental quality" of high density neighborhoods. Actual evidence for the effects of urban crowding on residents' attitudes toward their locales, however, has been minimal. In this chapter, the national survey data add new information to this important debate.

I introduce the topic by examining some general American sentiments about the noticeable impact of neighborhood density. Questions asked of the national sample of the NORC Continuous National Survey in 1973–74 provide some clues in this respect. Next, the opinions of urbanologists are reviewed as a source for the generation of hypotheses.

Before examining the effects of urban crowding on attitudes toward the neighborhood environment, it is essential to gain some perspective on historical trends and present levels of neighborhood density in the United States. The basic unit examined here is the census tract, which, despite problems of definition and measurement, is the only available uniform and widely used measure for urban neighborhoods. The United States Census Bureau does not regularly collect information on tract densities, so that tracts are not a source for data on trends and correlates of density, as they were for household crowding in chapter 3. As a result, this portion of the analysis must rely heavily on the census tracts sampled in the national surveys. There is an inherent weakness to this approach, since the surveys are representative samples of people in the United States, not neighborhoods. Additionally there are no data on neighborhood density that would allow comparison of the distributions of densities gathered through the survey sampling against a broader sample of densities. At best, the distributions and correlates of density in the two national samples can be compared for similarities, and information of a more macro nature (i.e., citywide and metropolitan-area-wide) can be reviewed to obtain some knowledge of historical trends in population densities.

The major issue addressed in this chapter is the impact of neighborhood density on residential satisfaction. Unlike some studies of "environmental quality," the analysis goes beyond the gross measures of neighborhood satisfaction. While it does attend to people's overall satisfaction with their neighborhoods, it also examines perceptions of specific local services, facilities, and environmental attributes. This provides a more comprehensive view of residents' attitudes toward their neighborhood environments and permits me to develop a much more complex argument concerning the role of neighborhood density in residential satisfaction.

Opinions about the Effects of Neighborhood Crowding

A number of viewpoints have been expounded on the impact of neighborhood density on local residents. There appears to be disagreement about the overall opportunities and problems that high densities create; moreover the perceived positive and negative effects of density seem to vary with the specific aspect of the neighborhood environment under consideration. I offer a perspective on this topic that is an extension of some of the more recent theoretical works in urban sociology.

Public Opinion

Individuals in both rural and urban areas throughout the United States made predictions about the impact of higher densities on their communities in a section of one of the national surveys (the NORC Continuous National Survey, cycle 11, N = 610). They were told "We're interested in knowing what you think would change in this community if the population were to grow rapidly," and they were given a list of twelve changes that might occur. Of course, the question was directed toward growth, and thus the responses reflect concerns other than changes in density, such as an increase in population size and land coverage. It is assumed, however, that the specific "change" items did tap some important attitudes (or prejudices) about high density, which is a central aspect of the package of factors associated with local growth.

The responses to these items are summarized in table 7.[1] One striking finding is that few "don't knows" are reported for the items asked, indicating that respondents were opinionated about issues related to population density. There also appears to be some consensus about the impact of growth and higher densities, because of either stereotypes or actual experiences.

The items showing the highest agreement concerned the likelihood of increased competition for resources as neighborhood densities increased. For example, 91 percent of those polled believed that "traffic congestion" would increase, 87 percent reported that community services would be "overloaded," and 73 percent felt that "overcrowding" would increase. In relation to these global feelings of greater competition for space and resources, a majority of individuals believed that unemployment and living costs would increase, that privacy would become a more precious commodity, and that the local area would lose some of its intimate and friendly character.

Despite these fairly strong negative opinions, individuals did expect some benefits to occur with higher densities. In particular, the expectation of more and better services and facilities was reflected in items concerning jobs, public institutions, transportation networks, and commercial facilities. Many respondents also saw growth and high density as leading to greater tolerance of individual differences, an attribute that may be considered as either good or bad.

Table 7

American Public Opinion on the Effects of
Increasing Neighborhood Population
(N = 610, March–April 1974, NORC national sample)

*"We're interested in knowing what you think would change in this commu-
nity if the population were to grow rapidly. If the population were to grow
rapidly would . . .*

	Yes	No	Don't Know
Taxes and the *cost of living* increase?	74%	23%	3%
The number of *jobs* increase?	55	40	5
Unemployment increase?	53	40	6
The number of *facilities* for public transportation (e.g., buses) increase?	57	35	8
Pollution and traffic congestion increase?	91	8	1
Ways to have *fun* (e.g., shops, restaurants, new people to meet) increase?	79	18	3
Less space and privacy for recreation, that is, would *overcrowding* increase?	73	25	2
Government *services* (e.g., schools, good roads) increase?	72	23	5
A less friendly, small town atmosphere, that is, would *unfriendliness* increase?	61	35	4
Be easier to keep your business to yourself—would *privacy* increase?	33	62	5
Would *overloading* of community services (e.g., schools, water, welfare) increase?	87	12	1
People of different opinions more easily accepted—would *tolerance* increase?	57	35	8

Thus, individuals seem to have mixed feelings about what would happen if the densities of their communities were to increase. Though seemingly contradictory, these statements may have some validity. [2] For example, more and better urban services may develop at higher densities, but competition for using them may become keener. In any event, the data indicate that people expect both costs and benefits to be associated with high density neighborhoods, and they seem to express a high level of agreement.

Urbanologists' Opinions

In chapter 1, I introduced the views of Philip Hauser and Amos Hawley, since their arguments captured the contemporary debate about costs and benefits of high density living. It is relevant at this point to reconsider their statements briefly.

Hauser (1968) stresses the impact that "population implosion" has had on creating a "chaotic society." He argues that crowding has increased disorganization and conflict. Hawley (1972), on the other hand, has focused on the positive aspects of high density environments. He cites benefits, particularly a more economical means of providing easy access to services for many more people. This, in turn, creates greater environmental diversity and stimulation, higher quality transportation and communication, and greater opportunities for individual goal attainment. In Hawley's view, and this reflects the human ecology perspective, these benefits are made possible largely through more dense residential conditions. Low density settlement patterns could not possibly provide individuals with a wide array of nearby benefits, particularly at such a low cost. In addition, according to Hawley (1972) there are few noticeable costs associated with high density urban environments; in this view, he stands in obvious disagreement with many stated predictions by urbanologists. Again, as with public opinion, one is left with contradictions concerning the overall value of high neighborhood densities.

I now offer some sociological speculations of my own in an attempt to synthesize these seemingly dissonant viewpoints. My underlying assumption is that high density neighborhoods on the average contain an array of costs and benefits for their residents. They probably provide a high opportunity for diversity and stimulation and offer various conveniences not as readily available in low density settings. For example, the presence of many people residing in a small area makes possible the development of diverse and specialized commercial and social activities (see Fischer, 1976). Those activities also become enhanced because of qualitative improvements in transportation and communication. On the other hand, these dense environments have certain potential drawbacks for individuals. Available services and land can be overloaded. Land and resources can become heavily congested as many people attempt to conduct their activities. The environment (e.g., housing, sidewalks, streets, parks) can become less pleasing aesthetically because of overuse and an inability to meet the high demand for maintenance. The neighborhood setting can be less satisfying for all of these reasons, and residents may experience a general heightening of displeasure due to conflicts over scarce resources and goal thwartings among neighbors (e.g., competition for on-street parking).

My hypothesis is that individuals perceive these attributes of high density neighborhood environments and thus can find both costs *and* benefits associated with their local area. Overall, though, I would expect global ratings of neighborhood satisfaction at high densities to be more negative for two reasons. I suspect that societal values deter most respondents from expressing overall approval of high neighborhood densities in an interview. Also, if it is correct to assume that people opt for high density settings to achieve access to desired services, the neighborhood environment per se may not be particularly satisfying to them (i.e., they like the location rather than the physical setting).

Several important predictions about "subgroup" effects flow from the ways that high density neighborhoods have been depicted here, and I will partially examine these issues toward the end of the chapter. First, satisfaction with the neighborhood setting should reflect individuals' life-styles, which vary along several personal and social dimensions, including the *life cycle*. For example, the elderly may place a high premium on accessibility to services, and the young single population may value diversity of facilities, but middle-aged adults with young children may value safe streets and a stable, predictable environment over the benefits of high densities. Whether people's present needs "fit" with their present environmental circumstances, including the neighborhood density, is thus a crucial issue to study (see Michelson, 1976, 1977). An important proposition to examine is whether satisfaction with the neighborhood environment varies along the life-cycle dimensions described above.

One could also expect variations due to *social position*. The benefits of varied and high quality services may not be as available to those with low economic resources, since the level of wealth in such high density areas may not be able to support such facilities (i.e., benefits in facilities may be available only to those with greater financial resources living at high densities). Also, individuals of low social position may be living at high densities due to constraints (i.e., a need for inexpensive housing), rather than choice, and may thus be less enthusiastic about their residences. In either case, the proposition to be examined is whether those with low social status in high density neighborhoods report more neighborhood dissatisfaction than others.

These hypotheses about attitudes toward the neighborhood are explored after examining in some detail the measure of neighborhood density, persons per residential acre. The statistical properties of this measure are evaluated for both of the national samples. A search for the major correlates of neighborhood density is also made, along with a brief perspective on historical trends of urban densities in the United States.

Distributions of and Properties Associated with Metropolitan Neighborhood Crowding

How can the neighborhood densities within metropolitan areas be characterized, and what factors are highly associated with persons per residential acre? More definitive answers to these questions demand a random distribution of United States census tracts, but the data available here dictate analyses of the national samples of households. There are weaknesses to this approach, but the purposes of this investigation are well served by examining the neighborhood densities of urban residents. To make matters somewhat more complicated, there is no widely accepted definition of an overcrowded neighborhood, as there is for household overcrowding. Such a task would be extremely difficult and beyond the abilities of the present study. Considering the many residential settlement patterns that could produce the same areal densities (e.g., mixed land use, single family homes, multiple-story apartment buildings), the difficulty in determining an overcrowded neighborhood is apparent. One of the few guidelines available for making such an appraisal is a study by Lansing et al. (1970), which found that densities over twelve housing units per acre created noticeable changes in residential dissatisfaction. Using that figure as an estimate of overcrowding (and assuming that average household size is three persons), then about 10 percent of the sample from each national survey lives in a neighborhood that could be described as very dense (i.e., at least thirty-six persons per residential acre). Of course, the approach taken in this book does not really require a determination of what should be considered overcrowded living conditions. Rather, it examines whether higher densities are associated with shifts in attitudes and social patterns. When data from the top 10 percent of the density distribution are discussed, therefore, they are used for illustrative purposes.

The distributions of neighborhood densities obtained from the national surveys are presented in table 8.[3] The densities experienced by metropolitan respondents range from fewer than 1 person per residential acre to over 275 persons per residential acre. The sampled neighborhoods thus contain between 100 and 175,000 persons per square mile (excluding nonresidential areas). The variation in densities experienced by the respondents is considerable, which is an obvious advantage in using these nationally based data. The

Table 8
Statistical Distributions of Persons Per Residential
Acre for Metropolitan Respondents

Persons per Residential Acre	1971 ISR Quality of Life (N = 1,361)	1973–74 NORC Continuous National Survey (N = 823; cycles 3 and 4)
Minimum	.01	.01
Mean	15.38	13.35
Standard deviation	27.91	24.95
Median	7.80	5.82
Maximum	275.26	239.71

national average of persons per residential acre obtained here was about 14 (or 9,000 persons per square mile), while the median density is around 7 persons per residential acre (or about 4,500 persons per square mile). No modal density was calculated; there did not appear to be a clustering around any particular neighborhood density, though a substantial percentage of the respondents lived at densities of 2 persons per residential acre or less (about one-third of the NORC and one-fourth of the ISR samples). In interpreting these figures, it must be remembered that the density measure used here includes sidewalk and street areas, which account for somewhere between 25 and 40 percent of the land in most neighborhoods. This is mentioned in order to avoid the false assumption that the average American lives on a quarter of an acre of land. This inclusion of public areas is acceptable and even preferable, given the strong interest of the present study in the contacts made possible by high neighborhood densities.

It is difficult for most people to imagine what these numbers represent, so I will give a few examples to illustrate the levels of neighborhood density experienced by these respondents. Two well-known cities come to mind that typify the average (mean) population density in the United States: Denver and Los Angeles. These cities have densities of between 5,000 and 6,000 persons per square mile. The reader might think of these sprawling cities, dominated by

neighborhoods with single family homes and low rise apartment buildings, when considering the national average (e.g.,
the Los Angeles–Orange County urbanized area—see
Woodhull, 1975:169–74). In comparison, the reader could
consider some major cities in the Southwest that have densities well below the national average (e.g., Phoenix, Albuquerque) and older cities in the Northeast that are well
above the national average (e.g., Boston, New York,
Philadelphia).

Next, what would the typical housing settlement patterns of these respondents be, given the available statistics on
neighborhood density? These can be calculated by excluding
approximately one-third of the land in the measurement of
persons per residential acre, and assuming that average
households in the United States include three persons. Using
these guidelines, one could imagine six households, each
with one-sixth of an acre of land and three persons, as one
settlement pattern typifying the mean American density.
Other possibilities exist involving multiple family dwelling
units, but the illustration used is particularly appropriate
given the large proportion (over 60 percent) of respondents
living in single family homes. In any event, the sample is
clearly picking up the weight of suburban developments in
small metropolitan areas. Given the median densities and the
types of land use that can be envisioned using the national
data, the sample seems to represent the continuing influence
of the suburban pattern in the United States.

The density distributions reviewed here provide some
interesting observations, though caution is in order when reviewing these samples of households. First, it appears that
metropolitan neighborhoods in the United States on the average are not very dense by world standards. Even the most
crowded Americans live at much lower densities than do citizens of major world cities such as Tokyo, Hong Kong, or
Calcutta. This provides support for the notion that there is
increasing diffusion of the urban population into outlying
areas of the metropolis and widely observed declines in density for the central cities (see Hawley, 1972). While a histori-

cal trend in the "leveling off" of density gradients may be occurring in urban areas, it should also be noted that the continuation of metropolitan growth means that fewer and fewer Americans are living at very low densities, or in areas characterized as rural (see Berry and Kasarda, 1977: chap. 8).

The data reported in table 8 also indicate a high degree of skew in both samples, which could affect correlations. This is a problem when conducting a multivariate analysis, and it necessitates special statistical tests (e.g., using the logarithm of density in separate equations) to ensure that the reported results are not affected by the measure's skew. Also, the distributions of densities for the two national samples are not as similar as might be preferred, perhaps due to chance or some variations in sample selection (e.g., selection of different cities as sample sites). In any case, it may be more difficult to replicate survey results, since the distributions of density are somewhat different. However, since no predictions of threshold effects or optimal densities are made, and since the variations are small anyway, this lack of similarity will probably not be an important factor in the analysis that follows.

Next, factors associated with neighborhood density were examined. Five tract-level and five individual-level factors that were available in both national surveys were selected for intensive analysis (see table 9). These ten variables were considered some of the basic characteristics of urban neighborhoods and individuals. Here, the search was not for "causes" of density, but rather for the factors most closely associated with living in a more crowded area. In fact, many of the characteristics could be considered causes of density as well as caused by density. Table 9 summarizes the results of this analysis.

By far, the strongest associate of neighborhood density was the population size of the metropolitan area: the larger the metropolis, the more dense the neighborhood of the respondent. This finding is consistent with the thinking of human ecologists. Population pressure puts increased demands on limited space and thus great competition for space would result in high neighborhood densities (since a high

Table 9

Factors Associated with Persons Per Residential Acre:
Zero-order Correlations and Explained Variance

	ISR (N = 1,361)	NORC (N = 823)
1. SMSA population size	.56	.43
2. Tract median income	−.18	−.24
3. Tract percentage black	.16	.22
4. Tract population size	.07	−.06
5. Tract area (residential acreage)	−.10	−.12
6. Ownership of the dwelling	−.26	−.33
7. Years in the neighborhood	.11	.06
8. Family income	−.05	−.10
9. Respondent's education	−.04	−.22
10. Respondent's age	.04	.05
Percentage of Persons-per-Residential- *Acre Variance Explained by Factors*		
Factors 1–3	36.9%	28.1%
Factors 6–10	9.1	16.4

demand and a low supply of space would make available land
expensive and subject to more subdivisions). Another explanation would be that the large metropolitan areas are older
and contain more crowded settlement patterns reminiscent of
the days before automobile travel. Evidence for the latter
proposition can be found in ISR interviewer reports. Buildings
in high density neighborhoods were rated as older. For
example, three-fourths of the individuals residing in
neighborhoods with densities of thirty-five persons per acre
or more lived in housing structures rated as twenty-five years
old or older.

A cross-tabular analysis of neighborhood density and
"type of urban place" added further evidence for the importance of community size.[4] Virtually all respondents living at
densities of twenty persons per residential acre or more lived
in the twelve largest metropolitan areas and metropolitan
areas of at least one hundred thousand persons. Those experiencing densities of thirty-five persons per residential acre
or more (i.e., 10 percent of the sample) were almost exclu-

sively (i.e., almost 80 percent) residents of the central cities of the twelve largest metropolitan areas. The interconnection of these factors, of course, makes it extremely difficult to separate the effects of urbanicity from those of local density, but I will attempt to control for community size in later analyses.

Other tract-level data indicated that lower incomes (measured in median income) are associated with higher neighborhood densities. This indicates that those with more *choice* (i.e., more economic resources) are somewhat less likely to locate in high density areas, while those with greater economic constraints tend to find lower rents in neighborhoods that contain more dwelling units per acre. It is no surprise, then, that larger percentages of disadvantaged groups (e.g., blacks) are also found in more crowded neighborhoods. The tendency for groups with fewer opportunities to live in high density areas is not, however, very strong. This is perhaps because some affluent people choose to live in luxury high-rise areas to obtain greater access to services. Judging from the ISR interviewers' evaluations of housing and neighborhood quality, though, the crowded neighborhoods of the more wealthy are superior in quality to others. Respondents comprising the top third of the income distribution (i.e., at least $15,000 per year) tended to have neighborhood housing rated as newer and in better condition than others living at the highest densities (i.e., thirty-five persons per residential acre or more). Despite these differences, there are similarities in all crowded areas (e.g., a high number of contacts) that are expected to affect environmental attitudes and interpersonal relations.

Population size and the acreage of the census tract are only marginally related to persons per residential acre. This adds assurance to the notion that neighborhood density is fairly independent of its components.[5] It is obvious from table 9 that the most important correlates of density are urbanicity and economic resources. These factors explain about one-third of the variance.

The individual-level factor that is most strongly associated with neighborhood density is ownership of the dwelling. Respondents who are homeowners are clearly more likely to live at lower densities. This actually points to the fact that neighborhoods of predominantly single family homes are less crowded than those with apartment buildings or mixed land uses. It is interesting to note that the size of this correlation may be reduced in subsequent decades as more cooperative apartments and condominiums become available. Analyses of other ISR items dealing with the type of dwelling (scaled from single family home to large apartment complex) and the number of stories in the resident's dwelling were also strongly related to neighborhood density (dwelling type, $r = .44$; stories, $r = .50$). For example, less than one-fourth of those residing in neighborhoods of thirty-five or more persons per residential acre live in duplexes and single family homes, while almost two-thirds live in structures with three or more stories.[6]

No other individual-level factors were consistently associated with neighborhood density. The length of residence in the neighborhood had a small positive relationship with neighborhood density in the ISR data, but this tendency was less pronounced in the NORC study. The respondent's education and income were negatively related to density in the NORC study, which seemed to confirm the results of tract-level analysis, but these associations did not appear in the ISR data. Finally, the age of the respondent was weakly related to the density of the residential area in both surveys, which could be expected from the earlier discussions of the "fit" between life cycle and life-styles associated with high densities. The relationship may actually be somewhat suppressed by the fact that respondents under thirty as well as the elderly may choose to live in high density areas (see later sections of this chapter). The five individual-level factors together accounted for only 9.1 percent of the explained variance in the ISR study, while faring much better (16.1 percent) in the NORC study (this discrepancy can be traced to the differential power of the socioeconomic variables).[7]

In summary, it appears that the size of the metropolitan area, the kinds of building structures within neighborhoods, and the economic resources of residents, in that order, are the strongest correlates of neighborhood density.[8] However, the overall ability to "explain" neighborhood density was less successful than the attempts with household crowding described in chapter 3. One reason is that no correlation for neighborhoods compares with the strong relationship between household size and persons per room. Perhaps also the density of residential areas cannot be explained by factors measured here, since it may involve historical circumstances surrounding the development of each area. Thus, specific land use patterns within each urban area may better explain neighborhood density than the present analysis of a national sample relying on a few variables.

Analysis of Residential Satisfaction and Neighborhood Density

In this section, the influence of persons per residential acre on attitudes toward the residential environment is examined. Since little work has been conducted on this topic,[9] the information provided by an analysis of the two national surveys is critical. Both overall satisfaction with the neighborhood and attitudes toward specific attributes of the residential environment are assessed. The latter involves an examination of items about the physical appearance, availability of mass transit, safety, institutions, and services in the neighborhood. Where possible, comparisons are made between findings in the ISR and NORC surveys.

Overall Levels of Neighborhood Satisfaction

It was predicted earlier that global ratings of residential environments would be somewhat more negative at higher densities. One reason was the prevalence of a cultural bias toward single family homes and against high density buildings—an attitude that is clearly part of "the American dream." This bias may be reinforced by the fact that many present-day adult urbanites have parents from less dense areas or themselves grew up in rural areas (e.g., few respondents grew up in the largest metropolitan areas). Thus, people in more dense areas would be predisposed to describe their neighborhoods less positively irrespective of environmental opportunities. In addition, the attributes expected to be a part of high density neighborhoods (e.g., congestion of streets, high numbers of contacts, noise, overcrowding) lead to negative appraisals of the environment, even if the location itself is presently preferred by the respondent.

Some might criticize these views as simplistic. First, they imply a level of homogeneity in environments and among residents of a given area that may not be found in any given census tract. In my opinion, the census tract is probably small enough in size and homogeneous enough in composition for the present purposes. There are probably tracts in the samples that would not meet these criteria, and they may suppress the size of correlations. Despite various criticisms of the use of tract data, the tract is presently the best approximation of "natural areas" available on a national basis. Another argument could be raised that it is not density, but rather factors associated with high densities (e.g., central cities, old housing, low status areas), that lead to lower evaluations of neighborhoods. This is an important problem and merits caution in interpreting the results in this chapter, all the more so because of the high colinearity between high densities and these other factors. Greater controls must be used in the analysis to separate the effects of other urban and social factors as much as possible.

Items were chosen from the ISR and NORC surveys on the issue of overall neighborhood satisfaction. The question in the ISR survey was worded, "All things considered, how satisfied or dissatisfied are you with this neighborhood as a place to live?" and was scaled from one (completely dissatisfied) to seven (completely satisfied). The NORC item asked, "Taking everything into account, how do you feel about living in this neighborhood?" and was scaled from zero (not at all satisfied) to four (completely satisfied). The ISR item had a zero-order correlation of $-.16$, while the NORC item showed a similar relationship with neighborhood density ($r = -.18$). As an illustration of this effect, about 40 percent of the ISR respondents were completely satisfied, while only about 25 percent living at thirty-five persons per residential acre or more reported the highest level of satisfaction.

Next, tests were made to determine if this relationship would remain strong after accounting for economic and life-cycle factors. Three variables used in the preceding section of this chapter were again chosen: the respondent's age, education, and ownership of the dwelling.[10] "Years in the neighborhood" replaced years in the dwelling unit, since this seemed to better reflect the respondent's exposure to the neighborhood environment. Also, "tract median income" was used instead of family income, since it is more relevant to account for the level of wealth in an area when considering neighborhood density and residential attitudes.[11] The beta weight for neighborhood density, with the inclusion of the five control variables in the final regression equation was $-.12$ ($p < .001$) for both surveys (see table 10).[12] Adding to the equations items that measured the level of urbanicity did not affect this finding. There thus appears to be a consistent and negative relationship between neighborhood density and overall neighborhood satisfaction.

The results of an earlier study by Marans and Rodgers (1973), who conducted a survey of 1,300 individuals throughout the nation, agree with the evidence presented from these national surveys. They found that people living at the lowest densities (measured in dwellings per acre) were the most satisfied with their neighborhoods, while those at the highest neighborhood densities were the least satisfied (Marans and Rodgers, 1973:220–21).

The desire to move, which can be viewed as another indicator of overall neighborhood dissatisfaction, was also examined. The NORC and ISR items mentioned in chapter 3, which deal with long-distance and short-distance moves, were used for this purpose. Neither was significantly related to density before or after controls. Despite somewhat higher levels of dissatisfaction, attitudes toward leaving the neighborhood are not affected by neighborhood crowding.

The analysis next considers specific attributes of

Table 10

Beta Weights for Residential Satisfaction Regression Equations:
NORC and ISR Comparisons[a]

	Neighborhood Density	Education of Respondent	Home Ownership	Years in Neighborhood	Tract Median Income	Respondent's Age
Overall neighborhood satisfaction						
ISR	-.12[c]	.03	.08[b]	.07	.16[c]	.15[c]
NORC	-.12[c]	.03	.12[c]	.02	.10[b]	.12[b]
Satisfaction with police department						
ISR	-.14[c]	.13[c]	.10[c]	.04	.21[c]	.17[c]
NORC	-.07	-.02	-.02	-.02	.09	.15[c]
Satisfaction with schools						
ISR	-.16[c]	.06	-.01	-.05	.17[c]	.18[c]
NORC	-.18[c]	-.11	.02	.03	.09	.05

[a]Beta weights and significance levels reported are for the final multiple regression equations.
[b]$p < .01$.
[c]$p < .001$.

neighborhoods, in order to determine what sources of complaints and praise are generated by dense neighborhood
environments.

Neighborhood Physical Appearance

Evidence concerning the aesthetic qualities of neighborhoods as perceived by their residents is considered first. No
comparable questions were asked in the ISR and NORC surveys,
but various items in these studies indicate poorer environmental quality at high densities, as expected.

The ISR study asked respondents to evaluate the residential buildings in their neighborhood. The item was worded,
"What about the condition of the houses in this neighborhood? Overall, would you say that they are very well kept up
[1], fairly well [2], not very well [3], or not kept up at all [4]. "
Of the few respondents who indicated the poorest level of
upkeep, almost half lived at densities of twenty persons per
residential acre or more. As expected, there was a positive
relationship between perceptions of poor housing conditions
and neighborhood density (r = .18). This relationship remained significant after controlling for the five factors mentioned earlier, though the economic status of the area did
diminish the association (beta weight = .09; p < .001). Residents of crowded neighborhoods tended to rate their physical
environments less favorably even when accounting for the
urbanicity of the sampling site in the equations. The findings
may reflect a tendency for structures in dense areas to appear
more overused, or it could perhaps indicate less concern for
neighborhood aesthetics by residents and landlords.

No questions concerning housing quality were drawn
from the NORC survey, though there were three items on attributes of the physical environment. Two questions were asked
in a section concerned with problems in the neighborhoods.
The general item was worded, "I'll read you some things that
are problems for some people in their neighborhoods. Please
tell me if they are a big problem [2], somewhat of a problem
[1], or not a problem [0] to you, in your neighborhood." Ratings for "litter and trash in the streets" strongly correlated

with neighborhood density (r = .24), and this relationship remained strong after introducing the five controls (beta weight = .16; p < .001). "The amount of noise in the area" was also highly associated with crowding (r = .23), even when accounting for the extraneous variables (beta weight = .20; p < .001). Next, in the context of items concerning facilities and services (which I discuss in greater detail later), people were asked about the availability of "trees, grass, and flowers in the neighborhood," scaled zero (not available), one (poor), two (fair), and three (good). This question was also associated with neighborhood density (r = −.30) and remained significant after the same five controls (beta weight = .23; p < .001).

In summary, consistent evidence was found that the aesthetic qualities of high density neighborhoods are evaluated more negatively. Crowded neighborhood conditions tend to lead to perceptions of poorer housing upkeep, more litter in the streets, more noise pollution, and less greenery. These findings persisted through controls for home ownership, socioeconomic status, life-cycle position, and tract economic characteristics, and held true after entering urbanicity into the regression equation.

Availability of Mass Transit

One statement often made by the proponents of high density living is that more compact residential settlements facilitate more economical and efficient forms of transportation, which allow easier access to a variety of desired local services (e.g., shopping, entertainment, health and welfare agencies). From the point of view of human ecology theory (see Hawley, 1951, 1972), inexpensive and convenient transportation services are made available by the existence of dense urban areas. Transportation planners also place great importance on the population density of an area when they are trying to determine the kind of mass transit to implement, the likelihood of sufficient riders to support a given system, and the frequency of service to be provided (Regional Plan Association, 1975). This section evaluates the availability of mass transit, the frequency of its use, and the level of satisfaction with services, to determine if this advantage of high density living is realized by the respondents.

A number of questions concerning the local public transportation system were in the ISR survey. First, individuals were asked, "Is there any local form of public transportation available to you here (not taxicabs)?" and responses were coded either one (no) or two (yes). Neighborhood density was associated with the presence of mass transit ($r = .28$), and this relationship was only slightly reduced by controls (beta weight = .20; $p < .001$). High density settlement patterns seem to allow and perhaps necessitate mass transportation. The quality of the transit system was evaluated in a question worded, "How good is the public transportation for the people who live around here?" and was scaled five (very good), four (fairly good), three (neither good nor bad), two (not very good), and one (not good at all). For those respondents having mass transit, the correlation between the quality of the system and neighborhood density was not high ($r = .13$) but remained significant after introducing the five control variables (beta weight = .10; $p < .001$). This indicates that public transportation is only somewhat more favorably evaluated in high-density areas. It should be remembered that all respondents having transit systems in their neighborhoods were asked to evaluate the quality of service; evidence exists that the actual users of mass transit are much more favorably disposed to it than are nonusers (see Baldassare and Wachs, 1977). The frequency of use of public transportation was ascertained in a question that asked, "How often do you use public transportation: almost every day [5], once a week or more [4], once a month or more [3], less than once a month [2], or never [1]?" About one-half of the most frequent users lived at densities of twenty persons per residential acre or more. This item was highly related to neighborhood crowding ($r = .39$), even after accounting for the five control factors (beta weight = .33; $p < .001$).

Several cautions should be noted about concluding from these findings that neighborhood density results in more and better public transportation. First, though the availability and use of mass transit were highly related to density, the perceived quality of the system was rated positively to a much lesser degree. The characteristics of respondents may have accounted for this finding. However, it is also possible that high density *forces* the development and use of mass transit, because of overload and congestion of public thoroughfares, and thus it may not necessarily be a good or desired form of mobility for residents. In fact, indications are that transportation policy is moving more toward constraining auto use as time goes on.[13] Second, one must remember that various aspects of public transportation systems are largely dependent on factors beyond the local area (e.g., the density of cities, counties, metropolitan areas) or the nature of land use in the surrounding communities (i.e., the location of trip destinations). In fact, controlling for urbanicity reduced the strength of the two relationships (i.e., existence, quality of mass transit) dramatically. Finally, the effects of density on the most popular and preferred form of transportation in the United States, namely the automobile, also need to be reviewed. This is done through an analysis of items from the NORC survey.

Along with questions concerning "neighborhood problems," which were cited in the discussion of neighborhood appearance, two questions were directly related to automobile travel. Respondents' evaluations of whether or not "streets were in poor repair" were weakly associated with neighborhood density ($r = .07$), and were insignificant when controls were applied (beta weight $= .03$; $p > .01$). In addition, individuals were asked whether they perceived "heavy traffic in the streets." Higher densities led to reports of traffic problems ($r = .18$), which persisted after consideration of the five control factors (beta weight $= .14$; $p < .001$), and even when urbanicity was considered. In examining these two items, it is evident that travel by automobile is no better for high density residents and, in fact, may be worse due to problems of road congestion.

Whether, on balance, high density neighborhoods have added conveniences in terms of the availability of transportation and easier access to desired services remains a question in my mind. It is apparent that there is a greater availability and use of mass transit, while travel by automobile seems somewhat more difficult due to traffic congestion. The general findings were unaffected by urbanicity, though it is difficult to discount this factor entirely. A more thorough analysis of this issue would require more detailed information on residents' daily movements and destinations than was presently available.[14]

Neighborhood Safety

Next, residents' attitudes about safety from crime are considered. The expressed concerns with the relationship between crowding and "pathology" (see chapter 1) suggest that high density living would result in more displeasure with this particular aspect of the local area.

First, attitudes toward the police department in the local community, using comparable items in the NORC and ISR surveys are examined (see table 10 above). It is assumed that they tap attitudes toward neighborhood safety, though they are obviously also relevant to the discussion on services that follows. The NORC item asked, "How satisfied are you with your local police department—are you completely satisfied [4], very satisfied [3], moderately satisfied [2], slightly satisfied [1], or not at all satisfied [0]?" This item was not strongly related to neighborhood density ($r = -.07$), nor was it significantly associated after life-cycle and socioeconomic controls (beta weight = $-.07$; $p > .01$). An ISR item asked, "How good do you think the relations are between the police and the people around here? Are they very good [5], fairly good [4], neither good nor bad [3], not very good [2], or not good at all [1]?" This item, obviously worded somewhat differently from the NORC question, produced a more negative appraisal of the police's role in the community in more dense urban areas ($r = -.20$; beta weight = $-.14$; $p < .001$). This may be indicative of greater crime problems, or it may reflect fewer positive encounters between police and citizens due to overload or resulting interpersonal adaptations (see chapter 6). Though crime and police activities may be somewhat affected by neighborhood densities, I must again caution that the quality of neighborhood attributes, such as police service, may be largely determined by extralocal forces.

The ISR study asked two more specific questions about fear of crime in the locality, and both indicated more negative appraisals in denser residential areas. One question was: "Would you say that it is safe to go out walking around here at night?" and was coded two (yes) or one (no). This item was significantly associated with neighborhood density ($r = -.24$) and remained strong after controls were instituted (beta weight $= -.17$; $p < .001$). As an illustration of this relationship, about half of the respondents living at densities of twenty or more persons per residential acre did not feel safe. Further support for this finding was observed through analyzing the question, "How important do you feel it is to lock your doors when you are going out of the house for just an hour or two? Would you say it is very important [1], somewhat important [2], not very important [3], or not important at all [4]?" Residents of high density neighborhoods reflected greater concern with locking doors ($r = .19$) even when the five factors including life cycle and economic status were considered (beta weight $= -.15$; $p < .001$).

Apparently, crime is feared more in crowded neighborhoods, and there is less confidence in the local police department. Whether the expressed fear of crime is rooted in reality cannot be ascertained through this survey analysis. Perhaps these attitudes reflect only the fact that high density residents know their neighbors less well (see chapter 6) and thus distrust them more. Data from areal studies (see review in Fischer et al., 1975) point toward more macro-level explanations. The correlation between crowding and crime, when properly controlling for percentage of blacks and poverty, though, is quite strong nonetheless. In any event, another area of residential dissatisfaction among high density respondents seems to be present, and it too is, at least statistically speaking, independent of urbanicity.

Institutions and Services

The quality of local services and institutions is now reviewed. The major issue is whether local facilities show signs of overload because of increased competition for their use in high density areas, or whether there are qualitative improvements in the delivery of services because of the increased demand and economizing factors associated with high densities.

First, institutions of learning within the local community are considered. An ISR question asked, "How do you feel about the quality of the *public* schools that the children around here go to—would you say that it is very good [5], fairly good [4], neither good nor bad [3], not very good [2], or not good at all [1]?" Lower evaluations of public school quality were consistently related to high neighborhood densities (r = −.19; beta weight = −.16; p < .001), indicating that the residents of dense areas were not as happy with these institutions as others. In the context of some NORC questions dealing with available services and facilities within the neighborhood, respondents were asked to rate their elementary, junior, and senior level schools one (poor), two (fair), or three (good). For the purposes of a comparison with the ISR item on schools, I chose to look at their responses to the question concerning senior high schools (see table 10): the correlation was sizable (r = −.19), and the significant relationship between dissatisfaction with high schools and residence in high density neighborhoods remained after controls (beta weight = −.18; p < .001). The responses on items concerning other levels of schooling were similarly high (even when controlling for urbanicity), giving consistent evidence that the educational needs of children were not met as well, according to adults, in high density environments.[15]

The "speed with which the fire department comes to the neighborhood when called" was also assessed in this series of NORC items. Though most people may not have had real experiences with this, their answers indicate an attitude toward a crucial neighborhood service. Slightly more positive evaluations were in evidence as density increased ($r = .08$), and the association remained when accounting for the five extraneous factors (beta weight = .10; $p < .01$). Though this is obviously not a strong relationship, it is interesting, given the neutral and negative evaluations of police actions and traffic congestion in the area (which would presumably slow down the time the fire department would take to respond to a fire). Two interpretations of this finding are offered. It is possible that fire stations are located closer to each other as density increases, therefore making the reaction time smaller. For example, a central city district with 5,000 people would be considerably smaller in area than one of comparable population in the outer suburbs. Another possibility is that firefighters may respond faster in light of the increased danger of lost lives when fire strikes high density areas (e.g., the vulnerability of high-rise-apartment dwellers). In any event, the finding provides some evidence for time savings or "economizing factors" supposedly associated with high density areas.

Finally, an ISR item concerning local taxation was examined. It was worded, "Would you say that the local taxes in (city or county) are very low [1], low [2], moderate [3], high [4], very high [5]?" It was not surprising to learn that those residing in dense areas reported higher taxes ($r = .17$) even after controlling for economic and life-cycle factors (beta weight = .15; $p < .001$). This finding, however, was largely explained away by adding urbanicity to the final regression equation (beta weight = .08; $p < .01$). It is unfortunate that questions were not addressed specifically to homeowners concerning the level of property taxes in their areas, since this may have indicated some of the economic costs of living on land that is in high demand. Whether the cause of the complaints is density or urbanicity, what is discouraging is that individuals who more readily complained about taxes also rated their neighborhood environments and services in a

more negative fashion. The flight from large central cities
with high density neighborhoods in the last few decades is
thus not surprising.

The Impact of Social Position and Life Cycle

Two critical issues are explored in this section. One is
the finding that the reported quality of high density
neighborhoods varies with economic resources. In other
words, the less affluent, high density resident inhabits a setting with fewer opportunities (and more noticeable costs)
than the wealthier resident of a high density neighborhoud.
Further, those with fewer economic resources are likely to
choose high density neighborhoods more because of constraints (e.g., affordable rents) than because of preferences
and are thus more likely to express dissatisfaction. The second issue is the mitigating role of life cycle in attitudes toward
high density neighborhood settings. It is hypothesized that
those whose life-cycle (or life-style) needs do not "fit" the
density of their surroundings will express more dissatisfaction. For example, middle-aged, child-oriented individuals are
probably less interested in the benefits of high density living
(e.g., diverse and numerous facilities, mass transit) and more
constrained by its costs (e.g., traffic in the street, safety of the
neighborhood). I suspect then that members of this group see
their neighborhood in more temporary terms (i.e., have more
desire to move); are less likely to choose the setting as a
preferred location (i.e., have fewer economic resources); are
more dissatisfied than the general population; and see themselves as "relatively deprived" (i.e., do not have the assets of
low density that are available to a good proportion of their
age cohorts).

Several questions from cycle 12 of the NORC survey are
used in this analysis, as well as a few items from the ISR
survey.[16] Social positions, or economic resources, were
explored by separating those respondents with family incomes of less than $10,000 from others. Life cycle was consid-
ered by separately analyzing individuals in the middle years

(thirty to sixty-four), a substantial number of whom had children living at home. The impact of gender on residential satisfaction is not examined in this section, because no sex differences worth mentioning were found and because no theoretical reasons for such an analysis were available.

It is obvious from earlier discussion in this chapter that low income respondents have a tendency to live at higher densities.[17] In addition, ISR interviewers' reports indicated neighborhoods with thirty-five or more persons per residential acre were more likely to be rated as "not very well kept" for low income individuals than for high income individuals. The NORC survey asked respondents to evaluate "the conditions of houses in this neighborhood" (scaled from one [not kept up well] to four [very well kept]). Though there was an association between poor housing quality and neighborhood crowding for the total sample, the size of the correlation was not larger for the less affluent group alone. Items measuring crime in the neighborhood also showed little variation among subgroups, while there was again a relationship with high density in the expected direction (one item asked if "it is safe to go out walking around here at night" and was rated yes or no; the other item asked "how important do you feel it is to lock your doors when you are going out for just an hour or two" and was scaled from one [not important] to four [very important]). There were also no subgroup differences in the likelihood that the respondent would "move out of this neighborhood in the next few years" (scaled from four [very likely] to one [not at all likely]), nor was this association significant for the total sample. Only one significant finding emerged from this subgroup analysis: the poorer respondents were somewhat more likely to report more overall dissatisfaction at high densities than the total sample ($r = .3$ versus $r = .2$).[18] In all, attitude differences of a specific nature were not found among economic subgroups, though interviewers rated low income, high density neighborhoods as inferior. It is possible that high density residents who are constrained in their choice of residence (i.e., lower income respondents) may be coping with their environment by not noticing its unpleasant attributes. Equally likely is the possibility that limited residential experiences may produce a different comparison level for the less affluent: they may not complain about specific environmental circumstances because the criteria for "good quality" may be different from those of a broader population (in addition, their knowledge of better alternatives may not be broad). It is important, however, that there are signs of higher overall dissatisfaction for the less affluent in high density neighborhoods, lending some support for the original hypothesis.

The same items were explored in search of life-cycle variations. Middle-aged people at high densities complained more than others about neighborhood housing quality ($r = -.3$), and this group reported a high preference for moving ($r = .3$). They did not, however, complain more about crime, nor were they more dissatisfied (overall) than the total sample. This life-cycle subgroup varied considerably from the elderly, who tended to be more affluent, less likely to move, more satisfied with neighborhood housing conditions, and more concerned about crime (they also expressed slightly more overall dissatisfaction). I conclude from these data that middle-aged people tend to find high density neighborhoods less to their liking than other age groups and seem to choose such environments more out of constraint than preference. Their overall dissatisfaction with the high density neighborhood may not be greater than that of others because they believe that they will leave the neighborhood fairly soon. In addition, the elderly may complain more about crime, and this in fact may reduce their overall satisfaction ($r = .4$ between crime concerns and dissatisfaction), because this negative attribute is very salient to a group that has mobility problems and feels physically vulnerable. Though the results overall tend to support the original hypothesis, the issue is obviously one of considerable complexity and subtlety.

This admittedly brief examination of a key topic has provided some encouraging evidence to support a body of literature in urban sociology (Gans, 1970; Fischer et al., 1977; Michelson, 1976, 1977). It also raises a number of important issues for future research. Obviously a number of objective measures of neighborhood conditions are needed, since such data would illustrate "real" differences in high density environments. These measures are required because respondents' perceptions of their areas may vary with their life experiences and knowledge of alternatives. In addition, it is possible that the objective circumstances of the middle-aged in high density settings are different from those of the elderly in dense neighborhoods in ways only partially illustrated by attitudinal data. Finally, I have only alluded to the impact of specific kinds of attitudes (e.g., preference for or likelihood of moving) on residential satisfaction at high densities, and future studies should consider such potentially relevant moderating variables more carefully. In fact, experimental data on "perceived control," or the ability to escape, high density environments suggest the importance of such an investigation (see Sherrod, 1974; Sherrod and Cohen, 1977; Baldassare, 1978). A number of factors thus point to the importance of further work of the nature suggested in this section.

Summary and Conclusions

This chapter introduced the use of the variable "persons per residential acre," or neighborhood density. The distribution of neighborhood densities in the national sample was fairly wide, though most metropolitan Americans reside at rather low densities by historical and cross-cultural standards.

The size of the metropolitan area was the best predictor of high density neighborhoods for the national survey respondents. Two explanations were provided, one relying on notions of "competition" from the human ecology literature and the other considering ecological patterns of older, more dense metropolises before the days of the automobile. Respondents from low income areas were also more likely to be residents of high density neighborhoods. There was some evidence that those with choice (i.e., the wealthier respondents) live either elsewhere or in higher quality crowded neighborhoods. Less affluent individuals either take advantage of the lower rents in high density living or are forced to reside in such neighborhoods because they lack alternatives. Home ownership was also a powerful determinant of high density living, apparently due to the prevalence of multiple-dwelling-unit structures. In all, the selected factors had less ability to "explain" residence in high density neighborhoods than in crowded households.

Questions from the NORC survey found a consensus on what individuals expect from high density areas. Several "costs" were cited (e.g., congestion, loss of privacy, over-loaded services) as well as "benefits" (e.g., more mass transit and recreational facilities). Overall, hypothetical evaluations were fairly negative.

Urbanologists' opinions seemed similarly mixed: proponents of high density found in crowded neighborhoods opportunities for increased diversity, facilities, transportation, and communication; opponents of high density cited disorganization, congestion, and overload of services. The view that high density neighborhoods provide both costs and benefits was examined by using the national survey data.

"Overall neighborhood satisfaction" items from both surveys indicated that high density neighborhoods were less liked, and controlling for intervening factors did not alter this relationship. The analysis of neighborhoods went further than most density studies by examining perceived attributes of the environments. Topics examined were: neighborhood physical appearances; availability of mass transit; neighborhood safety; and institutions and services. The results leaned heavily in the direction of negative evaluations of high density neighborhoods. Crowded neighborhoods were consistently rated as less attractive. Public transit was more available, heavily used, and somewhat more favorably evaluated, while traffic congestion was a more serious problem in crowded neighborhoods. The general public felt less safe in high density residential areas; dissatisfaction with police and fears of crime surfaced in this analysis. The quality of local institutions and services was worse at high densities in all but one case: firefighting services were reported as more responsive. One caution voiced throughout the chapter was that the quality and quantity of neighborhood services are partially dependent on extralocal forces (e.g., the city and metropolis). Controlling for urbanicity did not significantly affect findings reported throughout this chapter, though it is difficult to separate this macro-level variable from crowding in the "real world." In essence, it is possible that many of the findings could be explained just as easily by factors associated with neighborhood density, such as central city location, age and quality of housing, mixed land use, and heterogeneity of the population. The summary of selected comparison items in table 10 shows that there is basic agreement between the findings of both surveys. In addition, the beta weights in table 10 indicate that economic and life-cycle factors are also significant determinants of neighborhood satisfaction. Here, as in Part II of this book (and in chapter 6 as well), it is obvious that all the factors considered do not explain a great deal of the variance.

In summary, it appears that individuals are more displeased with high density neighborhoods than with low density neighborhoods. The perceptions of the respondents, which may or may not reflect objective conditions, indicate that the purported benefits of high density living may have been overstated by its proponents; for residents these benefits are overshadowed by the costs.

Despite these flaws, some individuals choose to reside in dense neighborhoods. There is, on the whole, a tendency for those with greater economic resources to have more residential space as well. Though the reason for this correlation could not be empirically explored, space is a valued resource because it increases privacy, reduces interference, and enhances predictability and control of local events. Still, the correlation is not perfect, and thus some people with greater residential opportunities choose to live at high densities. The possibility that variations in economic resources provide qualitatively different high density neighborhoods was explored, and some evidence suggested that more affluent residents tend to be more satisfied with their surroundings (or poorer

residents less satisfied). People with greater economic resources may be able to manipulate high density settings to
drastically reduce their costs and increase their benefits (e.g.,
using doormen and soundproofing to reduce interference).
This is one possible explanation for "choice" of high density
settings.

Perhaps people also choose such settings because of the
way they rank environmental attributes. For instance, they
may view certain dense neighborhood factors (e.g., accessibility to services) as more salient than the problems associated
with high density (e.g., crime and congestion). Inevitably,
this points to the fact that different densities provide opportunities for people to pursue various kinds of life-styles.
Life-cycle factors seem particularly relevant here. Young
adults may thrive on easy access to diverse activities in dense
areas: they may not be as concerned with crime as the elderly
or as concerned with the conditions of schools as parents of
young children. Family-oriented individuals may weigh
these factors differently, since they have greater neighborhood needs for safety, security, predictability, and control of
the local environment. Still others, such as the elderly, the
poor, and the handicapped, may locate (by choice or constraint) in areas of low rent and easy access to public transportation. The issue of life-cycle variations in reactions to high
density was partially examined and given some preliminary
support. I share with others involved with urban issues (see
Fischer et al., 1977; Gans, 1970; Michelson, 1976, 1977) the
view that factors such as the ability to choose and manipulate
settings and the fit between individual needs and environmental attributes are critical. It was clear from the analysis,
however, that objective data on neighborhood conditions
should be systematically collected in future studies. In addition, a closer examination is needed of attitudes (e.g., ability
to move) and psychological and social conditions as mod-
erators of satisfaction with high density neighborhoods.

6. Residential Crowding and Social Contacts

This chapter discusses the influence of high density residential environments on social relations, particularly individuals' nonfamilial social interactions. Whereas chapter 4 considered relations among relatives in the dwelling, the focus here is on friends, organizational affiliations, neighbors, and casual acquaintances.

As I noted earlier, several urban theorists believed that high population density leads to deterioration in social relations. A review of the contributions of Simmel and Milgram is worthwhile before I present a critique and revised interpretation of the "social overload" model. More thorough theoretical discussions of urban underinvolvement and social disorganization can be found elsewhere (see chapter 1; Fischer, 1976).

The writings of Georg Simmel (1905) and Stanley Milgram (1970) on the subject of social life best depict the issue of urban overload. For present purposes, readers should especially note their concern with the astronomical number of contacts that occur in the daily life of the urbanite. The term *contacts* refers here to the mere presence of others within an individual's sensory range, and not necessarily a verbal exchange or nonverbal recognition. These authors consider the degree of social stimulation potentially available as psychically unhealthy. Thus, an overload of the nervous system may occur that could produce severe mental problems if precautions are not taken to contain the number of social stimuli. An analogous situation would be the danger of blowing a fuse in the home by plugging in too many electrical appliances. Both of these authors (see also Wirth, 1938) believed that most individuals avoid overload by developing "coping mechanisms." The most common strategy is "social withdrawal." In other words, urbanites limit the *number* of contacts that they respond to, as well as their *involvement* in social relations. The result is a visible "urban" life-style, which places a premium on keeping relations superficial, functional, and impersonal. This coping pattern, though presumably successful in a gross sense, has other psychological implications. It creates difficulties for conducting meaningful social relations in dense urban settings and increases the probability of a generalized social withdrawal and alienation.

Another view on this topic was recently provided in a paper by Cohen and Spacapan (1977). To summarize, they assert that situations, such as overcrowding, that cause high attentional demand leave the individual fatigued and unable to attend to subsequent stimuli. Though these authors have no place for the coping strategies mentioned by Simmel and Milgram, their predictions are quite similar, since the cognitive fatigue produced by high levels of contact also leads to social withdrawal in a very general sense (see also the review in Baldassare, 1978).

My views on this subject differ from those of the authors above, particularly because I disagree with the mechanistic or deterministic tone of those discussions. The empirical predictions I offer come from a perspective on human interrelationships that draws in part on concepts from exchange theory. The basic questions that I ask throughout this analysis are: How do individuals experiencing residential crowding decide which contacts should become "social," and how do they differ in their ability to implement strategies to conduct desired social relations?

Neighborhood Density and Social Contacts

A perspective on human choice and adaptive abilities is provided that permits specific predictions about the effects of macro-level residential crowding on social patterns. These ideas are partially tested through analysis of the national survey data, and the results substantiate the claims made in the theoretical discussion. Suggestions for subgroup analysis are made, along with some exploratory analyses in a later section.

A Theory of Specialized Withdrawal[1]

Implicit in any discussion of population density is, of course, the notion of many individuals sharing a common area. Émile Durkheim (1893 [1964]) and others mentioned earlier discussed the fact that contacts increased with proximity to others and a greater number of people per area. Even considering that residential space is divided and that human movement is nonrandom, higher densities still create higher levels of potential contacts, since individuals in low density areas also live in housing units and schedule their time in urbanized societies. High levels of potential or real contacts create an information management problem for the individual. My point of departure from theorists such as Milgram and Simmel concerns the strategy that most individuals use to alleviate the problem of overload due to high neighborhood densities.

In order to best describe the kinds of coping strategies that might be acceptable to individuals, I must analyze the contacts that occur in the daily life of an urbanite. First, there are encounters with family and friends—interrelationships that are usually highly valued, very intimate in nature, and potentially personally rewarding. Then there are more limited kinds of relationships that occur on a fairly regular basis—contacts with acquaintances from church, the PTA, or various other voluntary associations, involving specific and narrower goals. Other contacts are only economic or contractual in nature, such as encounters with grocery clerks or waitresses. Lastly, there are contacts that are not as regularly scheduled, purposeful, or predictable, such as saying hello to neighbors, gazing at passersby on a street corner, or being confronted by strangers. In modern urban societies, many kinds of social contacts may occur, ranging, for example, from an encounter with a best friend or lover to examining the outstretched hand of a street beggar. Moreover, individuals perceive that these potential contacts have *costs* and *rewards* attached to them, and they therefore *value* these contacts to varying degrees. An individual might find it highly desirable and important to have contacts with intimates, while considering it less valuable and perhaps even dangerous to respond to a stranger's remarks in a dark alley. Thus, my notion of social exchange involves the belief that individuals consciously decide which relations to participate in and to avoid on the basis of their potential value. This theory has important ramifications for revising the "urban overload leads to social withdrawal" model.[2]

Specifically, the next issue that arises is: How do individuals respond to the possibility of numerous contacts created by living in overcrowded neighborhoods?[3] Unlike Simmel and Milgram, I do not believe that most people cope with the problem of overload by randomly "turning off" encounters and generally "tuning down" their inputs and receptivity to relationships. Conducting this strategy in an unsystematic and random fashion would lead to a situation in which individuals would not *maximize their utilities,* and thus it is improbable to me that people would act in this manner. In other words, given a situation of too many contacts, why would people avoid encounters with friends, or become more impersonal in their intimate relationships? A more rational, less risky strategy, which would obviously maximize the pleasure they receive from social relations is available. Given that individuals can discriminate important from unimportant social ties, it is hypothesized that they would minimize the *less valued contacts* in order to reduce the total number of personal contacts to an acceptable level. Thus, they would also be able to maintain time and energy for their valued social relations. This would reduce the possibility of interference with important aspects of their social lives due to neighborhood crowding. In effect, when contacts are ignored or marginally attended to, in order to avoid overload, reductions in attention would occur in less rewarding and less potentially costly encounters. The strategy used to cope with increasing levels of neighborhood density, labeled here *specialized withdrawal,* seems one more reasonably to be expected from humans attempting to maximize the pleasure they receive from social interactions.

This theoretical discussion has stressed learning a strategy through experiences with situations involving too many contacts; other forms of learning may take place as well. A resident of a dense area may "model" the social behaviors of others and thus exhibit the strategy others use without ever experiencing overload (i.e., vicarious learning). An individual might also learn how to respond by the way he or she is treated by others—for example, when violating rules or understandings about how to handle "casual" encounters in a dense neighborhood. This suggests an important point: that individuals may exhibit the social patterns described here because of "social pressures" and not always because they choose a particular strategy. Differences in the "generation"of the strategy could result in variations in well-being, satisfaction with the residence, and satisfaction with social life. Unfortunately, this issue could not be explored in the data analysis that follows.

The notion of specialized withdrawal is tested through a reexamination of past empirical findings and an analysis of data from the two national surveys. Based on the ideas discussed in this section, the following hypotheses are offered: (1) that individuals' *friendships* are not affected (quantitatively or qualitatively) by the neighborhood densities in which they reside; (2) that *group affiliations,* of both a formal and an informal nature, are unaffected by crowding within urban residential areas; (3) that *casual encounters* (e.g., neighborliness, responses to relative strangers) are deemphasized in numbers and intensity as density increases. The latter, relatively unimportant encounters are reduced when people need to limit their attention to contacts at high neighborhood densities (i.e., the presence of unacceptable numbers of contacts leads to partial or full withdrawal from these kinds of stimuli). The assumption is also made that the changes in social relations due to higher neighborhood densities do not have only "local" effects (i.e., within the residential setting) but also have implications for social contacts in general. The length of exposure to density may be important, though it is considered here that these coping strategies by most adults are learned by some method after a short amount of time.

Evidence of Specialized Withdrawal

Based on the hypotheses developed, this discussion divides interpersonal relations into three areas: friendships, formal group affiliations, and casual relationships. Evidence from the national surveys and past empirical studies is provided.

Friendships Few researchers have examined the effects of neighborhood density on social interactions, including friendships. As part of the Toronto Crowding Study, Alan Booth (1974) prepared a report entitled "Crowding and Social Participation," which dealt with this issue. He examined the effects of neighborhood density on the number of friends regularly contacted and the number of neighborhood friends regularly contacted. For both males and females, he reported no significant relationships when socioeconomic and life-cycle factors were taken into account.

In an earlier study, I used the Detroit Area Survey to examine the relationships between important social ties and neighborhood crowding. This mid-1960s survey involved approximately one thousand men in the Detroit Metropolitan Area, who were asked questions concerning their friendships and "social networks." An item concerning the "number of friends" showed no indication of a significant effect of neighborhood density (i.e., persons per square mile within 1960 census tracts). In addition, residential crowding had no effect on the amount of time respondents spent socializing (Baldassare, 1975a).

In the next phase of the analysis, I wanted to determine whether neighborhood density had only *local* effects; that is, are only the relationships that occur within the residential setting harmed in some way? I looked at the relationships that the respondent reported with those of his best friends (up to three could be listed) who were residents of his neighborhood. Not only was the number of best friends who lived within the neighborhood unrelated to density, but the characteristics of those relationships (as measured by intimacy and frequency of contacts) did not vary with persons per residential acre within census tracts. These results remained after a series of stringent controls for life-cycle and socioeconomic characteristics of the individual and the urban area (Baldassare, 1975b). It seemed evident from this analysis that close neighborhood friendships were also not disturbed by density.

Another study considered the characteristics of the social networks of these Detroit men. I looked at a variety of indicators of the depth and breadth of their best friendships *irrespective* of local boundaries. For example, I examined the intimacy and frequency of social contacts they had with their friendship circles, the degree to which their friends knew each other, and the extent to which their close associations showed a variety of purposes (i.e., multiplex) rather than simply one. Again, there were no indications that living at high neighborhood densities affected these permanent and important social ties (Baldassare, 1977).

With previous studies in mind, new data from one of the national surveys are examined (see table 11).[4] Certain attributes of the Detroit data had made further tests crucial (e.g., its sampling a decade ago of only white males in one metropolitan region). The analysis in this section is limited to the ISR Quality of Life data set, since the NORC Continuous National Survey had no item on friendships. Again, my primary interest was in the quality and quantity of existing friendships.

The question dealing with the *quantity* of these intimate social ties was worded: "Would you say that you have a good many very good friends [1] that you could count on if you had any sort of trouble, an average number [3], or not too many very good friends [5]?" In analyzing the responses of United States metropolitan residents, it was obvious that neighborhood density had no impact (r = .04) even after accounting

for areal and individual-level factors, such as home ownership, age, education, years in the neighborhood, and tract
median income (beta weight = .03).

A question that dealt with the *quality* of existing friendships asked: "All things considered, how satisfied are you
with your friendships—with the time you can spend with
friends, the things you do together, the number of friends
you have, as well as the particular people who are your
friends?" It was scaled from one (completely dissatisfied) to
seven (completely satisfied). Here also, there was a very low
zero-order correlation between this item and neighborhood
density (r = −.03), which persisted when controlling for the
five factors mentioned earlier (beta weight = −.04).

In addition, several items were used from summary sections of the questionnaire, which asked people to assess the
importance, satisfaction, and dissatisfaction associated with
this part of the life domain (i.e., friendship).[5] In all cases, the
zero-order correlations were .05 or below, and the partial correlations (and beta weights) were similarly low.

It seems safe to summarize by stating that, in both the
national survey data and the earlier analyses, no evidence
was found to support the argument that important social ties
are disturbed—in number or quality—by the density of the
neighborhood environment. If residential crowding does
produce overload, then it seems that individuals are able to
maintain their valued relationships under those conditions, at
least according to the data sources thus far explored.

Group Affiliations Participation in voluntary associations
is another area in which to measure the avoidance of social
contact by individuals living in high urban densities. Again,
little evidence exists on this subject aside from the work of
Booth (1974) and myself (Baldassare, 1975a, 1975b).

Booth's Toronto Crowding Study asked individuals
about their level of participation in voluntary associations. He
found no relationship between neighborhood crowding and
organizational affiliations, even after various factors were accounted for through multivariate techniques.

Table 11
Beta Weights for Social Contacts Regression Equations: Selected Items for Neighborhood Density[a]

	Neighborhood Density	Respondent's Age	Home Ownership	Years in Neighborhood	Education	Tract Median Income
Friendships						
Number of friends (ISR)	.03	-.01	-.07	-.09[b]	-.03	-.01
Quality of friends (ISR)	-.04	.10[b]	.03	.08	.02	-.02
Group affiliations						
Number of groups (ISR)	-.06	.04	.15[c]	.11[c]	.32[c]	.06
Quality of groups (ISR)	-.08[b]	.13[c]	.06	.04	.06	-.07
Participation in neighborhood groups (NORC)	.07	.03	.13[c]	.08	.18[c]	.10[b]
Meet with neighbors in groups (NORC)	.06	-.02	.09	.06	.16[c]	.08
Neighbors' interest in area (NORC)	-.03	.27[c]	.17	-.10	.15[b]	.10
Casual encounters						
Poor quality neighbors (ISR)	.15[c]	-.17[c]	-.12[c]	-.06	-.09[c]	-.08[b]
Poor quality neighbors (NORC)	.11	-.32[c]	-.15[b]	-.17[b]	.08	-.10
Quantity of neighbors known (NORC)	-.10[b]	.05	.18[c]	.16[c]	-.01	.004
Neighbors friendly (NORC)	-.08	.05	.06	.03	-.004	-.04
Shun meeting new people (ISR)	.12[c]	.20[c]	.04	-.04	-.01	-.01

Respondent suspicious (ISR)	.16[c]	.11[c]	.001	-.03	-.04	-.05
Respondent insincere (ISR)	.14[c]	.05	-.01	-.02	-.12[c]	-.01
Respondent uninterested (ISR)	.05	.04	.004	-.05	-.27[c]	-.10[c]

[a]Beta weights and significance levels reported are for the final multiple regression equations.
[b]p < .01.
[c]p < .001.

In my use of the Detroit Area Survey, I also examined items concerning participation in formal groups. "The Effects of Density on Social Behavior and Attitudes" (Baldassare, 1975a) analyzed relationships between the number of persons per square mile within census tracts and the number of social organizations to which respondents belonged. Though the zero-order correlation was significant ($r = -.13$), the relationship diminished when life-cycle and socioeconomic factors were taken into account (partial $r = .03$). In a later study that examined only neighborhood interactions, I considered the degree of attachment to community groups. Again, while there was a significant relationship between density and not belonging to neighborhood organizations ($r = .10$), this association became negligible after controls (beta weight = .002). The results of these studies indicated little support for the notion that neighborhood crowding diminishes participation in formal groups.

Further data on organizational affiliations are introduced through the use of both national survey instruments. The ISR survey asked questions about participation in certain kinds of formal groups (e.g., neighborhood improvement associations, community centers, social groups). None of these items had a zero-order correlation with neighborhood density above .02, nor did the same controls instituted during the analysis of friendships indicate any suppressor effects. However, analysis of the number of types of groups (e.g., neighborhood, church, political) that respondents belonged to revealed a slight decrease in this measure of social contacts as density increased ($r = -.11$), though even this finding was substantially reduced after controls (beta weight = $-.06$). Finally ISR items concerned with satisfaction, dissatisfaction, and the importance deriving from this life domain were considered. The importance and dissatisfaction items were related at .02 and below, both before and after controls. Satisfaction with organizational affiliations was somewhat reduced by neighborhood density ($r = -.08$; beta weight = $-.08$; $p < .01$).

Three of the NORC items were relevant to the topic of involvement and participation in neighborhood groups. Two were from cycles 3 and 4 (N = 823) and the other was from cycle 12 (N = 437). The first two items asked respondents if they had "ever done any of the following in this neighborhood: formed or attended neighborhood organizations, met with other interested people" (answered yes [1] or no [2]). In both cases the zero-order correlation between these items and neighborhood crowding was −.02; the controls for the five life-cycle and socioeconomic factors did not alter these results (beta weights were .07 and .06; p > .05). The third NORC item asked respondents "how interested are most people around here in neighborhood problems: very interested [1], somewhat interested [2], or not at all interested [3]?" This item showed a fairly good association with density (r = −.13), though the five controls "explained away" this finding (beta weight = −.03).

This analysis of neighborhood attachment and formal group participation, along with past studies, provided no sufficient support for the notion that overload due to neighborhood crowding disturbs voluntary associations.

Casual Encounters Lastly, encounters perceived as less permanent and rewarding are considered. It was predicted earlier that these potential contacts would most likely be affected by a strategy to avoid social overload in high density neighborhoods. Since I have already shown that friendships and formal group participations are uninjured by residential crowding, it remains to be seen if the data can substantiate the claim that individuals reduce (or are less responsive to) casual encounters in order to preserve their more rewarding social contacts. If not, then it seems that density has no measurable effects on interpersonal behavior.

One of the first tests of this notion was made through the analysis of an item in the Detroit Area Survey of 1965–66 concerning how well individuals know their neighbors (Baldassare, 1975a). Using this as a measure of how much effort individuals put into casual contacts, I found a clear decrease in neighborliness associated with neighborhood crowding (r = −.12). This persisted after individual-level life-cycle and socioeconomic controls (partial r = −.11), though it disappeared after controlling for tract median income. This finding of lower levels of neighboring at high urban densities was in agreement with past evidence (see Lansing et al., 1970; Michelson, 1973). Also, a study by Fischer (1973) used SMSA population size (which is strongly associated with neighborhood density in both national surveys—see chapter 5) and found neighboring to decrease as urbanism increased. One study with contrary evidence was conducted by Kasarda and Janowitz (1974), though its survey was conducted in another culture (i.e., Great Britain) and did not sample respondents in the London area.

In another use of the Detroit Area Study (Baldassare, 1975b), I examined how the interviewer was treated by the respondents (i.e., in a hostile or friendly manner, as reported by the interviewer). This was considered another indication of how casual contacts would be attended to at varying levels of neighborhood crowding. There seemed to be a tendency for respondents at high urban densities to be less friendly in this situation (r = −.10), though this finding did not stand up to rigorous tract-level and individual-level controls. However, an earlier study by Davis (1975) also indicated less responsiveness to interviews by residents of dense neighborhoods.

These so-called casual encounters were examined through the use of the large-scale national surveys, which contained a variety of items on neighboring and respondent behavior during the interview. The ISR study contained one item that asked individuals to evaluate "the people who live around here. As neighbors, would you say they are very good [1], fairly good [2], neither good nor bad [3], not very good [4], or not good at all [5]?" Only about one-fourth of the respondents living at thirty-five or more persons per residential acre rated their neighbors as "very good" compared to half of the total sample. This neighboring item was highly related to the density of the area (r = .18) despite stringent controls (beta weight = .15; p < .001). This was replicated in an item from cycle 12 of the NORC study (N = 437), which asked, "What about the people who live around here? As neighbors, would you say they are very good [1], fairly good [2], neither good nor bad [3], not very good [4], or not good at all [5]?" This item was also significantly associated with neighborhood density (r = .14), even after the five life-cycle and socioeconomic factors were taken into account (beta weight = .11; p < .03). Because these questions only indirectly measure interactions with neighbors, through evaluations of them, other items were examined as well.

The NORC study, in cycles 3 and 4 (N = 823), asked several other questions more directly concerning relations with neighbors. One was, "How many of your neighbors do you know well enough to stop and talk with—none [0], some [1], most [2], all [3]?" Approximately 12 percent of those residing at thirty-five or more persons per residential acre knew none of their neighbors, while only 5 percent of the total sample knew none. This item correlated with the measure of areal crowding at −.15, and remained significant after controls (beta weight = −.10; p < .01). It raises some interpretational problems, since it could be reflecting the greater proportion rather than greater numbers of unknown neighbors (in other words, high density areas have more neighbors available). Another NORC item asked if individuals thought their "neighbors were friendly [3], neither friendly nor unfriendly [2], or unfriendly [1]." This item was not as highly correlated with neighborhood density (r = −.08), though it remained steady after controls (beta weight = −.08; p < .05). In all, the evidence indicates a reduction in neighboring and less positive attitudes toward neighborliness in crowded residential areas.

Moving away from neighboring per se, an ISR item asked about interest in meeting new people. This seemed to be another indicator of the willingness to expend energy in the direction of casual contacts. The question was worded, "How interested would you say you are in meeting new people and making friends? Would you say you are very interested [1], somewhat interested [3], not very interested [5]?" Again, there appeared to be less willingness to engage in these kinds of casual encounters at high neighborhood densities (r = .11), which persisted after the use of the five control variables (beta weight = .12; p < .001). Approximately one-third of those living at the highest densities (i.e., thirty-five or more persons per residential acre) were "very interested" in comparison to almost half of the total sample.

Several responses by the interviewer concerning the treatment he or she received from the respondent were also reviewed for evidence of specialized withdrawal. The interviewer rated "How suspicious did the respondent seem to be about the study before the interview" at a score of one (not at all), three (somewhat), or five (very suspicious). The question, "How sincere did the respondent seem to be in his [her] answers?" was scaled one (completely sincere), three (usually sincere), and five (often seemed to be insincere). Finally, interviewers were asked, "Overall, how great was the respondent's interest in the interview?" and their responses were rated one (very high), two (above average), three (average), four (below average), and five (very low). At high neighborhood densities there was a tendency for the respondent to show greater suspicion (r = .17; beta weight = .16; p < .001), and to be perceived as less sincere in the interview situation (r = .14; beta weight = .14; p < .001), though no less interested (r = .07; beta weight = .05). Half of those living at the highest densities (i.e., thirty-five or more persons per residential acre) were suspicious (i.e., somewhat or very) compared to about one-fourth of the total sample. Half of the respondents considered "often insincere" were residents of neighborhoods with densities of twenty or more persons per residential acre. The results from two questions thus provide evidence of decreased input for casual encounters at high densities, while the evidence from the third item does not.

In sum, along with the negative findings reported in the sections on friendships and group affiliations, evidence of decreased social contacts in the sphere of casual encounters at high neighborhood densities was found (see table 11). Neighboring, the desire to engage in novel social contacts, and the treatment of strangers (i.e., interviewers) all indicated that social withdrawal does occur among the less lasting and rewarding contacts of more crowded urbanites. This lends some credence to hypotheses built around the concept of specialized withdrawal.[6]

Household Crowding and Social Contacts

Though Part III has thus far been concerned exclusively with the impact of neighborhood density on social patterns and attitudes, the effects of household crowding on social relations are now explored. This is because enhancement of significant human relationships is a central problem and should thus be considered for both levels of residential crowding. In addition, "contact management" and its ramifications are important components of crowded homes as well as high density neighborhoods. Both the theories and the hypotheses offered in this section differ considerably from those previously mentioned in this chapter, because of differences in the socioenvironmental settings of the home and neighborhood alluded to in chapter 1 and further explicated in chapter 4. The impact of adults' social position in the home is reviewed later and suggestions are offered for further subgroup analyses.

A Theory of Status and Space Use

As stated from the outset, any environment can have too many potential contacts due to an overabundance of people in relation to the available space, and thus the home is not immune to this problem. In essence, living in a crowded household could mean that residents are suffering intrusion or interference at an unacceptable level. This can produce problems with internal dwelling relations (see chapter 4) and withdrawal from relations with outsiders. Moreover, the problem of allocating the dwelling space for socializing is generally aggravated with more persons per room. Though not all social activities occur within the home, at some point in the development of intimate ties (at least in American culture) it is appropriate to entertain acquaintances at home. Because of the overabundance of intradwelling contacts and the lack of adequate household space, the quality and quantity of extradwelling social contacts should be adversely affected by household crowding.

However, if one examines the structure of social relations within most dwellings, it becomes clear that these predictions may be based on simplistic notions. The home is often a social setting for individuals who have lived together over a period of time as a group with culturally prescribed roles and relationships (i.e., the family). Individuals within it have varying degrees of status and power. For example, parents generally have influence over the actions of their children. In some cases, adult males have household decision-making capabilities while in other instances adult females do.

Of particular importance is the existence of a status hierarchy under conditions of potentially high contacts and scarce space within the home. Those with power in the family (usually parents) can devise and implement a strategy to maintain their social relations and perhaps those of others in the home at a desired level. This means that adults will attempt to control the activities of the group within the dwelling, so as to minimize social overload for themselves and perhaps others. In addition, they can usurp the household space they need from others in order to maintain their social functions. They have the option of conducting their social activities elsewhere as well. This viewpoint may seem to downplay fairness on the part of parents, placing primary emphasis on their needs to maintain order and normal levels of social interaction. My prediction is that space will be obtained and the control of disruptive actions (i.e., overload) will be achieved by those with power in the crowded home. Whether they act primarily in their own self-interest or for the entire family's successful functioning (as they perceive it) is not evident from this viewpoint. In general, adults' social relations are probably not significantly disrupted by household crowding. Thus, there would be no effects of household crowding on their friendships, group affiliations, or casual encounters for the national samples of adults.

Of course, power differentials in the home have the potential of causing the experience of household crowding to be different for children. Relatively speaking, they usually lack control over the residential environment. Their ability to maintain social contacts of high quality is thus more likely to be impaired. For example, their social position may make it more difficult for them (in some cases) to obtain the space they need for intradwelling socializing, and their in-dwelling time may be more subject to personal disturbances and lack of privacy. Further, their actions are more controlled than adults', and thus their ability to conduct interactions outside the home may be constrained. Unfortunately, the sample does not allow a test of this notion.

Evidence of No Adult Effects

The empirical findings concerning the effects of household crowding on social relations are now reviewed. Older studies, along with newer data from the national surveys, are used to test the notion that household crowding has no significant impact on adults' social ties. One problem with assessing past evidence is, again, that few rigorous studies of residential crowding and social interaction have been performed. In all, the data discussed here provide little support for the idea that a lack of household space hinders the social activities of adults.

Robert Mitchell's (1971) study of high density living in Hong Kong involved this topic to a minor extent. Of particular relevance, he found that living in crowded households led to less entertaining of neighbors. This is the only finding reported in this section that indicates any sort of social withdrawal due to a shortage of space per person. However, its generalizability should be questioned, since the study occurred outside North America, heightening the possibility of cultural misinterpretations. Unfortunately, no item of this nature was available in the United States national surveys.

A relevant study in North America was the Toronto Crowding Study conducted by Alan Booth (1976). He found no association between objective measures of household crowding and survey items concerning friendships and group affiliations, after controlling for extraneous factors (e.g., life cycle, ethnicity, socioeconomic status). These findings remained stable even when Booth examined the responses of males and females separately. Only one item indicated a negative impact of perceived (i.e., subjective) household crowding, and this was evident in only the female portion of the sample: females reported fewer contacts with relatives at higher levels of *perceived* household density. It should be stated, however, that Booth and his associates did not account for the number of children living within the residence, which is highly related to the amount of crowding in the dwelling and is also likely to be a hindrance to the visiting patterns of females. In addition, the problem of causality is again met in discussing subjective crowding: does a surplus of family contacts and a lack of outside contacts make one feel more crowded, or does feeling more crowded cause a decrease in social contacts?

As part of a larger analysis reported in a paper entitled, "Residential Density, Household Crowding, and Social Networks" (Baldassare, 1977), I examined the effects of household crowding (i.e., persons per room) on relations with neighborhood acquaintances. This used a national sample selected by Norman Bradburn and his associates in conjunction with their Neighborhood Integration Study (see Bradburn et al., 1970). The data gave no indication that household crowding in any way inhibited the social relations of adults. The number of persons per room had no bearing on the respondent's number of friends living in the neighborhood, the number or kinds of social contacts with neighbors, or the place in which socializing with neighbors occurred. This finding was consistent, both before and after controlling for life-cycle and socioeconomic factors.

The findings on household crowding and social contacts from the analysis of the two national surveys are now reviewed. The questions used were the same as those in the previous section on neighborhood density. No attempt is made to give separate accounts of the associations between household crowding and the three kinds of social contacts previously outlined (i.e., casual encounters, group affiliations, friendships), since the hypothesis does not indicate a need for these distinctions.

First, household crowding and social activities are considered using the ISR Quality of Life survey. After controlling for the same five life-cycle and socioeconomic factors that were used in the last section, there were no indications that high persons-per-room ratios were disruptive to social ties (see table 12). This examination included all of the previous items on friendships, organizations, and casual encounters mentioned earlier in conjunction with the ISR study. Data from the NORC Continuous National Survey indicated similar results, since adults' social lives were in no way hampered by the densities they experienced in their homes when other factors were taken into account.[7]

The effects of "subjective" household crowding on social contacts were also considered. Using the items on perceived crowding discussed in chapter 3, I found no indication that the "feeling" of living in a crowded dwelling was related to the quality and quantity of social contacts.

In summary, the density of the dwelling had no noticeable impact on relations with people outside the family (see table 12). There could be effects on the social lives of children, though this assumption remains untested due to limitations in the data collected (i.e., the exclusion of individuals under eighteen years of age). Evidence from previous studies has alluded to the problems children have in obtaining household space for their own social activities under conditions of dwelling-space scarcity (see Mitchell, 1971; Davis et al., 1974). So, the present study only reports the social effects of crowding for those who have the most control over space and activities in the home. A fuller exploration of the household or population may not present as positive a picture of individuals' abilities to adapt their social relations to scare spatial re-

Table 12

Beta Weights for Social Contacts Regression Equations: Selected Items for Household Density[a]

	Household Density	Respondent's Age	Home Ownership	Years in Neighborhood	Respondent's Education	Tract Median Income
Friendships						
Number of friends (ISR)	.01	-.004	-.07	-.08	-.03	-.01
Quality of friends (ISR)	-.06	.07	.04	.07	.01	-.02
Group affiliations						
Number of groups (ISR)	.04	.05	.17[c]	.10[c]	.32[c]	.07
Quality of groups (ISR)	-.03	.11[b]	.08[b]	.03	.06	-.06
Participation in neighborhood groups (NORC)	.09	.06	.11[b]	-.09	.19[c]	.10[b]
Meet with neighbors in groups (NORC)	.02	-.01	.07	.07	.16[b]	.08
Neighbors' interest in area (NORC)	-.02	.26[c]	.12	-.11	.15[b]	.10
Casual encounters						
Poor quality neighbors (ISR)	.01	-.16[c]	-.16[b]	-.04	-.08[b]	-.09[b]
Poor quality neighbors (NORC)	.03	-.31[c]	-.17[c]	-.17[c]	.08	-.12
Quantity of neighbors known (NORC)	.01	.05	.21[c]	.15[c]	.01	.02
Neighbors friendly (NORC)	.05	.06	.09	.03	.01	-.03

Shun meeting new people (ISR)	.04	.22[b]	.01	-.02	.001	-.02
Respondent suspicious (ISR)	.02	.12[c]	-.04	-.003	-.03	-.06
Respondent insincere (ISR)	.01	.05	-.05	-.200	-.11[c]	-.02
Respondent uninterested (ISR)	.02	.06	-.01	-.04	-.27[c]	-.11[c]

[a]Beta weights and significance levels reported are for the final multiple regression equations.
[b]$p < .01$.
[c]$p < .001$.

sources. To partially meet this need for further research, the next section considers the impact of household crowding on adult males and females in the home.

The Impact of Social Position or Role

This section considers whether or not attributes of the individual have a moderating effect on the association between residential crowding and social contacts. Specifically, males and females are considered separately in order to determine if one gender has an advantage over the other in making the necessary adjustments and optimizing social ties under conditions of household crowding and high neighborhood densities. In addition, suggestions are made for other kinds of subgroup analyses that could not be pursued in this study.

I do not consider differences in gender to be a highly significant factor for social ties under dense residential conditions. It is unlikely that the sex of the respondent has an impact on the ability to conduct valued interpersonal relations and "turn off" less valued ones (i.e., specialized withdrawal). Perhaps females in high density neighborhoods will be less able to reduce their involvement in unwanted encounters (or more likely to be bothered by others) because of their relatively weaker social position, though such an interpretation seems oversimplified (e.g., they can probably manipulate situations in other ways, such as staying indoors more or going out in groups). Perhaps females in the crowded home, because of their role and status, are less able to obtain needed space for entertaining, less able to leave the home to engage in social contacts, and more vulnerable to the effects of overload. Again, I believe that their abilities to socialize are not especially affected by household crowding, since they can exert a considerable degree of flexibility and influence in the home to maintain, in most cases, an optimal level of contact in a long-term sense. In summary, I expect few if any subgroup differences of this nature to emerge, though the topic is of considerable importance and should be examined. All the items from the ISR survey found in this chapter are used in this analysis. Zero-order correlations between the residential crowding variables (household crowding, neighborhood density) and the dependent variables (friendships, group affiliations, casual encounters) for each gender are considered, as well as the beta weights in a final regression equation that included the five life-cycle and socioeconomic control variables and one or the other of the residential crowding measures.

First, neighborhood density was examined, and in general no large differences were found between the subgroups. Friendships and group affiliations showed no impact of residential crowding for either gender, though males tended to be slightly less satisfied with their organizational affiliations than females (for reasons that may have more to do with different styles of answering questions, or different experiences with the phenomena, than with density). Concerning casual encounters, similar responses were given for the neighboring item, but females tended to be slightly more suspicious of the interviewer and less interested in meeting new people than were males (they also tended to appear less interested in the interview itself). This may indicate greater concern about safety and crime among females at high densities and may not necessarily be a sign that women have difficulty reducing the level of contacts. On the other hand, it may indicate that those with a weaker social position do have a harder time reducing unwanted or undesired contacts. This issue should be further examined in future studies, since it may point to special problems of women living in high density neighborhoods.

The same items were reviewed for evidence of the differential impact of household crowding. There were no variations between subgroups for items concerning friendships, group affiliations, or casual encounters. This result was replicated when considering husbands versus wives, which seemed to reflect potential social and role position differences in the home better. Only one finding was worth noting when perceived crowding was examined instead of objective crowding. Wives' friendships seem to be slightly disrupted by perceived household spatial inadequacies, while husbands' friendships were not. Though a variety of interpretations could be offered for this finding, it is possible that displeasure with the dwelling's spatial features may cause women in this sample to be less willing to entertain friends (i.e., crowding heightens embarrassment and consequently lessens home invitations by them; see also discussions on subgroup differences in Part II). It may also be an expression of less "usable" space for some women's needs and thus an indication of the impact of their social or role position. Further studies should examine whether there are sex differences in the amount of household space available for private and social purposes, as well as determining if crowding per se makes certain subgroups decrease their social involvement more than others. The former proposition was the only one given some support in this study.

The present analysis provided only limited evidence of sex differences and examined possible routes for future studies that may not be constrained by examining secondary data. I would also suggest that more studies be conducted to determine whether people whose values or backgrounds limit their ability to make adjustments such as specialized withdrawal (e.g., people who value neighboring and casual contacts, rural dwellers) suffer social or psychological decrements or express more residential dissatisfaction from crowding. It would be significant to determine if those who cannot devise strategies to keep the level of social contacts manageable, due to either ineptness or other social and psychological factors, experience more general effects of neighborhood crowding. Regarding family adaptations that may allow social functioning to remain at an acceptable level, it would be important to note if those in transient positions in the home (i.e., boarders), or those living in crowded households with nonrelatives, or those living in families with weak or illegitimate power structures report less socializing. At the very least, these subgroup studies of household crowding must contain measures of "home entertaining" at the group and individual level (similar to Mitchell, 1971) and should include children (i.e., possibly the lowest social position) to assess these issues properly.

In summary, there is only very limited evidence that females' social ties are more affected by crowding than males' social ties. This issue should be further examined in the future, along with other subgroup analyses considering the social, psychological, and value-oriented differences among individuals.

Summary and Conclusions

This chapter reviewed theory and evidence regarding the effects of residential crowding on social relations. Overall, little evidence would suggest that high densities in homes or neighborhoods disturb the most important social activities of their residents. The respondents did not show social patterns that would be predicted from the cognitive fatigue or general withdrawal models. The social overload argument was restated and several new avenues for analyzing and predicting the effects of residential crowding were explored.

First, in attending to the relationship between neighborhood density and social encounters, the kinds of contacts experienced by urbanites were carefully explored. It was evident that these associations could be ranked by degree of importance, or potential for rewards, and that this had implications for high density or socially overloaded conditions. As predicted, the data indicated that only the less valuable (i.e., casual) contacts are affected by situations in which crowded urbanites are forced to "turn off" and "tune down" their relations with others. The more rewarding and important social activities (i.e., friendships and formal groups) are unchanged.

In considering household crowding and social contacts, the social order of the typical dwelling was noted. This led to the view that those with power (i.e., adults) are able to control space and activities in the home in order to optimize their social contacts. The data provided no evidence of disturbed social activities due to dwelling-unit density. The results gave necessary information but were not sufficient to establish validity for the statements about the control over space.

The theories reported here stressed that most human beings under conditions of high density can use social and personal resources to obtain desired social goals and reduce the negative effects of crowding. The present data allude to the abilities of human beings to adapt through problem solving and social structure. Future studies must provide more concrete evidence of the coping strategies inferred from these findings.

The view of the mechanisms for adjusting to crowding was not totally positive. The strategy of specialized withdrawal, while protecting the individual from the more serious circumstance of overload, may create a less-than-desirable social atmosphere for many urbanites. For example, the quality of urban life suffers, in terms of relationships with both insiders (i.e., neighbors) and outsiders (i.e., strangers), especially those who value casual encounters (e.g., due to socialization or the lack of primary ties). People who lack the ability to manage their contacts in the home or neighborhood adequately—for example, those in weaker social positions (e.g., children) or those with psychological deficits—may be less able to make the necessary adjustments to maintain their important social ties. Little evidence was found for this, though here only the impact of gender was considered, and thus it was urged that future research examine this issue more carefully. Again, the general notion is that most people can find strategies to ensure fairly "normal" human social patterns under conditions of residential crowding, yet coping costs in some respects.

Part IV—Conclusions

7. Reevaluating the Issue of Residential Crowding

This final chapter[1] has three purposes. First, I consider the most widely discussed and perhaps the most significant topic in the density literature: the effects of residential crowding on pathology. I cast the problem in a way that differs from past approaches and use the national survey data to help support my arguments. The evidence I evaluate suggests that the commonly expressed thoughts about a link between density and well-being are not substantiated and that more complex models need to be evaluated. Next, I give a brief and general review of the contributions and problems of the present study, and I suggest topics for future research. I then make some concluding remarks on the need to consider space as a resource and, in particular, on the special problems of space management and contact management, which I characterize as central problems in modern urban society.

Residential Crowding and Pathology:
Another Look at a Popular Topic

Why has the mental and physical well-being of individuals been a critical issue in past discussions of residential crowding? Foremost, this is because research on animals reported dramatic behavioral problems and illnesses among caged, crowded populations. In particular, of course, the widely noticed work of John Calhoun (1962) was extremely influential in forcing a consideration of the relationship between high density living and psychophysiological abnormalities (see also Christian et al., 1960). The frightening and spectacular results of nonhuman studies probably led some social scientists to believe that they might find such bizarre problems among humans (e.g., high aggression, low fertility, high mortality). Coincidentally, the United States was undergoing an "urban crisis" during the 1960s. The riots and social disorder that struck many major cities a decade ago seemed to defy all reasoning, and, as social scientists searched for answers, several looked to the possible consequences of over-crowded living conditions. The theoretical model that de-veloped from the animal studies and current events was a simple one: crowding leads to stress, which leads inevitably to pathology.

Unfortunately, as stated earlier, the reports of animal experiments tended to misguide some of the work of social scientists. For instance, researchers would attempt merely to replicate earlier nonhuman studies instead of giving proper consideration to social theories or human living conditions. Such analyses sometimes overlooked human abilities to or-ganize and control dense settings, and they did not consider that the actual densities experienced in urban America were not comparable to the physical circumstances in the animal studies. The importance of density was often overestimated because these models disregarded the fact that economic re-sources are highly predictive of well-being and that spatial and economic resources are often highly correlated. In gen-eral, crowding models based on work with animals tended to express simplistic ideas about the impact of crowding on human pathology. They ignored, among other things, impor-tant differences among species and environments. For vari-ous reasons, then, these models had weak predictive power, as I shall report later in this chapter.

Crowding research on pathology has leaned heavily on two methods in the past. The use of the experimental method gave researchers the ability to approximate the studies of caged animals that they so often tried to replicate. In addi-tion, sociologists with urban expertise found data on neighborhood crowding and areal rates of deviance and pathology in good supply. These two methods are, of course, subject to criticism in terms of reliability and validity (see Baldassare and Fischer, 1977). Unfortunately, few studies sampled households, and even fewer directly assessed the impact of both housing and neighborhood densities on an individual's well-being. In this chapter, some new thoughts and survey data contribute relevant information to this crucial issue.

Past Evidence and New Hypotheses

Aside from the methodological problems and theoretical issues I have just raised concerning the literature on crowding and pathology, the research findings themselves do not offer convincing evidence of a link between the two. While one study finds deleterious effects, others may find no effects, and yet others find positive effects associated with high densities. In addition, there have been strong controversies over the proper measurement of both pathology and crowding, and there is little consensus on the extent to which multivariate techniques are needed (and how they are to be used). All that can be said about the studies of well-being to date is that consistent findings have not emerged. If replicability is the ingredient needed to show the reliability and validity of trends, then I would argue that there is no association between density, mental health, and physical health (see reviews in Fischer et al., 1975; Fischer and Baldassare, 1975; Freedman, 1973, 1975; Freedman et al., 1975).

Because of my particular theoretical orientation, I am neither surprised nor disappointed to find little sound evidence for the hypothesized link between residential crowding per se and pathology. I have stressed throughout this book that most people can develop strategies to overcome the effects of residential crowding, and that these effects are basically problems of social overload and lack of needed space. Overt signs that these adaptations actually take place were not measured in the survey data, though it was clear from this analysis that important social ties remain intact and family relations are only marginally affected by conditions of residential crowding. It was argued that adults can control activities and space use in crowded homes and thus minimize family frictions. These management abilities would prevent the disturbance of most important social exchanges and allow the individual to avoid psychic problems associated with overcrowding (e.g., frustration, overload). Concerning neighborhood overcrowding, I suggested the existence of a process called specialized withdrawal. Basically, this involves the protection of primary social ties in times of potential social overload by eliminating (or deemphasizing) contacts that are less important to the individual. The kinds of adaptations outlined here seem to ensure an adequately normal social life for most individuals in crowded residential environments, while minimizing the psychological consequences of over-stimulation and other problems related to overcrowding.

Although dense environments may be disliked and may have qualitative effects on certain kinds of relationships, the general hypothesis regarding well-being is that serious effects will not be found from crowding, since various strategies are available to most people to reduce its impact. Unlike an ar-gument that crowding has no impact on individuals, my model places strong emphasis on people's real and perceived abilities to control their residential environments (see the lit-erature reviewed in Baldassare, 1978). Thus, certain sub-groups, namely those with less social power (e.g., children, the poor, women, the elderly, the physically or mentally handicapped) could suffer (additional) psychological prob-lems from the effects of crowding. The latter notion is par-tially explored at the end of this section.

Evidence from the National Surveys

Since items from the national surveys covered topics in the general category of "pathology," they can be used to test the proposition that household crowding and neighborhood crowding do not have independent effects on well-being. Furthermore, unlike the past attempts outlined earlier, the methods used here allow examination of individuals' re-sponses to their actual residential conditions.

First, the issue of physical health is explored through the use of these surveys (see tables 13 and 14).[2] An item in the NORC survey (N = 852) asked, "Compared to other people of your age, would you say that your health is very good [1], good [2], fair [3], poor [4], or very poor [5]?" and was coded

Table 13

Beta Weights for Household Density and Pathology Regression Equations:
NORC and ISR Comparisons[a]

	Household Density	Education of Respondent	Home Ownership	Years in the Dwelling	Family Income	Age of Respondent
Physical health						
ISR	-.03	-.18[c]	-.04	-.004	-.09[b]	.21[c]
NORC	.002	-.12[b]	-.01	.01	-.14[c]	.15[c]
Mental health						
ISR	.04	-.07	.000	.01	-.12[c]	-.11[b]
NORC	-.01	-.05	-.02	-.07	-.09	-.08
Happiness						
ISR	.07	-.002	-.08[b]	.02	-.15[c]	.06
NORC	.01	-.05	-.11[b]	.01	-.02	-.04
Life satisfaction						
ISR	.02	.01	-.08[b]	.04	-.16[c]	-.08
NORC	.04	.03	-.13[c]	.03	-.06	-.01

[a]Scales run from high to low on the dependent measures. Beta weights and significance levels reported are for the final multiple regression equations.
[b]$p < .01$.
[c]$p < .001$.

Table 14

Beta Weights for Neighborhood Density and Pathology Regression Equations: NORC and ISR Comparisons[a]

	Neighborhood Density	Education of Respondent	Home Ownership	Years in Neighborhood	Tract Median Income	Age of Respondent
Physical health						
ISR	.05	-.21[c]	-.05	-.02	-.02	.24[c]
NORC	-.01	-.15[c]	-.04	.02	-.08	.18[c]
Mental health						
ISR	-.03	-.10[c]	-.01	-.02	-.09[b]	-.10[b]
NORC	-.02	-.06	-.05	-.02	-.06	-.08
Happiness						
ISR	.08[b]	-.05	-.07	.04	-.10[c]	.03
NORC	.07	-.06	-.10[b]	.03	.003	-.05
Life satisfaction						
ISR	.01	-.04	-.10[b]	-.04	-.07	-.04
NORC	.04	.01	-.14[c]	.05	.004	-.03

[a]Scales run from high to low on all the dependent measures. Beta weights and significance levels reported are for the final multiple regression equations.
[b]p < .01.
[c]p < .001.

as shown in brackets. Several ISR (N = 1,361) questions dealt with health issues, including one that was worded: "Of course most people get sick now and then, but overall, how satisfied are you with your own health?" and was ranked from one (completely satisfied) to seven (completely unsatisfied). The relationships between these variables and persons per room and persons per residential acre were not significant (i.e., r ≤ .08), particularly when extraneous variables (i.e., age, years in residence, education, home ownership, and income) were accounted for through multiple regression techniques.[3]

Next, data on the mental health of individuals living at various densities are examined. An ISR question stated: "Some people have so many problems in their everyday life that they worry they might have a nervous breakdown. Do you worry about this?" and was coded two (yes) or one (no). A section of the NORC survey asked people several questions about "how they were feeling these days." Among other things, they were asked if they were feeling either restless, depressed, or upset, and responses were coded two (yes) or one (no). For these items no zero-order correlations with crowding variables were above .08 and their beta weights were small and insignificant (i.e., about .05; p > .01).

"Satisfaction with life" was examined using an item from each national survey. The ISR question asked, "How satisfied are you with your life as a whole these days?" and was scaled from one (completely satisfied) to seven (completely dissatisfied). This time, the zero-order correlations between the two density variables and this item were below .06, and control factors diminished this association to a beta weight below .03. A similar NORC item in cycles 11 and 12 was worded, "Generally speaking, how satisfied would you say that you are with your life as a whole—completely satisfied [0], very satisfied [1], moderately satisfied [2], slightly satisfied [3], or not at all satisfied [4]?" This item had a slightly higher correlation with household crowding (r = .05) and neighborhood density (r = .08), though the beta weights were insignificant and identical (beta weight = .04; p > .10).

Lastly, a measure of the general level of "happiness" expressed by the respondents was used to determine if residential crowding had effects on this element of well-being. An ISR question asked, "Taking all things together, how would you say things are these days—very happy [1], pretty happy [3], or not too happy [5]?" Those living at high neighborhood densities did report more unhappiness ($r = .12$; beta weight $= .08$; $p < .01$). An attempt was made to duplicate this result through the analysis of a similarly worded NORC item coded from one (very happy) to three (not too happy). A similar zero-order correlation was found ($r = .11$), though an insignificant beta weight (.07; $p > .01$) resulted. It should be noted that these relationships, when controlling for other factors, are not very large. Also, the failure to obtain significance using both surveys does not add validity and reliability to this finding. For both survey items, in addition, there was no meaningful relationship between household crowding and happiness: the zero-order correlations were nonsignificant, as were the beta weights.

The majority of the items reviewed were not significantly associated with the measures of residential crowding when controlling for other factors (see tables 13 and 14). Of course, reporting insignificant effects may merely indicate that the items on pathology have no validity. The best indication of the adequacy of these self-evaluations is the fact that they are significantly related to expected factors, such as age and education. Thus, the conclusion is that the negative findings are not due to an inability to measure mental and physical health, happiness, and satisfaction with life.

This exercise confirms the general notion that the issue of pathology as currently stated, which has attracted so much attention in the density literature, lacks both conceptual and empirical grounding. Perhaps overcrowding has no effect on humans at all and thus no impact on overall well-being. I would argue, based on the thoughts of Spencer (1895), Durkheim (1893 [1964]), and the school of human ecology (Hawley, 1950), that density and increased social contacts facilitate and necessitate complex social organizations and the scheduling of roles and activities in space. Thus, control or organization can often alleviate the gross problems associated with well-being that one would expect to occur with overcrowding. For now, it seems obvious that the typical treatment of pathology and crowding should be replaced by a more comprehensive and complex view of humans in crowded environments. I allude to this in the analysis of subgroup effects and discuss it further in the reviews toward the end of this chapter.

An Investigation of Subgroup Effects

Scattered evidence in the crowding and pathology literature suggests that certain kinds of individuals may be more vulnerable to the impact of high density situations. Studies of children in crowded homes have found not only social deficits (Davis et al., 1974; Mitchell, 1971) but also impairments in well-being (Rodin, 1976; Booth and Johnson, 1975). The argument is made by Gove et al. (1977) that mothers in crowded homes are placed in a taxing role position, which has implications for their mental health. Data gathered in social psychology experiments suggest that perceived loss of control makes crowding in a laboratory room psychically disturbing (Sherrod, 1974). In this section, I supply further information on the impact of residential crowding on well-being for special groups within the general sample of NORC respondents (cycles 11 and 12).

To my knowledge, there has been no systematic study of individuals living at high neighborhood densities who vary in economic resources, life cycle, or psychological attributes. Such a study would be extremely worthwhile, particularly given the emphasis of this book on needed abilities for managing (and manipulating) interpersonal relations and spatial resources. However, in order to test those ideas properly, it would probably be necessary to do the following: select a sample of *high density* residents who vary along those dimensions; collect information on self-selection or "drift," to ensure that the physical environment has a real impact on well-being (e.g., that the data are not showing only that the mentally ill of low incomes reside at higher densities); provide measures of attempts to cope with crowding; and measure relevant indices of well-being. Unfortunately, the present subgroup analysis can only partially explore the issue at hand. Here, the relationship between neighborhood density and well-being was measured through a series of items mentioned in the last section (i.e., whether or not the respondent recently felt restless, depressed, upset, excited, bored, elated, lonely, pleased, proud), and the metropolitan sample was separated into three kinds of subgroups for examination. *Economic resources* seemed to be an important indicator of the ability to control crowded environments; thus respondents with family incomes of less than $10,000 were separated from those with more. *Stage of life cycle* represents two important factors of relevance to this discussion: middle-aged people at high densities may show signs of general dissatisfaction with life, due to the lack of fit between their environment and their needs, and may experience feelings of relative deprivation; and the elderly, due to a variety of physical problems, may be further strained by the cost of coping (or may be unable to cope) in crowded neighborhoods. Therefore respondents were separated into three age groups: individuals over sixty-five, under thirty, and thirty to sixty-four. *Psychological attributes*, such as existing neuroses or psychoses, may cause individuals to suffer ineptness and powerlessness that decrease the effectiveness and implementation of coping strategies: for that reason, respondents who feel "depressed" or "restless" and live in high density neighborhoods may have more serious deficits in well-being.

Though the relationship between neighborhood density and pathology was minimal for the total sample, some associations were significant within subgroups. This finding lends support to the notion that crowding is a significant factor, though in more complex ways than previously imagined. Some of the highlights of this brief exploration follow. When considering differences in life cycle, the under-thirty group seemed unaffected by neighborhood density, while the elderly were more "lonely" and "depressed" at high densities, and the middle-aged individuals were less "pleased" and "proud." Though the evidence is obviously crude (i.e., in measurement of the variables and the statistical approach used here), it does point to the kinds of deficits that were anticipated. Less affluent people living in high density situations did not show more restlessness or depression, though they were less proud, pleased, and excited about things than the more affluent respondents. People varying along the psychological dimensions mentioned in the previous paragraph also tended to be less proud and pleased. Of course, this very preliminary analysis of subgroup effects raises more questions than it answers. However, in at least one case, that of life-cycle variations, it points to promising avenues for future research.

The impact of household crowding on well-being could vary with social status in the home and the ability of the family structure to manage space and activities. The latter factor was unavailable in the survey data, and gender was the only available measure of potential variations in social position. As indicated in other chapters, I do not expect sex differences between adults in the home to be highly indicative of inequities in allocation of space or variations in the ability to avoid certain contacts in the home. The status of children in the home would probably be more vulnerable to spatial and social problems associated with overcrowding, thus resulting in possible deficits in well-being for that subgroup. Unfortunately, such an investigation was impossible with the present data. An examination of gender subgroups indicated no variations in well-being with higher levels of household crowding, supporting my original speculations.

My rather swift treatment of this topic should not be taken as a sign of its unimportance or simplicity. Rather, I am responding to limitations in the available data and the research design, and my overarching concern with general knowledge about residential crowding in urban America, rather than intensive analyses of subgroups. Perhaps more than any topic mentioned thus far, the well-being of individuals with specific attributes residing in high density homes and neighborhoods has direct and immensely important policy and planning implications. It is disturbing, particularly given some recent statements that "high density is not a problem," that so little work of this nature has been done. Obviously, this item should receive high priority in the near future and needs to include the impact of residential crowding on individuals with multiple handicaps (e.g., age, health, income, psychological state).

New Directions for Studies of Residential Crowding

The suggestions offered for future research on residential crowding are colored by impressions of the state of crowding research and the successes and failures of this study. Today, this area is largely the domain of environmental psychologists and very few sociologists. As a result, research on crowding has not been sufficiently concerned with sociological theories and strictly social phenomena. In many cases, the work thus lacks relevance to urban life. My bias, then, has been toward developing sociological issues within a field largely dominated by psychological concerns. This would advance knowledge on two fronts, since the sociological perspective ought to be incorporated within the study of crowding and because crowding is extremely relevant to numerous issues in sociology.

There is a great need for theory to guide research on residential crowding. As I indicated earlier, many researchers have placed undue emphasis on biological and environmental determinism. This tendency has eroded only recently, as psychologists studying crowding have begun to delineate models stressing cognitive, learning, and personality processes (see Rodin, 1976; Stokols, 1972b, 1978; Cohen, 1977). These are healthy and exciting developments in a field previously stunted by a theoretical vacuum. There remains, at least in my mind, a need to supplement these explanations with ideas from sociology and social psychology, to add depth and relevance to the complex issues surrounding crowding in residential environments.

For example, in this book I have used assumptions from *exchange theory* and *human ecology.* Assuming that people calculate the costs and benefits of residential environments and encounters in order to maximize their utilities, one can develop empirically testable hypotheses about the social and psychological impacts of neighborhood density. By analyzing the existence and use of power and control in families, hypotheses can be developed about how dwelling residents cope with overcrowding, and which individuals are likely to implement and decide on which strategies. By considering the positive and negative aspects of population density, as predicted by human ecology theory, one can develop hypotheses about the residential satisfaction likely to be expressed by individuals with differing environmental needs. There have also been some recent and promising uses of concepts from *role theory* and *symbolic interactionism* (see Ellis, 1974; Smith, 1971; Ball, 1973; Lym, 1975; Silverman, 1976). They alert us to the meanings people attach to space and the roles they expect to perform in specific settings. These concepts provide a somewhat different perspective on the problems that crowding creates for social interactions. Clearly, a view of human crowding that includes the power relations among individuals, their roles and prescribed activities, the strategies they use to obtain their goals, and the symbolic meaning they attach to the space they occupy would be a major contribution to present theoretical development and the future of crowding research.

Equally important are *research designs* and techniques suited to produce definitive answers to those questions. To some extent, crowding research has experienced a movement out of the laboratory and into the field over the last several years. This new wave of studies lacks the validity that large random samples of urban residents would provide, and too few substantive issues are usually examined. Large-scale social surveys, including responses of individuals living in a variety of residential circumstances, would be a most useful way to study the broad range of questions emerging in the field of crowding. Naturally, such data should be supplemented by contextual information on residential crowding and other characteristics of the social and physical environment. The present study used this approach, and lessons were learned that should help to improve future studies. Secondary analysis was a useful way to test some general propositions about the impact of residential crowding on attitudes and social patterns. It was not, however, well suited to answering more complex questions about individuals' attempts to reduce the potential problems associated with crowding, nor was it capable of fully exploring subgroup effects. Clearly, interview schedules need to be designed to produce data on people's adaptations to their spatial and social limitations, as well as the adjustments they have made over time. The skew that was present in the measures of household and neighborhood density, indicating that few people in fact reside at very high densities, also points to the fact that a possible approach in the future may be to sample *densities* rather than households. In addition, it will be necessary to sample children and perhaps other theoretically relevant subgroups in future studies.

Several important *substantive issues* have been overlooked in the past, probably because of the attention given to the link between crowding and pathology. I have tried to address that imbalance in the present study by concentrating on residential attitudes and social life. In addition, despite all the studies on well-being, it is obvious that this area of great practical and theoretical importance deserves more thought and carefully constructed research. In particular, individuals having certain social and psychological characteristics that may limit their ability to control and organize their residential surroundings may be psychically and physically affected by overcrowding. This question could be explored only partially in the present study. Future studies may have to be narrower and more intensive and will probably demand special sampling designs (or quasi-experimental designs) as well as measures of present environmental, social, physical, and psychological conditions.

A minimal amount of time has been devoted to studies of residential attitudes: perceptions of crowding, global satisfaction with the home or neighborhood, preferences and reasons for mobility, and satisfaction with specific attributes of residential environments (see, e.g., Marans and Rodgers, 1973). This constellation of attitudinal variables points to a need to better understand the effects of household and neighborhood crowding on the "quality of life," in the interest of both academic pursuits and practical concerns about how to provide settings that are satisfactory to residents. I found that household crowding was noticed by many and led to feelings of housing dissatisfaction and a preference to move. Higher neighborhood densities were less favored, though there were a few positive aspects of those settings. Absent from this analysis were objective measures or hard data on the physical attributes of homes and neighborhoods (e.g., available facilities, services, design, trees). Future studies would do well to consider those additional factors both as mediating and as dependent variables. Some evidence suggested that individuals who vary in life cycle or social position have different attitudes about "specifics" in their settings. That issue is of considerable importance and needs future attention. Data on expectations, perceived alternatives, residential experiences, and abilities to alter the present environment favorably would be critical to the discussion.

The study of social processes was given considerable emphasis here because of questions I raised about the need to manage space and contacts in high density residential settings. Future studies might concern family structure and concentrate on role performance, frictions due to loss of privacy, family adaptations to spatial shortages, and the allocation and differentiation of space in crowded homes. The effects of household crowding and of resulting group strategies on family members who may not have direct authority over space use (e.g., children, nonfamily residents) or who may have more demands and responsibilities (e.g., women) in this "primary environment" (Stokols, 1976) should be considered in more detail than I have done. For now, it appears that household crowding leads to mild family problems and no serious disruptions. These issues apparently demand in-depth interviewing with several household members and long-term field studies in the home.

Few researchers have concentrated on the wide range of extrafamilial relations that could be affected by the high levels of social contact associated with neighborhood and urban crowding: friendships, organizational affiliations, support networks, neighboring, behavior toward strangers, and casual encounters. I have reported information suggesting a deterioration of "nonessential" social relations in conditions of high neighborhood density. Detailed descriptions of neighborhood socializing are absent from the data now available, and evidence for the strategy of specialized withdrawal is indirect. Finally, models that link various substantive issues (environmental attitudes, social patterns, well-being) would provide a highly sophisticated view of human crowding phenomena. I doubt that they can be fully tested with data collected at one point in time.

In the near future, research on population density will have to take two other directions. First, aside from the pioneering work of Hall (1966) and Mitchell (1975), *cross-cultural* studies of crowding have not been developed. Whatever paradigm one operates under, eventually such studies need to be conducted: ethological and psychological explanations would predict similarities, while social structural and social psychological (e.g., expectations) theories would predict varying responses to population density. In my opinion, these studies would be useful because they would point to various cultural factors that limit individual and group adaptations to overcrowding (e.g., the amount of privacy required for certain activities, the ability of the family to control its members, the level of desired neighboring and social stimulation). Second, studies of *population growth* and decline should be conducted in the same neighborhoods or households over lengthy time periods. They would reveal changes that occur in social and environmental quality with population density and provide valuable information on the ability of social structural and organizational forces to aid individuals in adapting to those changes.

The study of residential crowding has come a long way in a relatively short period of time. If it is to answer the profoundly important academic and practical issues that are ahead, it must not lose sight of the need for further theoretical development, the problems in research design, and the broad range of substantive issues that require investigation. I present a perspective on space, contacts, and crowding in the last section that highlights the importance of furthering knowledge in this area.

Space as a Resource and Crowding as a Social Issue[4]

This investigation ends with some general comments on the importance of questions concerning high density living conditions. My purpose is to address any lingering doubts that the reader might have about the relevance of the major factors considered in this book. The discussion is on an abstract level, though an attempt is made to provide examples from everyday experiences in modern urban society.

A perspective presented in this study is that *space is a resource*. In other words, it has value for humans, as money, time, or food do. Space is prized because it allows individuals to conduct activities that are desired; thus the allocation of space can cause conflict or competition unless rules and regulations are provided. A major function of society is to provide a framework for distributing space among its participants. It seems evident that in most social groups space is distributed so that those who have advantages in other resource categories (e.g., money, political power) have more space or greater ability to choose the space they want. Examples of this phenomenon abound and are evident in the occupational world. The president of a company can choose the site of the business, select an office in a building, and more than likely take the greatest amount of office space for personal use. Similar correlations between social status and space can be found in residential environments as I indicated earlier. The study of space and its use by humans thus is crucial because space is a valued entity that reflects the social order. It also has symbolic or communicative value, since it informs people of other attributes of an individual. Moreover, a lack of space, due to either low status or high competition (i.e., crowding) has extremely significant consequences, since it can constrain opportunities, goals, and activities.

I have also stressed the idea that *humans value social contacts* and that factors associated with modern life (density, population size, heterogeneity) necessitate some attempt to regulate social encounters. Few people want to be isolates, yet most also lack the desire or ability to socialize with every human they meet. Thus, a key element is the ability to choose those contacts that are the most pleasurable to the individual, while avoiding those that drain time and energy. Again, I believe that the distribution of this valued good (i.e., choice of contacts) varies along other obvious status dimensions. For example, the corporate president mentioned in the last paragraph has a secretary to screen phone calls and visitors; the executive's ability to visit or speak with friends and associates in the course of a day would make a salesperson or factory worker envious. In the same way, those with higher status and more resources are more able to maintain and develop the friendships they want and to manipulate their residential environments in ways that reduce unwanted disturbances. For instance, those who can afford transportation may have a citywide network of friends, in contrast to those who are able to maintain friendships only on their residential block (e.g., suburban housewives without cars; the inner city poor without carfare). An inability to regulate contacts successfully, or to choose those that are most wanted, can thus limit a person's experience of positive events. Of course, the combination of acquiring needed space and regulating social contacts as desired provides heightened opportunities for fulfilling one's goals (that is, assuming that the abilities to control contacts and obtain space are indicative of possession of other social and personal resources).

I have argued in this book that humans are not typically "overcome" by high density, as one would expect from reports of animal studies, because in general they can adapt by organizing their space and reducing their contacts to minimize the more harmful impacts. These ideas may seem like armchair speculating; yet control of space and activities already exists in modern urban societies, and it is clear how important that regulation is to people's well-being. It would be hard to imagine the chaos that would exist if society did not set aside land specifically for streets, sidewalks, commerce, industry, parking, and housing. Equally hazardous would be activities such as driving or walking across the street in dense areas without the aid of traffic lights and signs. Queuing in grocery stores or movie theaters is an important social mechanism for avoiding social contacts and conflicts in overpopulated settings. The point is that the urban individual's use of space and contact with others is highly controlled; it follows that adaptations to high density living may exist at the personal and small group level, like those in obvious evidence at the societal level.

It could be argued that the controls necessitated by density that I outlined in the previous paragraph are "good," since they allow the society to function smoothly and protect individuals from harmful events. While this is probably so, what further adaptations will be needed to cope with the tremendous world population expected in the next century? What will be the cost to individual freedom of choice in a world (or in specific countries) short on habitable space and high on potential contacts, aggravated, perhaps, by shortages of key resources such as energy? Will human life be characterized by even more control and organization of activities, at the personal, group, and societal levels? In addition, will the scarcity of space place even wider gaps between those who have already acquired necessary resources and those who have not, on local, national, and international levels? Can planners, policymakers, and social scientists have a say in the distribution of this resource or at least implement "coping strategies" for those who lack substantial ability to manipulate their crowded environments? It would be wise to begin asking these more futuristic and global questions about crowding now, as well as exploring the present problems associated with household and neighborhood crowding. Barring unforeseen events, the issue of crowding will become even more significant in coming decades.

Notes

Notes to Chapter 1

1. For a good example of how and why a planner uses housing-unit density as a measure of overcrowding, see Osborn (1956).

2. Donald Foley, personal communication. Also see Chapin (1957: chapter 12) for a discussion of the place of density in land use planning.

3. Allan Jacobs, personal communication. Chapin (1957:346–48) states that density restrictions are usually based on standards that are widely accepted, though local variations are considerable. The rationale for the standards, usually health and safety considerations, is rarely well stated or tested.

4. Additionally, the so-called FIRE organizations (finance, insurance, real estate) may, perhaps, seek center city locations for their main offices because the density of the commercial area facilitates face-to-face communication and coordination among organizations and thus allows more efficient and speedy functioning.

5. For a review of Durkheim's sociological theories, and the historical and philosophical period in which they developed, see Robert Nisbet, *The Sociology of Émile Durkheim* (1974). For discussions on the concept of community and the "decline of community" argument, see Claude Fischer et al., *Networks and Places* (1977), particularly chapters 1 and 10.

6. For other reviews by the author, see Baldassare (1978), Fischer et al. (1975), and Baldassare and Fischer (1977).

7. See review by Baldassare (1975c).

Notes to Chapter 2

1. Two previous publications (Baldassare and Fischer, 1977; and Fischer et al., 1975) contribute to this review and critique of past crowding research.

2. An entire issue of a widely read journal was devoted to "crowding in real environments" (see *Environment and Behavior*, June 1975). One reported study was conducted in a department store and train station (Saegert et al., 1975), another in a college dormitory (Baum et al., 1975), yet another in a children's psychiatric facility (Wolfe, 1975), another among sailors aboard ship (Dean et al., 1975), and the last among confined prisoners (D'Atri, 1975). Despite the apparent limitations of findings produced in such abnormal settings, the authors took great liberties to explain the relevance of their results to crowding theories, presumably because they used "real," as opposed to contrived, crowded settings.

3. The best overall discussion of the theory and method behind this approach is probably found in Hawley (1950). Another valuable review of the field of human ecology has been prepared by John Kasarda (1974), along with enlightening defenses of the method by Leo Schnore (1958, 1961), and a critique by William Michelson (1976:3–32).

4. I have argued against using the ecological approach in discussions of average household crowding in urban areas (see Galle et al., 1972) and against the implementation of gross areal measures, such as national densities (see Booth and Welch, 1973; Factor and Waldron, 1973). The former use can lead to inappropriate discussions of individual effects (i.e., ecological fallacies) and erroneous discussions of causation, unless control variables have been very carefully selected. The latter use aggregates data to a very high (and very error-prone) degree.

5. Two anthropological field studies conducted in nonurban societies have also related the population density of areas to the responses of individual inhabitants (cf. Munroe and Munroe, 1972; Draper, 1973).

6. An exception is the British national study reported by Kasarda and Janowitz (1974), which unfortunately eliminated the London area and thus also narrowed the range of possible densities.

7. The alternative, conducting a new survey that was broad in scope and sample selection, was financially unfeasible.

8. Those interested in the more technical aspects of the sampling procedure should consult Campbell et al., (1976: Appendix A) and Kish and Hess (1965).

9. For further information, consult Murray (1974), and King and Richards (1972).

10. For further information on this procedure, see the National Planning Data Corporation catalog (1974b) and its paper entitled "Population Density Report" (1974a).

11. As I discuss in chapter 5, neighborhood density often occurs in conjunction with multiple dwelling units (e.g., high rise buildings). The assumption here is that density per se and not building type affects the attitudes and actions of respondents. In reality it would be difficult to separate these two factors (as it is difficult statistically) but theoretically it seems easier to think of causal arguments related to neighborhood density than to the types of buildings in a particular area. In a sense, I indirectly controlled for building type through the use of the control variable "home ownership" in this study.

12. This study relies on racial composition as a measure of the heterogeneity of an area, though a factor with broader meaning would also be a useful control variable. No tract-level statistics seemed well suited, and the respondents' assessments of the similar-

ity of their neighbors seemed unreliable. It is unfortunate that the potential importance of heterogeneity, mentioned long ago by Wirth (1938), remains relatively unexplored.

13. All of the analyses use the Statistical Package for the Social Sciences Version 6.0 (see Nie et al., 1975).

Notes to Chapter 3

1. Elsewhere when cycles 3 and 4 of the Continuous National Survey are used, the comparability with the census and Quality of Life distribution is very similar.

2. The sample size for cycles 11 and 12 of the Continuous National Survey was 1,268. All 852 SMSA residents had data for "number of rooms" and "number of household members," so there are no missing cases for the ratio variable *persons per room*. The sample for the Quality of Life study was 2,164, while the number of SMSA residents was 1,361. This latter number differs slightly from other reported data from this survey, since my listing included residents of areas that were newly defined as SMSAS in 1970, while others are working with 1960 SMSA designations. There was one missing case in the "number of rooms" variable, accounting for an N of 1,360.

In all tables and reported statistics in this book, unless otherwise indicated, I used the provided weighting variable to account for sampling underrepresentations. However, for the sake of realism, the unweighted N is reported. I also use the unweighted N in calculating significance levels, so as not to inflate the chances of reaching significance by using large NS. No differences were found using weighted versus nonweighted data.

3. I examined data from the *Annual Housing Survey, 1974*, which included a sample of 50,000 all-year-round occupied housing units in metropolitan areas. There were fewer overcrowded dwellings in 1974 than in 1970 (i.e., approximately 5 percent), which seems to suggest the hypothesis of a continuing downward trend. However, I am not sure that the difference of two or three percentage points within the four-year period is one that can be relied on, given differences in methodology and instruments between the census and the housing survey. It does, however, in my estimation give considerable support for the interpretation of the yearly declines in household density found here (see U.S. Bureau of the Census, 1976a:2).

4. There are no apparent discrepancies in the measurement of number of rooms or number of household members in the two surveys. Both excluded bathrooms and hallways in counting the rooms, along with various kinds of unfinished and unfurnished space in the home. The distributions of the rooms and persons variables also seemed similar for the two surveys.

5. An analysis of data from the *Annual Housing Survey, 1974* basically supports this finding (U.S. Bureau of the Census, 1976b:5, 7).

6. This raises the question of whether children should count as one person each, since they contribute largely to what is considered household crowding. Though children do not have full-grown bodies, they probably demand as much (if not more) space for their household activities. Thus, I agree with the existing census definition.

7. In an early project report concerning the NORC data, Morgan and Murray (1974) used the same item on satisfaction with the dwelling. In assessing the effects of number of persons and number of rooms on all of the respondents of cycles 1 and 2, they reported a significant relationship between these household measures and the satisfaction item. For some unexplained reason, they did not, however, use "persons per room." Campbell et al. (1976:249–56) also examined housing satisfaction using the ISR data. Using the entire national sample, they basically replicate my results, though they used "number of rooms" and "rooms per person," placing a higher premium on space than on social factors in their discussions. They also used "size of rooms," which they considered a housing attribute instead of a subjective measure, finding, as is supported here later, that it is a good predictor of housing satisfaction.

8. The five control variables used in this section were a compromise between what needed to be controlled and what was available in both surveys. The general opinion has been widely held by sociologists for decades that socioeconomic conditions affect a wide range of attitudes and sometimes represent very different personal experiences. The use of family income and respondent's educational level, instead of a measure of occupational prestige, stems from a general dissatisfaction with scales based on the socioeconomic position of the head of the household (usually the male) rather than the respondent. Life-cycle factors seemed related to household crowding, so age, years in the dwelling, and home ownership were used to account for those effects. The latter two variables are also important in that they control for the amount invested (in terms of time and money) in a particular residence, which may account for attitude differences. Also, the home ownership variable helps to rule out apartment versus house attitude differences, which may account for certain apparent crowding effects. These control factors had, on the whole, little effect on existing statistical relationships between residential attitudes and household crowding, though some of the factors did have effects of their own.

9. These and other items concerning satisfaction with the dwelling unit were left separate, rather than being combined into an index of housing dissatisfaction. Since the items were not highly

correlated with each other, and since they stressed various aspects of the housing environment, it seemed better to analyze and report them separately.

10. The NORC leisure satisfaction item read: "How satisfied are you with the things you do in your leisure time or for recreation?" and was scaled from four (completely satisfied) to zero (not at all satisfied). The ISR leisure satisfaction question stated: "Overall, how satisfied are you with the ways you spend your spare time?" and was scaled from one (completely satisfied) to seven (completely dissatisfied). The NORC item was recoded here to scale both items in the same direction. The housework question, asked of female ISR respondents, was worded: "Different people feel differently about taking care of the home. I don't mean taking care of the children, but things like cooking, sewing, and keeping house. Some women look at these things as just a job that has to be done; other women really enjoy them. How do you feel about this?" The scale ranged from one (unqualified liking) to seven (unqualified disliking), though the form of this question was originally open-ended and required reading.

11. Additional tests confirmed the reliability of the reported findings. Using the logarithm of the household crowding measure, which reduces the skew of this variable, did not affect any of the findings reported from the regression equations. Dependent variables were tested from the ISR data in order to determine if the building that housed the dwelling unit (i.e., the number of stories and the type of structure) or the presence of children in the unit affected any of the findings. Again, no change occurred in the basic conclusions. Percentage of blacks and median income of the census tracts in which the respondents lived also had no effect on the association between household crowding and housing dissatisfaction.

To ensure that results could be attributed to persons per room (the ratio variable) and not the numerator (i.e., number of persons) or the denominator (number of rooms) comprising this measure, the numerator, the denominator, and the ratio variable were entered into a regression equation after the five control variables for each dependent variable studied in this section. In every case in which significant associations were reported except one (i.e., the NORC housing satisfaction measure) the beta weights for household crowding were larger than the beta weights for number of persons or number of rooms. While this seems to establish the independent importance of the persons-per-room measure, it must be noted that the colinearity between these measures makes this or any other "proof" tenuous. However, most statistical evidence is in favor of placing more importance on the ratio variable. The ability to replicate through various survey items in two national surveys lends further support to this conclusion. Conceptually speaking, household crowding better accounts for housing dissatisfaction, since it captures the amount of space available per individual in a residential setting better than other factors.

12. My review of the mobility literature was aided by two sources: Fischer and Stueve (1977) and Stueve (1976).

13. Using the logarithm of household crowding in the equations instead of actual persons per room did not significantly change any of the results. The additional ISR controls outlined in note 11 above also did not alter the association between mobility and persons per room. The beta weights for "persons" and "rooms" were also smaller than the beta weight for "persons per room" when these variables were present in an equation with five control variables. The relation between the NORC mobility item and persons per room did not change when controlling for "persons" and "rooms." This replicates an early analysis by Morgan and Murray (1974) of the first and second cycles of this interview. They based their conclusions on a cross-tabulation between the "here/elsewhere" question and a four-level grouping of household crowding (not an interval variable) using the entire national sample.

14. Using the logarithm of household crowding in place of actual persons per room did not change these results nor did the additional ISR controls outlined in note 11 above. For the NORC item, I entered into the regression equation with "persons," "rooms," and the five control variables, the household crowding measure: the beta weight for "persons per room" was higher than for the two variables comprising it. When the same procedure was carried out for the ISR item, the beta weight for "persons per room" was smaller than that of its numerator and denominator. Assessing all of the data, though, household crowding is associated with perceived crowding in and of itself, since the bulk of the evidence points in that direction.

15. I purposely avoided discussions of neighborhood crowding and dwelling discontent. My theoretical understanding of satisfaction with the dwelling and crowding in the home addresses itself only to relations between dwelling inhabitants, and most of the associations were weak anyway.

16. It could be argued that "social" explanations of the effects of household crowding call for data analyses that exclude people who are living alone. These data are not reported, since I wanted to account for all metropolitan respondents. However, a separate analysis excluding solitaries in the ISR survey yielded very similar results concerning housing discontent. When single person households are excluded from the analysis, some of the zero-order correlations between persons per room and the control variables change, and these changes have implications for the determinants of persons per room. While life-cycle factors (e.g., age, length of residence) do

not vary greatly, the relationship between two socioeconomic factors (dwelling ownership and education) gain strength slightly, and the association between family income and household crowding becomes a marginal negative association (i.e., less than −.1) rather than a marginal positive association (i.e., less than +.1). The unexpected marginal association between better incomes and more household overcrowding found earlier thus seems partially determined by the existence of poor, single person households of low density, as I argued in an earlier section. However, this analysis of two or more person households again stresses the greater importance of life-cycle factors than socioeconomic conditions.

17. It has been assumed that "feeling overcrowded" encompasses one kind of subjective measure, but there should probably be several different kinds of perceptual crowding items. For example, consider two categories of subjective crowding: aesthetic and reactional. What is measured in the national survey could be considered aesthetic crowding, since it indicated an incongruence between a spatial norm and the real density condition within the respondent's home. This is substantially different from reactional crowding, which indicates emotional distress (e.g., feeling thwarted, vulnerable, anxious, distracted) due to socio-spatial conditions (cf. Stokols, 1976). Perhaps once a certain threshold of aesthetic crowding is reached a degree of reactional crowding begins, or maybe both lead to reported environmental dissatisfactions but with varying final results. In any case, some distinction between subjective measures that merely indicate an awareness or appreciation of density levels (cognition) and those that illustrate a degree of despair and a need for action is in order (experience or evaluation). I have addressed only the aesthetic side of perceived crowding in this chapter.

18. It should be stated, however, that a relatively small percentage of the variance was explained for each dependent variable. For example, the five control variables, objective crowding, and subjective crowding accounted for 20 percent of the variance of the dwelling satisfaction items. After the inclusion of the five controls, household crowding accounted for an average of 2 or 3 percent, and after including all of those factors in a regression equation, the subjective crowding measure explained on the average another 5 percent of the variance. Variance in the preferred mobility item in the ISR survey was explained about 16 percent by all seven variables: about 5 percent of the variance was explained by a combination of persons per room (1.3 percent) and subjective crowding (3.9 percent) after accounting for the control variables. The factors contributing to the prediction of household crowding were reviewed in an earlier section of this chapter. Despite these low percentages, I still place considerable importance on the impact of household crowding on

dwelling discontent, because the findings were fairly consistent throughout and because a large number of other carefully chosen explanatory factors were even poorer predictors.

Notes to Chapter 4

1. I thank Carol Silverman for helping me develop the conceptualization of family life and household crowding reported here. The effects of neighborhood density on family life are not discussed, because the hypotheses are related to intradwelling dynamics and because none of these measures was significantly related to persons per residential acre.

2. The NORC survey had no items concerning family life. No comparable surveys were available for analysis, so the data in this chapter are limited to the ISR survey.

3. It should be noted that Stokols (1976) is referring to subjective crowding, not an objective measure of household density (e.g., persons per room).

4. This analysis was helped by personal communications with William J. Goode and study of his earlier writings (Goode, 1972, 1973).

5. They rely on neither persons per room nor area per person as the measure of household crowding. See Booth and Edwards (1976) for a discussion of the index they used, which may in fact place their findings in doubt.

6. Two other reports of crowding and family relations conducted in the United States do not discuss the effects on the husband–wife relationship (Choldin et al., 1975; Davis et al., 1974).

7. A comparison of this subsample against the total sample of metropolitan residents indicates only minor differences in the distribution of the persons-per-room variable. As expected, on the average, married individuals found themselves slightly more crowded (mean = .67; median = .62), probably due to the exclusion of individuals living alone.

8. Using the logarithm of household crowding had no effect worth noting in this analysis. In addition, the neighborhood density variable was minimally associated with these items. Lastly, cross-tabulations were used to assess the possibility of serious curvilinearity or threshold effects, but no such patterns were evident.

9. The first two items were scaled from one (very well) to four (not well at all), the third item was scaled from one (all the time) to five (hardly ever), and the fourth was scaled from one (never) to five (very often). This index was created by the ISR staff in the following way: it is the mean of the four items, with the first two items being adjusted for smaller means and standard deviations (by multiplying

by a constant). One item containing missing data was allowed in the creation of the index.

10. The "importance of a happy marriage" item was scaled from one (extremely important) to five (not at all important). The satisfaction and dissatisfaction with marriage items were scaled from seven (high) to one (low).

11. See note 7 in chapter 3 concerning the choice of the five control variables used in equation 1. The variable "number of children in the dwelling," asked in equation 2, was selected on the basis of common sense notions and previous findings (Clausen and Clausen, 1973) concerning family size and the quality of husband–wife relations. Finally, the effects of subjective crowding needed to be accounted for, since other studies alluded to its importance (Booth and Edwards, 1976; Gasparini, 1973).

12. Additional regression runs were used to ensure the reliability of these findings. First, I should note that "length of marriage" was not a control variable in the reported analysis, since it was highly related with age. When used, though, it did not significantly affect any of the reported findings. Finally, "number of persons" and "numbers of rooms" were added to equation 1 in order to determine the effects of the numerator and denominator of persons per room. In the cases of significant associations reported in this section, the ratio variable had larger beta weights than either "persons" or "rooms."

13. In another study conducted in an American married-student housing project, Choldin et al. (1975) found the opposite: *fathers* left the homes in order to escape the housing density. Even this adaptation, which may not apply generally, results in fewer parent–child interactions and perhaps a lesser degree of parental control. Davis et al. (1974) found, in possible agreement with Mitchell, that children could not bring their friends into the home if they lived under crowded conditions. This could also mean that they were forced to play outdoors more, though this alternative was not specifically investigated.

14. They also report more sibling quarrels with greater household crowding (based on reports from the parents, not the children).

15. Because this subsample dealt with households with at least a parent and child present, the distribution of the persons-per-room variable was substantially different from that for the total sample (mean = .80; mode = 1.0; median = .75).

16. See Clausen and Clausen (1973) on the significance of family size.

17. An examination of the zero-order correlations between the family life and crowding items for *all* metropolitan respondents yielded no significant relationships.

18. Additional data analyses indicated that using the logarithm of household crowding did not alter any of the reported findings, nor did accounting for "rooms" and "persons" in regression equations modeled after those mentioned in previous sections. Cross-tabulations indicated no apparent curvilinear relationships or threshold effects.

Notes to Chapter 5

1. The responses of only metropolitan respondents differed very little on these questions.

2. See, for example, Hawley (1950, 1972).

3. I used NORC cycles 3 and 4 (N = 823) here, since they contained the items on the neighborhood environment used throughout most of this chapter. See chapter 2 for discussion of how neighborhood density was calculated.

4. The NORC and ISR urbanism scales mentioned throughout the chapter were in different formats. The NORC variable scored type of community in the following manner: (1) large central city, (2) medium central city, (3) suburb, large central city, (4) suburb, medium central city, (5) unincorporated in SMSA. The ISR variable scored urbanism as follows: (1) central cities of twelve largest SMSAS, (2) suburbs with 1960 population of 2,500 to 100,000 within twelve largest SMSAS, (3) cities with 1960 population over 100,000 excluding those coded one above, (4) cities with 1960 population of 10,000 to 100,000 excluding those coded two above, (5) places with 1960 population of 2,500 to 10,000 excluding those coded two above, (6) rural places in an SMSA with a 1960 population of less than 2,500, (7) rural places not in an SMSA but in an adjacent area. Of course, the NORC scale was based on 1970 census data, while the ISR involved 1960 computations. The ISR thus contained some error, since some respondents' areas changed categories (e.g., some coded "rural" were actually SMSA residents according to the 1970 census).

5. The opposite signs found in the weak correlations with population size in the two surveys are somewhat disturbing. However, the distribution of this variable in both surveys was quite similar, ruling out the possibility of systematic error. No reasons can be given for this finding, which may be accounted for by differences in the surveyed neighborhoods.

6. These ISR items mentioned in this section were not available in the NORC survey, thus limiting the comparative analysis to that shown in table 10.

7. Other findings deserve attention. For example, the density of the county was highly associated with the density of the census tract

(r = .84) for the ISR survey. In addition, gross density (persons per acre) was almost perfectly associated with neighborhood density (r = .99). This may indicate that the survey organizations take into consideration the homogeneity of land use in the selection of sampling areas, though I have no way of knowing about decisions of that sort. In an earlier study of Detroit (Baldassare, 1975a), I found less of a relationship (r = .51) though those data were much more selective in defining residential land.

8. In studies conducted within metropolitan areas, the correlation between tract median income and areal density is often much higher. For example, an analysis of a Detroit survey reported a relationship of about −.5 (Baldassare, 1975a). While density and income are highly related *within* metropolitan areas, they are not *across* metropolitan areas; this is because the dense tracts are more likely to be located in large metropolises, where the standards of living (and thus incomes) are usually somewhat higher in general. I do not consider this to be a major problem, though others might suggest adjustments of income to reflect differences in cost of living. For present purposes, it is assumed that densities and incomes have substantially similar meanings across metropolitan areas. For evidence of rising standards of living (as opposed to costs of living) with urban size, see Alonso and Fajans (1970).

9. Morgan (1975) and Campbell et al. (1976) used some of the data reported here to examine the association between urbanicity and residential satisfaction. The present data analysis indicates that the relationship between neighborhood density and residential satisfaction is stronger for most of the reported significant relationships.

10. See note 8 in chapter 3 concerning the rationale for using these variables.

11. The correlation between tract median income and family income was .48 in the ISR study and .44 in the NORC survey.

12. Throughout, separate regressions were also conducted using the logarithm of density with the five control variables, because of the skew of the independent variable. The few cases in this chapter where there was a significant difference are reported in the discussions of the items affected. Further, I accounted for the numerator (population) and denominator (area) of neighborhood density, using the methods outlined in note 11 in chapter 3; none of the reported relationships was affected by this added control. In addition, the presence of children (using the ISR data) did not account for any important statistical differences, when added to the regression equation with the five control factors and density. Lastly, an examination of cross-tabulations from the ISR study indicated no curvilinear relationships, so this possibility was ignored.

13. Martin Wachs, personal communication.

14. Unfortunately, the items involving commuting time and convenience of location were subject to variations between actual densities and the logarithm of density, perhaps due to the distributions of the independent and dependent variables. For this reason, they were dropped from the analysis.

15. Elementary schools: r = −.19, beta weight = −.15 (p < .001); junior high schools: r = −.14, beta weight = −.15 (p < .001).

16. The distribution of neighborhood density for the 437 NORC respondents was similar to the statistical properties found in table 8 (mean = 13).

17. The mean density of lower income respondents was eighteen persons per residential acre. Significantly, the neighborhood densities of black respondents were on the average twice as high as those of whites, perhaps indicating the combined effects of economic and social disadvantages.

18. This item was worded similarly to the NORC neighborhood satisfaction measure mentioned earlier, though here it was rated on a seven-point scale.

Notes to Chapter 6

1. I am grateful to Heidi Buettell for inventing the term *specialized withdrawal*, which describes this urban adaptation better than my previous attempts. She also offered helpful comments and personal testimonies on this topic.

2. In regard to social exchange theory, see *The Social Psychology of Groups* (1959), by Thibaut and Kelley, in addition to Blau (1964) and Homans (1974). Stanley Milgram at times seems to express the notion of specialized withdrawal, though he also indicates that overload has generalized effects on urban social life (Milgram, 1970:1464).

3. Naturally, environmental settings that are smaller or larger in size can also contain an overabundance of social contacts, leading to the possibility of overload. I will not discuss those possibilities, but rather assume the following: The experience of neighborhood density is critical to strategies used to conduct social relations, since individuals spend a good portion of their time under neighborhood residential conditions.

4. Throughout this analysis, neighborhood density was used, though an attempt was made to ensure that using the logarithm of density and controlling for "population" and "area" produced the same results. In almost all cases, they did. Accounting for the presence of children in the home did not alter the findings either, and there were no signs of curvilinearity.

5. See chapter 3 for the format of these items.

6. I also examined the effects of urbanicity and SMSA population size on casual encounters. In most cases, neighborhood density had a higher zero-order correlation than did other measures of urbanism. Of course, there is a body of literature on the impact of urbanicity on neighboring (see, e.g., Fava, 1959). Those findings are in general agreement with the notion that higher density settings are less neighborly. See also Reiss (1959), whose findings are similar to those reported in this chapter, though for rural–urban differences.

7. The statistical distributions for the crowding variables in cycles 3 and 4 combined were similar to those reported in other chapters (e.g., cycles 11 and 12 in chapter 3). In addition, regression equations (1) evaluated the effects of the numerator and denominator of persons per room, and (2) used the logarithm of household crowding instead of actual persons per room. Also, cross-tabulations were analyzed to search for curvilinear relationships. None of the results contradicts the findings in the text.

Notes to Chapter 7

1. A version of this chapter was presented at the meetings of the American Sociological Association in Chicago, September 1977. However, it did not include the subgroup analysis or the concluding remarks, which were prepared for present purposes.

2. Again, I searched for effects when using the logarithms of the density variables, examined the issue of curvilinearity, and searched for explanations due to the numerators and denominators of household and neighborhood crowding. None of these controls affected the findings reported in the text.

3. As in earlier chapters, the control variables for household crowding were the respondent's age, years in the dwelling, family income, dwelling ownership, and educational level. The control variables for neighborhood density were the respondent's age, years in the neighborhood, dwelling ownership, and educational level, and the tract median income. Adding a dummy variable for "the presence of children in the home" had no effect. These controls were used throughout this chapter. In addition, subjective household crowding had no effect on well-being when controlling for extraneous factors.

4. I expressed some of these ideas in two earlier works (Baldassare, 1977, 1978).

References

Abu-Lughod, J., and M. Foley
1960 "The consumer votes by moving." Pp. 134–78 in A. Foote et al., Housing Choices and Housing Constraints. New York: McGraw-Hill.

Aiello, J. R., Y. M. Epstein, and R. A. Karlin
1975 "Effects of crowding on electrodermal activity." Sociological Symposium 14 (Fall): 43–57.

Alonso, W., and M. Fajans
1970 "Cost of living and income by urban size." Working Paper Number 128, Institute of Urban and Regional Development, Berkeley.

Altman, I.
1975 The Environment and Social Behavior. Belmont, Calif.: Brooks-Cole.

Anderson, E. N.
1972 "Some Chinese methods of dealing with crowding." Urban Anthropology 1 (Fall): 141–50.

Ardrey, R.
1966 The Territorial Imperative. New York: Atheneum.

Baldassare, M.
1975a "The effects of density on social behavior and attitudes." American Behavioral Scientist 18 (6): 815–25.

1975b "Residential density, local ties and neighborhood attitudes: Are the findings of micro-studies generalizable to urban areas?" Sociological Symposium 14 (Fall): 92–102.

1975c Book review: Oscar Newman's "Defensible Space." Contemporary Sociology 4 (4): 435–36.

1977 "Residential density, household crowding, and social networks." Pp. 101–15 in C. S. Fischer et al., Networks and Places. New York: Free Press.

1978 "Human spatial behavior." Annual Review of Sociology, Volume 4. Forthcoming.

Baldassare, M., and S. Feller
1975 "Cultural variations in personal space: Theory, methods, and evidence." Ethos 3 (4): 481–503.

Baldassare, M., and C. S. Fischer
1977 "The relevance of crowding experiments to urban studies." Pp. 273–85 in D. Stokols (ed.), Psychological Perspectives on Environment and Behavior. New York: Plenum Press.

226 REFERENCES

Baldassare, M., and M. Wachs
1977 "The role of personal factors in responses to BART's environmental impacts." Unpublished paper.
Baldwin, J., and J. Baldwin
1973a "Interactions between adult female and infant howling monkeys." Folia Primatologica 20: 27–71.
1973b "The role of play in social organization: Comparative observations on squirrel monkeys." Primates 14: 369–81.
Ball, D.
1973 Microecology: Social Situations and Intimate Space. New York: Bobbs-Merrill.
Barker, R.
1968 Ecological Psychology. Stanford: Stanford University Press.
Baum, A., R. E. Harpin, and S. Valins
1975 "The role of group phenomena in the experience of crowding." Environment and Behavior 7 (2): 185–98.
Beasley, R. W., and G. Antunes
1974 "The etiology of urban crime: An ecological analysis." Criminology 11 (4): 439–61.
Berry, B., and J. Kasarda
1977 Contemporary Urban Ecology. New York: Macmillan.
Bickman, L., A. Teger, and T. Gabriele
1973 "Dormitory density and helping behavior." Environment and Behavior 5 (4): 465–90.
Biderman, A., M. Louria, and H. Bacchus
1963 Historical Incidents of Extreme Overcrowding. Washington: Bureau of Social Science Research.
Blackshaw, M., P. Blockhine, and M. Lebegge
1959 "Utilization of space in dwellings." Geneva: United Nations Publication.
Blau, P.
1964 Exchange and Power in Social Life. New York: John Wiley.
Booth, A.
1974 "Crowding and social participation." Unpublished paper.
1976 Urban Crowding and Its Consequences. New York: Praeger.
Booth, A., and J. Edwards
1976 "Crowding and family relations." American Sociological Review 41 (2): 308–21.
Booth, A., and D. Johnson
1975 "Effects of crowding on child health and development." American Behavioral Scientist 18 (6): 736–49.
Booth, A., and S. Welch
1973 "The effects of crowding: A cross-national study." Paper

presented at the American Psychological Association meetings, Montreal.

Bradburn, N., S. Sudman, and G. Glockel
1970   Racial Integration in American Neighborhoods. Chicago: National Opinion Research Center.

Brail, R., and F. S. Chapin
1973   "Activity patterns of urban residents." Environment and Behavior 5 (2): 163–90.

Calhoun, J.
1962   "Population density and social pathology." Scientific American 206: 139–48.

Campbell, A., F. Converse, and W. Rodgers
1976   The Quality of American Life. New York: Russell Sage.

Carnahan, D., W. Grove, and O. R. Galle
1974   "Urbanization, population density, and overcrowding: Trends in the quality of life in urban America." Social Forces 53 (1): 62–72.

Cassel, J.
1971   "Health consequences of population density and crowding." Pp. 462–78 in National Academy of Sciences, Rapid Population Growth, Volume 2. Baltimore: Johns Hopkins University Press.

Chapin, F. S.
1951   "Some housing factors related to mental hygiene." Journal of Social Issues 7 (1, 2): 164–71.
1974   Human Activity Patterns in the City. New York: John Wiley.

Chapin, F. S., Jr.
1957   Urban Land Use Planning. New York: Harper.

Chevan, A.
1971   "Family growth, household density, and moving." Demography 8 (4): 451–58.

Choldin, H., E. Jacobsen, and G. Yahuke
1975   "Effects of crowded dwellings on family life." Sociological Symposium 14 (Fall): 58–75.

Chombart de Lauwe, P. H.
1961   "The sociology of housing methods and prospects of research." International Journal of Comparative Sociology 2 (1): 23–41.

Christian, J., V. Flyger, and D. Davis
1960   "Factors in the mass mortality of a herd of sika deer." Chesapeake Science 1: 79–95.

Clark, W., and M. Cadwallader
1973   "Locational stress and residential mobility." Environment and Behavior 5 (1): 29–42.

Clausen, J., and S. Clausen
1973   "The effects of family size on parents and children." Pp. 185–208 in J. Fawcett (ed.), Psychological Perspectives on Population. New York: Basic Books.
Clausen, J. A., and M. L. Kohn
1954   "The ecological approach in social psychiatry." American Journal of Sociology 60: 140–51.
Cohen, S.
1977   "Environmental load and the allocation of attention." In A. Baum, J. Singer, and S. Valins (eds.), Advances in Environmental Research. Norwood, N.J.: Lawrence Erlbaum Associates. In press.
Cohen, S., and S. Spacapan
1977   "The after effects of stress: An attentional interpretation." Unpublished paper.
D'Atri, D. A.
1975   "Psychophysiological responses to crowding." Environment and Behavior 7 (2): 237–52.
Davis, D. L.
1975   "The shadow scale." Sociological Review 23: 143–50.
Davis, D. L., K. Bergin, and G. Mazin
1974   "When the neighbors get noisy we bang on the walls: A critical exploration of density and crowding." Paper presented at the American Sociological Association meetings, Montreal.
Day, A. T., and L. M. Day
1973   "Cross-national comparisons of population density." Science 181: 1016–23.
Dean, L. M., W. M. Pugh, and E. K. Gunderson
1975   "Spatial and perceptual components of crowding." Environment and Behavior 7 (2): 225–36.
Desor, J.
1972   "Toward a psychological theory of crowding." Journal of Personality and Social Psychology 21: 79–83.
Draper, D.
1973   "Crowding among hunter-gatherers: The !Kung Bushmen." Science 177: 301–2.
Durkheim, E.
1893   (1964) The Division of Labor in Society. New York: Free Press.
Ehrlich, P.
1968   The Population Bomb. New York: Ballantine.
Ellis, W. R.
1974   "The environment of human relations: Perspectives and problems." Journal of Architectural Education 27 (2, 3): 11–54.

Eoyang, C.
1974 "Effects of group size and privacy in residential crowd-ing." Journal of Personality and Social Psychology 30 (3): 389–92.

Evans, G., and W. Eichelman
1975 "Preliminary models of conceptual linkages among proxemic variables." Environment and Behavior, forth-coming.

Factor, R., and I. Waldron
1973 "Contemporary population densities and human health." Nature 243: 381–84.

Fava, S.
1959 "Contrasts in neighboring: New York City and a suburban county." Pp. 122–30 in W. Dobriner (ed.), The Suburban Community. New York: Putnam.

Feller, S., and M. Baldassare
1975 "Theory and methods in urban anthropology: Contri-butions toward the study of American cities." Council of Planning Librarians Exchange Bibliography, Num-ber 899.

Fischer, C. S.
1972 "Urbanism as a way of life: A review and an agenda." Sociological Methods and Research 1: 187–242.
1973 "On urban alienation and anomie." American Sociological Review 38 (June): 311–26.
1975 "Toward a subcultural theory of urbanism." American Journal of Sociology 80 (May): 1319–41.
1976 The Urban Experience. New York: Harcourt Brace Jovanovich.

Fischer, C. S., et al.
1977 Networks and Places. New York: Free Press.

Fischer, C. S., and M. Baldassare
1975 "How far from the madding crowd?" New Society 32: 531–33.

Fischer, C. S., M. Baldassare, and R. J. Ofshe
1975 "Crowding studies and urban life: A critical review." Journal of the American Institute of Planners, forthcom-ing.

Fischer, C. S., and A. Stueve
1977 "The 'authentic community.'" Pp. 163–86 in C. Fischer et al., Networks and Places. New York: Free Press.

Fogel, R. W., and S. Engerman
1974 Time on the Cross, Volume 1. Boston: Little, Brown.

Foote, A., J. Abu-Lughod, M. Foley, and L. Winnick
1960 Housing Choices and Housing Constraints. New York: McGraw-Hill.

Freedman, J. L.
> 1972a   "Conceptualization of crowding." Pp. 497–509 in S. M. Mazie (ed.), Population Distribution and Policy, Volume 5. Washington: Government Printing Office.
> 1972b   "Population density, juvenile delinquency, and mental illness." Pp. 511–23 in S. M. Mazie (ed.), Population Distribution and Policy, Volume 5. Washington: Government Printing Office.
> 1973   "The effects of population density on humans." Pp. 209–38 in J. Fawcett (ed.), Psychological Perspectives on Population. New York: Basic Books.
> 1975   Crowding and Behavior. San Francisco: W. H. Freeman.

Freedman, J. L., S. Heska, and A. Levy
> 1975   "Population density and pathology: Is there a relationship?" Journal of Experimental Social Psychology 11: 539–52.

Freedman, J. L., S. Klevansky, and P. Ehrlich
> 1971   "The effects of crowding on human task performance." Journal of Applied Social Psychology 1: 7–25.

Freedman, J. L., A. Levy, R. Buchanan, and J. Price
> 1972   "Crowding and human aggressiveness." Journal of Experimental Psychology 8: 528–48.

Galle, O., and W. Gove
> 1974   "Crowding and behavior in Chicago: 1940–1974." Unpublished paper.

Galle, O., W. Gove, and J. McPherson
> 1972   "Population density and pathology: What are the relations for man?" Science 176: 23–30.

Gans, H.
> 1970   "Urbanism and suburbanism as ways of life." Pp. 70–84 in R. Gutman and D. Popenoe (eds.), Neighborhood, City, and Metropolis. New York: Random House.

Gasparini, A.
> 1973   "Influence of the dwelling on family." Ekistics 216: 344–48.

Goode, W. J.
> 1972   "Presidential address: The place of force in human society." American Sociological Review 37: 507–19.
> 1973   "Violence between intimates." Pp. 145–97 in W. J. Goode, Explorations in Social Theory. London: Oxford University Press.

Gove, W., M. Hughes, and O. Galle
> 1977   "Overcrowding in the home: An empirical investigation of its possible pathological consequences." Unpublished paper.

Greenfield, R. J., and J. F. Lewis
1969 "An alternative to a density function of overcrowding." Land Economics 45: 282–85.
Griffitt, W., and R. Veitch
1971 "Hot and crowded: Influences of population density and temperature on interpersonal affective behavior." Journal of Personality and Social Psychology 17: 92–98.
Hall, E. T.
1966 The Hidden Dimension. New York: Random House.
Hauser, P. M.
1968 "The chaotic society: Product of the social morphological revolution." American Sociological Review 34 (February): 1–19.
Hawley, A.
1950 Human Ecology. New York: Ronald Press.
1971 Urban Society. New York: Ronald Press.
1972 "Population density and the city." Demography 9: 521–29.
Heimsath, C.
1977 Behavioral Architecture. New York: McGraw-Hill.
Hollingshead, A., and R. Redlich
1958 Social Class and Mental Illness. New York: Wiley.
Homans, G.
1974 Social Behavior: Its Elementary Forms. New York: Harcourt, Brace and World.
Hutt, C., and M. Vaizey
1966 "Differential effects of group density on social behavior." Nature 209: 1371–72.
Ittleson, W., H. Proshansky, and L. Rivlin
1970 "The environmental psychology of the psychiatric ward." Pp. 419–39 in H. Proshansky, W. Ittleson, and L. Rivlin (eds.), Environmental Psychology. New York: Holt, Rinehart and Winston.
Jacobs, J.
1961 The Death and Life of Great American Cities. New York: Random House.
Johnson, D. R., A. Booth, and D. Duvall
1975 "Social determinants of human crowding." Unpublished paper.
Kasarda, J.
1974 "The ecological approach in sociology." Unpublished paper.
Kasarda, J., and M. Janowitz
1974 "Community attachment in mass society." American Sociological Review 39 (3): 328–39.

Katz, R.
  1961   "Residential densities." Council of Planning Librarians Exchange Bibliography Number 18: 1–20.
Keyfitz, N.
  1966   "Population density and the style of social life." Bioscience 16: 868–73.
King, B. F., and C. Richards
  1972   "The 1972 NORC national probability sample." National Opinion Research Center, University of Chicago.
Kish, L., and I. Hess
  1965   "The Survey Research Center's national sample of dwellings." Institute for Social Research, Number 2315, University of Michigan.
Lansing, J., and W. Ladd
  1964   The Propensity to Move. Washington: Government Printing Office.
Lansing, J., R. Marans, and R. Zehner
  1970   Planned Residential Environments. Ann Arbor: Institute for Social Research.
Law Week
  1975   United States Law Week 44 (August 26): 2093.
Lawrence, J. E.
  1974   "Science and sentiment: Overview of research on crowding and human behavior." Psychological Bulletin 81 (10): 712–20.
Levy, L., and A. N. Herzog
  1974   "Effects of population density and crowding on health and social adaptation in the Netherlands." Journal of Health and Social Behavior 15 (3): 228–40.
Lewis, O.
  1961   The Children of Sanchez: Autobiography of a Mexican Family. New York: Random House.
Lipowski, Z. J.
  1975   "Sensory and information inputs overload: Behavioral effects." Comprehensive Psychiatry 16 (3): 199–221.
Long, L.
  1972   "The influence of number and ages of children on residential mobility." Demography 9 (3): 371–82.
Loo, C.
  1972   "The effects of spatial density on the social behavior of children." Journal of Applied Social Psychology 2: 372–81.
  1973   "Important issues in researching the effects of crowding on humans." Representative Research in Social Psychology 4: 219–26.

1975   "The psychological study of crowding." American Behavioral Scientist 18 (6): 826–42.

Lorenz, K.
1966   On Aggression. New York: Bantam.

Lym, G.
1975   Images of Home at Peabody Terrace. Unpublished doctoral dissertation, Harvard University.

Marans, R. W., and W. Rodgers
1973   "Evaluating resident satisfaction in established and new communities." Pp. 197–227 in R. W. Burkhell (ed.), Frontiers of Planned Unit Development. New Brunswick, N.J.: Center for Urban Policy Research, Rutgers University.

Meier, R. L.
1962   A Communication Theory of Urban Growth. Cambridge: M.I.T. Press.

Merton, R. K.
1951   "The social psychology of housing." Pp. 163–217 in W. Dennis (ed.), Current Trends in Social Psychology. Pittsburgh: University of Pittsburgh Press.

Michelson, W.
1973   "Environmental change." Research Paper Number 60, Center for Urban and Community Studies, University of Toronto.
1976   Man and His Urban Environment. Reading, Mass.: Addison.
1977   Environmental Choice, Human Behavior and Residential Satisfaction. New York: Oxford University Press.

Michelson, W., D. Belgue, and J. Stewart
1973   "Intentions and expectations in differential residential selection." Journal of Marriage and the Family 35 (2): 189–96.

Michelson, W., and K. Garland
1974   "The differential role of crowded homes and dense residential areas in the incidence of selected symptoms of human pathology." Research Paper Number 67, Center for Urban and Community Studies, University of Toronto.

Milgram, S.
1970   "The experience of living in cities." Science 167: 1461–68.

Mitchell, R. E.
1971   "Some social implications of high density housing." American Sociological Review 38: 18–29.
1974   "Misconceptions about man-made space: In partial defense of high-density housing." The Family Coordinator 1: 51–56.

1975 "Ethnographic and historical perspectives on relationships between physical and socio-spatial environments." Sociological Symposium 14 (Fall): 25–40.

1976 "Cultural and health influences on building, housing, and community standards." Human Ecology.

Morgan, D. J.

1975 "Subjective indicators of the quality of life in U.S. communities." Unpublished report, National Opinion Research Center.

Morgan, D. J., and J. R. Murray

1974 "A potential population density distribution and its dynamics: The expressed preference for residential location." Unpublished report, National Opinion Research Center.

Morgan, L. H.

1881 Houses and House Life of the American Aborigines. Washington: Government Printing Office.

Morris, D.

1967 The Naked Ape. New York: Dell.

1969 The Human Zoo. New York: Dell.

Morris, E. W., and M. Winter

1975 "A theory of family housing adjustment." Journal of Marriage and the Family 37 (1): 79–88.

Munroe, R. L., and R. H. Munroe

1972 "Population density and affective relationships in three East African societies." Journal of Social Psychology 88: 15–20.

Murray, J.

1974 "Continuous National Survey." NORC Report Number 125, University of Chicago.

National Planning Data Corporation

1974a "Population density report." Ithaca, N.Y. Mimeograph.

1974b National Planning Data Corporation Catalog. Ithaca, N.Y.

Newman, O.

1973 Defensible Space. New York: Macmillan.

Nie, N. H., C. Hull, J. Jenkins, K. Steinbrenner, and D. Brent

1975 SPSS: Statistical Package for the Social Sciences. New York: McGraw-Hill.

Nisbet, R.

1974 The Sociology of Émile Durkheim. New York: Oxford University Press.

Osborn, F. J.

1956 "Housing densities." Paper presented at the Town and Country Planning Association National Conference.

Park, R.
　1915　(1969) "The city: Suggestions for the investigation of human behavior in the urban environment." American Journal of Sociology 20 (5): 477–512.

Plant, J. S.
　1960　"Family living space and personality development." Pp. 510–20 in N. W. Bell and E. F. Vogel (eds.), A Modern Introduction to the Family. New York: Free Press.

Proshansky, H., W. Ittleson, and L. Rivlin
　1970　"Freedom of choice and behavior in a physical setting." Pp. 173–83 in H. Proshansky, W. Ittleson, and L. Rivlin (eds.), Environmental Psychology. New York: Holt, Rinehart and Winston.

Rainwater, L., and W. Yancey
　1967　The Moynihan Report and the Politics of Controversy. Cambridge, Mass.: M.I.T. Press.

Regional Plan Association
　1975　"Where transit works: Urban densities for public transportation." Regional Plan News 99 (August): 1–23.

Reiss, A. J.
　1959　"Rural–urban and status differences in interpersonal contacts." American Journal of Sociology 65: 182–95.

Riemer, S.
　1943　"Sociological theory of home adjustment." American Sociological Review 8 (June): 272–78.
　1945　"Maladjustment to the family home." American Sociological Review 10 (October): 642–48.
　1947　"Sociological perspectives in home planning." American Sociological Review 12 (April): 155–59.

Robinson, W. S.
　1950　"Ecological correlations and the behavior of individuals." American Sociological Review 15: 315–57.

Rodin, J.
　1976　"Density, perceived choice and response to controllable and uncontrollable outcomes." Journal of Experimental Social Psychology 12: 564–78.

Ronnigen, J.
　1973　"Residential densities." Council of Planning Librarians Exchange Bibliography Number 416: 1–43.

Ross, M., B. Layton, B. Erickson, and J. Schopler
　1973　"Affect, facial regard, and reactions to crowding." Journal of Personality and Social Psychology 28: 69–76.

Rossi, P.
　1956　Why Families Move. Glencoe, Ill.: Free Press.

Sabagh, G., M. Van Arsdol, and E. W. Butler
   1969   "Some determinants of intra-metropolitan mobility: Conceptual considerations." Social Forces 48 (1): 88–98.
Saegert, S., E. MacKintosh, and S. West
   1975   "Two studies of crowding in urban public spaces." Environment and Behavior 7 (2): 159–84.
Schmitt, R.
   1957   "Density, delinquency and crime in Honolulu." Sociology and Social Research 41: 274–76.
   1963   "Implications of density in Hong Kong." Journal of the American Institute of Planners 29: 210–17.
   1966   "Density, health and social disorganization." Journal of the American Institute of Planners 32: 38–40.
Schnore, L. F.
   1958   "Social morphology and human ecology." American Journal of Sociology 63: 620–34.
   1961   "The myth of human ecology." Sociological Inquiry 31 (2): 128–49.
Schorr, A.
   1966   Slums and Social Insecurity. Washington: Government Printing Office.
   1970   "Housing and its effects." Pp. 319–33 in H. Proshansky, W. Ittleson, and L. Rivlin (eds.), Environmental Psychology, New York: Holt, Rinehart and Winston.
Sherrod, D.
   1974   "Crowding, perceived control, and behavioral aftereffects." Journal of Applied Social Psychology 4 (2): 171–86.
Sherrod, D., and S. Cohen
   1977   "Density, personal control, and design." In J. Aiello (ed.), Crowding and Design. New York: Plenum Press. In press.
Silverman, C.
   1976   "Jurisdiction and privacy: The effects of differential control over living space." Unpublished paper.
Simmel, G.
   1905   (1969) "The metropolis and mental life." Pp. 47–60 in R. Senmett (ed.), Classic Essays on the Culture of Cities. New York: Appleton.
Simmons, J.
   1968   "Changing residence in the city." Geographical Review 58: 622–51.
Smith, D.
   1971   "Household space and family organization." Pp. 62–69 in D. Davies and K. Herman (eds.), Social Space: Canadian Perspectives. Toronto: New Press.

Smith, S., and W. Haythorn
1972 "Effects of compatibility, crowding, group size and leadership on stress anxiety, hostility and annoyance in isolated groups." Journal of Personality and Social Psychology 22: 67–79.

Sommer, R.
1969 Personal Space: The Behavioral Basis of Design. Englewood Cliffs, N.J.: Prentice-Hall.

Speare, A.
1974 "Residential satisfaction as an intervening variable in residential mobility." Demography 11 (2): 173–88.

Spencer, H.
1895 The Principles of Sociology. New York: Appleton.

Stokols, D.
1972a "On the distinction between density and crowding." Psychological Review 79 (3): 275–77.
1972b "A social psychological model of human crowding phenomena." Journal of the American Institute of Planners 38: 72–84.
1976 "The experience of crowding in primary and secondary environments." Environment and Behavior (6): 49–86.
1977 "Origins and directions of environment–behavioral research." Pp. 5–36 in D. Stokols (ed.), Perspectives on Environment and Behavior. New York: Plenum.
1978 "Environmental psychology." Annual Review of Psychology 29: 253–95.

Stokols, D., W. Ohlig, and S. Resnick
1977 "Perceptions of residential crowding, classroom experiences, and student health." Human Ecology, forthcoming.

Stokols, D., M. Rall, B. Pinner, and J. Schopler
1973 "Physical, social and personal determinants of the perception of crowding." Environment and Behavior 5: 87–115.

Stokols, D., T. Smith, and J. Proster
1975 "Partitioning and perceived crowding in a public space." American Behavioral Scientist 18 (6): 792–814.

Straus, N.
1944 The Seven Myths of Housing. New York: Knopf.

Street, J. M.
1969 "An evaluation of the concept of carrying capacity." Professional Geographer 21 (3): 104–7.

Stueve, A.
1976 "The consequences and contingencies of residential mobility." Unpublished paper.

Stueve, A., K. Gerson, and C. Fischer
1977 "The structure and determinants of attachment to place."

Pp. 139–61 in C. Fischer et al., Networks and Places. New York: Free Press.

Sundstrom, E.
1975   "Toward an interpersonal model of crowding." Sociological Symposium 14 (Fall): 129–44.
1977   "Crowding as a sequential process: Review of research on the effects of population density on humans." In A. Baum and H. Epstein (eds.), Human Responses to Crowding. Hillsdale, N.J.: Lawrence Erlbaum Associates. Forthcoming.

Suttles, G.
1972   The Social Construction of Communities. Chicago: University of Chicago Press.

Taeuber, C., P. N. Ylvisaker, L. Wolffe, F. Hyde, and B. Hankw
1972   Density: Five Perspectives, A ULI Special Report. Washington: Urban Land Institute.

Thibaut, J., and H. Kelley
1959   The Social Psychology of Groups. New York: Wiley.

Tonnies, F.
1887   (1957) Community and Society. East Lansing: Michigan State University Press.

U.S. Bureau of the Census
1966   "Reasons for moving: March 1962 to March 1963." Current Population Reports, Series P–20, Number 154.
1971   Census of Population and Housing: 1970. General Demographic Trends for Metropolitan Areas, 1960–1970, U.S. Summary. Washington: Government Printing Office.
1972   Census of Housing: 1970. General Housing Characteristics, Final Report HC (1)–A1, U.S. Summary. Washington: Government Printing Office.
1976a   Annual Housing Survey, 1974. Part A: General Housing Characteristics. Washington: Government Printing Office.
1976b   Annual Housing Survey, 1974. Part C: Financial Characteristics of the Housing Inventory. Washington: Government Printing Office.

U.S. Department of Housing and Urban Development
1974   Housing in the Seventies: A Report of the National Housing Policy Review. Washington: Government Printing Office.

Valins, S., and A. Baum
1973   "Residential group size, social interaction and crowding." Environment and Behavior 5: 421–39.

Wallace, A. F.
1952   Housing and Social Structure. Philadelphia: Philadelphia Housing Authority.

Wicker, A.
1974 "Theoretical developments pertaining to personal space and crowding: Comments." Paper presented at the Western Psychological Association meeting, San Francisco.

Wicker, A., and S. Kirmeyer
1977 "From church to laboratory to national park: A program on excess and insufficient populations in behavior settings." Pp. 69–96 in D. Stokols (ed.), Psychological Perspectives on Environment and Behavior. New York: Plenum Press.

Wilner, D., R. Walkey, T. Pinkerton, and M. Tayback
1962 The Housing Environment and Family Life. Baltimore: Johns Hopkins University Press.

Windle, C., B. Rosen, M. Goldsmith, and J. Shambaugh
1975 "A demographic system for comparative assessment of needs for mental health services." Evaluation 2 (2): 73–76.

Winsborough, H.
1965 "The social consequences of high population density." Law and Contemporary Problems 30: 120–26.

Wirth, L.
1938 "Urbanism as a way of life." American Journal of Sociology 44: 1–24.

Wolfe, M.
1975 "Room size, group size, and density." Environment and Behavior 7 (2): 199–224.

Woodhull, J.
1975 "Urban density and mass rapid transit." Pp. 169–74 in A. D. Emerson (ed.), Transpo LA: Economic Leverage for Tomorrow, Proceedings: Fourth Annual Symposium. Hollywood: Western Periodicals Company.

Yarrow, M.
1963 "Problems of methods in parent–child research." Child Development 34: 219–26.
1968 Child Rearing: An Inquiry into Research Methods. San Francisco: Jossey-Bass.

Zlutnick, S., and I. Altman
1972 "Crowding and human behavior." Pp. 44–58 in J. Wohlwill and D. Carson (eds.), Environment and the Social Sciences. Washington: American Psychological Association.

Index

Abu-Lughod, J., 84
Activities, personal, 67, 91, 99, 104
 importance of, 67, 94, 99–100, 102, 123
 intrusions into, 98, 99–100, 102. *See also* Family strategies; Intrusions
 separating in space, 13, 19
 space for, 95, 206, 207. *See also* Space, use of
Adaptations to crowding, 21, 34–35, 46, 51, 61, 94, 121–122, 193, 194, 203
 cultural, 100–101, 102
 differences in ability to make, 34–35, 96, 122, 186, 188, 200, 201
 family, 33, 97, 100–101, 105, 121–122, 123, 186, 205
 group, 41, 206, 209
 human, 29, 39, 163, 165–166, 188, 192, 208–209
 personal, 46, 83, 203, 204, 206, 209
Adjustments, 7, 15, 78, 87, 91, 103, 122, 184–187
Adults, 96–97
 power of, 33, 62–63, 104–105. *See also* Power differentials in family
 See also Social contacts, of adults
Aesthetics, neighborhood, 60, 134, 147–148, 159
Age and density, 58, 73, 74, 75, 76–77, 80, 92, 135, 140, 142, 145, 146, 170, 183–184, 195, 196, 197, 198, 214, 223
Aggression, 9–10
Aiello, J. R., 21, 40
Albuquerque, N. M., 138
Alonso, W., 221
Altman, I., 21, 25, 36
Anderson, E. N., 24, 100–101, 102, 103
Animal research, 9–10, 20, 37, 38–40, 40–41, 42–43, 191–192. *See also* Experiments
Annual Housing Survey, 213, 214
Anomie, 18, 20
Antunes, F., 47
Architecture, 13–15, 23
Ardrey, Robert, 9

Areal studies, 37, 45–47, 152, 212
Automobile travel, 140, 150–151, 158

Baldwin, J., 39
Ball, D., 203
Baltimore, study in, 78–79
Barker, R., 25
Baum, A., 21, 44
Beasley, R. W., 47
Bedrooms, number of, 14, 122
Berry, B., 139
Bickman, L., 44
Biderman, A. 13
Biological approaches, 9, 16–17, 20
Biological determinism, 202
Blacks, 7, 58, 140, 141, 152, 222
Blackshaw, M., 14
Blau, Peter, 29, 222
Block measure, 56
Booth, Alan, 48, 73, 75, 87, 108, 113–114, 167, 169, 180, 199, 212, 218, 219
Boston, 138
Bradburn, Norman, 180
Brail, R., 67
Buettell, Heidi, 222
Building, multiple-dwelling, 142–143, 159, 212

Cadwallader, M., 84, 85
Calcutta, 138
Calhoun, John, 9–10, 38, 40–41, 191
Campbell, A., 52, 212, 214, 221
Carnahan, D., 69, 70
Carrying capacity, 12
Cassel, J., 13
Casual encounters, 102, 162, 166, 170–171, 173–177, 179, 180, 181, 182–183, 185, 186, 187, 188, 206, 223
Census, U.S. Bureau of, 13–14, 55, 68, 69, 70, 71–72, 73, 84, 129, 213
Census tract as natural area, 129–130, 144
Chapin, F. Stuart, 15, 67, 79, 98
Chapin, F. Stuart, Jr., 211
Chevan, A., 84
Chicago, study in, 108, 113

Design Dave Comstock
Composition Viking Typographics
Lithography Malloy Lithographing
Binder Malloy Lithographing
Text Palatino
Display Univers '59'
Paper 50 lb Glatfelter Natural
Binding Holliston Roxite B 51507